Routledge Library Editions

PRINCIPLES OF PUBLIC FINANCE

ECONOMICS

Routledge Library Editions – Economics

PUBLIC ECONOMICS
In 5 Volumes

I	Principles of Public Finance	*Dalton*
II	Problems of Economic Planning	*Durbin*
III	The Economic Theory of Fiscal Policy	*Hansen*
IV	An Expenditure Tax	*Kaldor*
V	The Principles of Economic Planning	*Lewis*

PRINCIPLES OF PUBLIC FINANCE

HUGH DALTON

Routledge
Taylor & Francis Group
LONDON AND NEW YORK

First published in 1922

Reprinted in 2003 by
Routledge
2 Park Square, Milton Park, Abingdon, Oxon OX14 4RN

Transferred to Digital Printing 2004

Routledge is an imprint of the Taylor & Francis Group

Printed and Bound in Great Britain

British Library Cataloguing in Publication Data
A CIP catalogue record for this book
is available from the British Library

Principles of Public Finance
ISBN 0-415-31397-X

Miniset: Public Economics

Series: Routledge Library Editions – Economics

Principles of Public Finance

BY

HUGH DALTON, M.A., D.Sc. (Econ.), M.P.

Sometime Reader in Economics in the University of London

ELEVENTH IMPRESSION

LONDON

GEORGE ROUTLEDGE & SONS, LTD.

BROADWAY HOUSE: 68-74 CARTER LANE, E.C.

1941

First Edition, December, 1922.
Second Edition, October, 1924.
Third Edition, May, 1926.
Fourth Edition, February, 1927.
Fifth Edition (enlarged, revised and reset),
January, 1929.
Sixth Edition, December, 1930.
Seventh Edition, August, 1932.
Eighth Edition, June, 1934.
Ninth Edition (enlarged, revised and reset), 1936.
Tenth Edition, January, 1939.
Eleventh Edition, May, 1941.

Publisher's Note.

This book has been translated into Arabic, Czech, Dutch, German, Japanese, Turkish and Urdu.

Printed in Great Britain by Butler & Tanner Ltd., Frome and London

PREFACE TO THE FIRST EDITION

THIS book contains the substance of lectures on the Theory of Public Finance delivered at the London School of Economics. It is designed, in Bacon's words, " to excite the judgment briefly, rather than to inform it tediously." I have aimed at setting out, without undue elaboration, the chief general principles which are applicable to the public finance of a modern community. For the study of first principles is a necessary preliminary to an effective discussion of practical problems, and should be helpful in providing a framework of general ideas, into which particular ideas and particular facts can be fitted, so as to appear, not as unique and isolated things, but in their true relation to a larger whole.

Though I may seem occasionally to have yielded a little to temptation, it is not my object in this book to advocate any detailed practical policy, but only to indicate some of the general considerations on which any sound policy must be based. Facts, in the field of public finance, are moving so rapidly at the present time, that realistic studies are soon out of date and the form, in which practical problems present themselves, is constantly changing. But there are certain general principles of which this is not true. Ignorance, or neglect, of these has caused, and is still causing, grave economic damage to the world. In the course of my argument, therefore, I have occasionally turned aside to criticise certain current opinions on questions of taxation, public expenditure and public debts, which I believe to rest upon errors of judgment and confusions of mind.

It has been customary with the majority of economists to adopt a somewhat negative attitude towards public expenditure. I have attempted to treat this part of the subject more positively and to exhibit the parallelism which exists between the theory of public expenditure and that of taxation.

I have made few references in the text to the writings of others. But for the benefit of readers, who wish to pursue the subject further, I have added a short note on books.

HUGH DALTON.

London School of Economics,
September, 1922.

EXTRACT FROM
PREFACE TO THE FIFTH EDITION

As compared with the First Edition of this book, the Second, Third and Fourth only showed a few minor verbal changes. But in this, the Fifth, Edition I have made larger alterations in the original text. . . . I have added two new chapters, XXIV and XXV; attached Notes, containing some elaborations which may bore "the general reader," to certain Chapters; lengthened and brought up to date the Note on Books; and provided an Index. The result is a somewhat longer book, though its general framework is unchanged. But I have tried not to sacrifice compactness, nor an eclectic brevity.

November, 1928.

PREFACE TO THE NINTH EDITION

I HAVE again given this book a very thorough revision. In the last few years we have seen strange sights in public finance and many men have had fresh thoughts. I have wished not to lengthen this book unduly, but, subject to this condition, I have taken account both of the new facts and the new ideas of this period. And I have been able to cut out much dead wood, both small twigs and larger branches. Chapter XXVI is new and many of the earlier chapters are substantially changed and, I hope, improved.

The boundaries of public finance are not clear cut. It is, for instance, very much entangled at some points with the theory of money and of industrial fluctuations, subjects on which thought is now very active, though opinion, even among certified economists, is still deeply divided. And tariffs, which belong to public finance, are closely related to other forms of trade restriction, which do not. Sometimes, therefore, I have had to cut short lines of argument which, if allowed to run on, would run too far afield.

October, 1935.

CONTENTS

PAGE

PART III.—PUBLIC EXPENDITURE.

PART IV.—PUBLIC DEBTS.

PART I

INTRODUCTORY

Chapter I

THE NATURE OF PUBLIC FINANCE AND THE MAIN DIVISIONS OF THE SUBJECT

§ 1. Public finance is one of those subjects which lie on the border line between economics and politics. It is concerned with the income and expenditure of public authorities, and with the adjustment of the one to the other. The " Principles of Public Finance " are the general principles which may be laid down with regard to these matters.

" Public authorities " include all sorts of territorial governments, from parish councils up to national, imperial and even international governments. They differ widely among themselves, of course, as regards the magnitude of the areas and populations which they govern, the range of functions which they exercise, their methods of obtaining income, the objects of their expenditure, and their financial relations with other public authorities, superior or subordinate to themselves. But in a broad survey of the subject these differences are only of secondary importance. In particular, there is no fundamental distinction between the public finance of " central " and of " local " authorities in such a country as Great Britain, or of the various grades of government in the hierarchy of a Federal Constitution.

§ 2. In modern civilised communities the income and expenditure of public authorities consist, almost exclusively, of money receipts and money payments. The word " finance " signifies " money matters " and their management, and public finance in its modern sense presupposes the existence of a money economy.

The expenditure of public authorities, indeed, consists practically without exception of money payments. But we may notice two sorts of public receipts which are not money receipts, namely (1) certain unpaid personal services, and (2) the payment of certain taxes otherwise than in money. Some unpaid services are rendered voluntarily to public authorities, others under legal compulsion. Examples of the former sort in this country are the services of Justices of the Peace and of elected members of local authorities. Examples of the latter sort, which have been called "labour taxes," are the services of jurors, the obligation resting upon all citizens under the English common law to assist in sweeping snow from the streets, in extinguishing fires and in helping the police to catch murderers and thieves. Likewise the "corvée" or forced labour, which is still imposed on coloured populations in certain colonies, chiefly for road-making and other public works. Another and more important form of compulsory service, which is still found, even in peace time, in most modern communities, is compulsory military service. But this differs from the corvée in that it is paid for, though at a very much lower rate than it would be necessary to offer, in order to secure an equal amount of voluntary paid service.

The payment of taxes in money has gradually superseded their payment in kind, for the same reason that a money economy has gradually superseded a barter economy, that is to say, on grounds of general convenience. But in this country there are a few exceptions of comparatively recent origin. Thus since 1909 the Death Duties of landowners may, with the consent of the Inland Revenue authorities, be paid in land,[1] though, when this proposal was first made in the House of Commons in 1906, it was ridiculed on the ground that, if it was accepted, distillers would next be asking to pay their Death Duties in whisky. Again, certain taxes may be paid by handing over certain public securities. Since 1919, for example, Death Duties may be paid in Victory Bonds, a convenient means of debt redemption, though somewhat expensive to the Treasury, since a £100 Bond, which was issued at 85 and until 1932 always stood below par in the market, is accepted as the equivalent of £100 of tax.

Since 1920, also, in the United States royalties, payable under leases of publicly owned oil-bearing lands, may be paid to the Federal Government in oil.[2]

§ 3. The main division in public finance is between public income and public expenditure, which form two symmetrical branches of the subject. Some writers have excluded public expenditure from the scope of public finance, but this is clearly illogical. Public debts are often treated as a separate branch of the subject and this is convenient, since they give rise to a number of special problems. On the other hand, receipts from public borrowings form part of public income, while payments of interest on, and repayments of the principal of, public debts form part of public expenditure. Similarly receipts from public assets, whether in the shape of annual income or of the proceeds of sales, form part of public income, while payments in respect of

[1] This provision, which might have been, and may still be, an important instrument for transferring land from private to public ownership, has hitherto been practically inoperative.

[2] Lutz, *Public Finance*, p. 132.

public assets, whether in the shape of expenses of management, or initial expenses of acquisition, form part of public expenditure. And these questions are related to the problem of balancing the budget.

Financial administration, again, raises a series of special problems and is often treated as a separate branch of the subject. It is not dealt with in this book, since the general principles which can be laid down with regard to it are comparatively few, and since their effective discussion presupposes in the reader a detailed acquaintance with existing financial systems. Financial administration, therefore, belongs to the stage of realistic study in public finance rather than to that of general principles.

Part II of this book is devoted to public income, Part III to public expenditure and Part IV to public debts and the balancing of the budget. Public assets are referred to at those points in the discussion, when they become relevant, but they are unfortunately much rarer and of much less practical importance than public debts. The two remaining chapters of Part I are concerned respectively with the fundamental principle which should govern all problems of public finance, and with the relation of public to private finance, and both these chapters have a bearing on the mutual adjustment of public income and public expenditure.

Chapter II

THE PRINCIPLE OF MAXIMUM SOCIAL ADVANTAGE

§ 1. In the sphere of public finance we are still greatly beset by the superficial views and shallow precepts of an earlier age. " The very best of all plans of finance," said J. B. Say, a hundred and thirty years ago, " is to spend little and the best of all taxes is that which is least in amount." He would still find many to agree with him. Much current discussion, and even much orthodox literature on this subject, starts from the negative assertion that " every tax is an evil." Credulous minds are thus biased in advance against all forms of public expenditure. This view is quite unscientific. It would be equally unscientific, but not more so, to start from the positive assertion that " all public expenditure is a good." It is not true that every tax is an evil. A tax on alcohol, which by raising its price diminishes its consumption, may be a positive good. For it was not a desirable state of things, when in the eighteenth century in England " a man could get drunk for a penny and dead drunk for twopence." Similarly, of course, it is not true that all public expenditure is a good. Expenditure on unnecessary wars is an obvious evil. Again, the large sums which have been paid in unemployment benefit and poor relief during recent years, without any appreciable attempt to reorganise our productive resources, indicate a grave failure of practical statesmanship. A somewhat similar reflection is suggested by the large payments of interest on War Debt. But it is not possible to pass a complete judgment upon any operation in public finance without balancing against one another both sides of the operation, the effects of the raising, and the effects of the spending, of public revenue.

It is idle to speak, as many do, of the " burden of taxation," regardless of the benefit of the corresponding public expenditure. No sensible person speaks of the " burden " of drawing cheques, regardless of the purposes for which they are drawn.

Historically the idea that all taxes are an evil appears as a deduction from the facile individualist doctrine that, outside the narrow sphere of its traditional minimum of activities, the State can do no right. But this doctrine is now seen to err on the side of simplicity. Historically also the idea is connected with the supposed distinction between " productive " and " unproductive " expenditure. It was imagined by early economists, including Adam Smith and Ricardo, that most of the private expenditure, which taxation checked, was " productive," while all public expenditure, which taxes paid for, was " unproductive." But this idea is fallacious, and the supposed distinction which it implies has long been discredited. The only economic test of the " productiveness " of any expenditure is its productiveness of economic welfare, and public expenditure on education and health, for example, is often productive of greater economic welfare than private expenditure on luxuries, or even on new capital goods.[1]

[1] See Ch. XVIII, and especially §7.

None the less, it is an ingrained habit with many "respectable authorities" on public finance,—statesmen and city magnates, no less than textbook writers—somewhat uncritically to deplore that growth of public expenditure which, independently of war and preparations for war, has been steadily proceeding in all civilised communities for many years past. A long series of Chancellors of the Exchequer have harangued successive Parliaments upon this theme with traditional gloom and set phrases of dismay. But a Chancellor of the Exchequer deprecating in the House of Commons expenditure sanctioned by the Cabinet, of which he is, or should be, one of the most influential members, is surely a slightly absurd, if not almost an unconstitutional, spectacle. For, if he has not considered the expenditure to be reasonably necessary, he should have resigned.

It is a truth not confined to public finance that "our great need is economy." But there is a sharp distinction to be drawn between false and true economy, between spending as little as we can, regardless of the results attained, and spending whatever is necessary in order to produce the best results attainable,—in short, between spending little and spending wisely.[1]

§ 2. If, therefore, public finance is to be treated as a branch of science, economic or political, and not merely as a string of catchpenny maxims, one funda-

[1] "Mere parsimony is not economy. Expense and great expense may be an essential part in true economy. Economy is a distributive virtue and consists not in saving but in selection. Parsimony requires no providence, no sagacity, no powers of combination, no comparison, no judgment. Mere instinct may produce this false economy in perfection. The other economy has larger views. It demands a discriminating judgment and a firm sagacious mind." (Burke *Works*, V., p. 229.)

mental principle must lie at the root of it. This we may call the Principle of Maximum Social Advantage. Most of the operations of public finance resolve themselves into a series of transfers of purchasing power. These transfers are made, by taxation or otherwise, from certain individuals to public authorities, and back again from these authorities, by way of public expenditure, to other individuals, some of whom, such as policemen or contractors, render services in return, while others, such as old age pensioners, do not.[1] This distinction between transfers in payment for services rendered, and transfers to which no services are related, is important in classifications of public expenditure. But it need not detain us here. As a result of these operations of public finance, changes take place in the amount and in the nature of the wealth which is produced, and in the distribution of that wealth among individuals and classes. Are these changes in their aggregate effects socially advantageous? If so the operations are justified; if not, not. The best system of public finance is that which secures the maximum social advantage from the operations which it conducts. This principle is obvious, simple and far-reaching, though its practical application is often very difficult. But the difficulty is inherent in the subject, and cannot legitimately be avoided by substituting a wrong principle for a right one, in order to arrive more easily at practical conclusions.

§ 3. In seeking to apply this principle we need to have before us certain tests of social advantage. The

[1] Sometimes the beneficiaries of public expenditure receive, not purchasing power, in the form of money, but specific goods or services, such as uniforms, education or medical treatment.

first which suggests itself is the need to preserve the community, assuming it to be worth preserving in its existing form, against internal disorders and external attacks. How this should best be done falls outside the scope of this discussion. But it is a question of wise public policy at home and abroad, and not merely of expenditure on armaments and police. If any community in its existing form is not worth preserving, it is the business of statesmen to change its form. And, in any case, it is their business to increase the welfare, both economic and non-economic, of its members.

This brings us to the more strictly economic tests of social advantage, with which this book is primarily concerned. The two chief conditions of an increase in the economic welfare of any community are, first, improvements in production, and second, improvements in the distribution of what is produced. Improvements in production resolve themselves into increases of productive power, so that a larger product per head of the population shall be obtained with a smaller effort, and improvements in the organisation of production, so as to reduce to a minimum the waste of economic resources, through misdirection and unemployment. Improvements in distribution resolve themselves into a reduction in the great inequality, which is found in most civilised communities, in the incomes of different individuals and families, and a reduction in the great variability, between different periods of time, of the incomes of particular individuals and families, especially among the poorer sections of the community. A reduction in inequality is desirable, in order that income may be distributed, at any given time, more in accordance with individual and family needs at that time, and with capacity to make good use of income. A reduction in variability is desirable, in order that there may be a greater stability, through time, in the economic life of the community, and particularly in the incomes and employment of individuals. Such reduction in variability is another aspect of the better organisation of production. To meet changes, through time, in individual and family needs, is a separate problem. All these are well accepted canons of economic improvement, and in so far as the operations of public finance can bring about improvement on the whole, such operations are justified.

It should be added that the statesman is a trustee for the future, no less than for the present. Individuals die, but the community, of which they form a part, lives on. The statesman, therefore, should prefer a larger social advantage in the future to a smaller one to-day.

§ 4. With these applications of the Principle of Maximum Social Advantage we shall be concerned in more detail later. But at this point a few negative conclusions may usefully be drawn, as correctives to certain popular arguments.

It is impossible " to make an estimate," as is sometimes suggested, " of what this country, taking its income into consideration, could really afford in the way of public expenditure." For what can be " afforded " depends partly on how the money is raised, and partly on how it is spent. We cannot afford the expense of an unnecessary war, or even of an unnecessary public department, however the money is raised. On the other hand we may be able to afford a considerable expenditure in various desirable directions, if the money is raised by one scheme of taxation, but not if it is raised by another. Unless hedged about with many qualifications and assumptions, the "taxable capacity" of a community is a phrase which has very little meaning.[1]

Again, it is not universally true that "private individuals spend money better than government does," and the general restriction of public expenditure cannot be defended on this basis. Gladstone, indeed, used to speak of "leaving money to fructify in the pockets of the people," as though it were a ripening cheese, and to defend this policy as preferable to the maintenance of taxation, even when the chief purpose of the latter was the more rapid reduction of national debt. But he and most of his generation were blind to the advantages of public expenditure on such objects as old age pensions, provision against sickness and unemployment, and the like. Amid the grave financial difficulties of the period through which we are passing we need to scrutinise more closely than usual the expenditure of private individuals, no less than of public authorities. This truth is not yet as widely emphasised as it should be. Thus in the early summer of 1920 I noticed one day the headlines of two newspapers, side by side. One pilloried "The Spendthrifts" and contained an article attacking the Government for paying large salaries to officials at the Ministry of Transport; the other advertised "Ascot Last Day," and informed me, with an air of regret for the good old days, that some ladies were wearing only four new dresses during the six days of that race meeting, instead of the six which were

[1] See Note on "Taxable Capacity" at the end of Ch. XII.

customary before the war. "Retrenchment" is a blessed word, but it should be applied to private no less than to public extravagance. It is not wisdom to cut down public expenditure simply in order that private individuals may have more to spend as they please.

On the other hand, it is not universally true, as some modern writers suggest, that "government spends money better than private individuals do," and the general expansion of public expenditure cannot be defended on this basis. It may often be true that, on the average, public spending out of the proceeds of taxation is of greater social advantage than the private spending, which would have taken place if the taxation had not been imposed. But it does not follow that it would be socially advantageous to increase public expenditure and correspondingly to diminish private expenditure. For it may not be the most useful parts of the former that will expand, or the most useless parts of the latter that will be cut off. A Government with more money to spend may spend it on projects which are not worth what they cost. A rich frequenter of Ascot, with more taxes to pay, may pay them, not out of what he spends on his wife's dresses or his own drinks, but out of what he might otherwise have invested in some useful enterprise, such as the building of working-class houses.

Finally, to take a misconception of another kind, "taxation for revenue only" is a shallow and mistaken precept. All taxes have effects besides the mere raising of revenue, and the best taxes are those which, in addition to raising the revenue required, have on the whole the best effects. It is the business of statesmen to investigate the effects of various alternative taxes, and to act upon the results of their investigations, not to set up for themselves a self-denying ordinance against possible well-doing. Yet so deeply is this precept embedded in the tradition of British financial policy that, for example, even Harcourt in 1894 disclaimed any "ulterior aims" in his reform of the Death Duties, though the ulterior *effects* of his policy were readily visible to all intelligent observers, who approved or disapproved of his policy according as they approved or disapproved of its tendency towards the gradual break up of large landed estates.

The persistence of the precept in this country may be accounted for, partly, by the Parliamentary conception, strengthened by the terms of the Parliament Act of 1911, of "Money Bills," as Bills which provide for the raising of revenue and for no other object and, partly, by a widespread opinion that the instrument of taxation should not be used for any other purpose, except that of raising revenue. But, as will be argued later, this narrow opinion has no logical basis. Thus it is sometimes thought to be a good argument against a protective tariff that it has other effects besides raising revenue. But this is, in fact, a very bad argument. For what opponents of a protective tariff need to prove is, not that it *has other effects*, for that is obvious, but that these effects are worse than those of some alternative method of raising an equal revenue. To this simple but comprehensive doctrine we continually return. Take account of all the probable effects, which can reasonably be foreseen, of any financial proposal which is under discussion ; strike a balance of probable gain and loss to the community ;

compare this balance with that of alternative proposals, and act upon the results of this comparison. Those who are oppressed by a sense of the difficulty of this calculus, should console themselves with the saying of the ancient Greeks that " it is not the easy things, but the difficult things, that are beautiful."

CHAPTER III

PUBLIC FINANCE AND PRIVATE FINANCE

§ 1. It is instructive to compare public with private finance, and this is the task of the present chapter. Broadly speaking, it is true to say that, while an individual's income determines the amount of his possible expenditure, a public authority's expenditure determines the amount of its necessary income. In other words, while an individual adjusts expenditure to income, a public authority adjusts income to expenditure. But to this broad statement there are qualifications.

To some extent an individual adjusts income to expenditure. If he marries, and especially if he makes himself responsible for a number of dependents, his estimate of necessary expenditure will rise and he may decide to increase his income by working harder and sacrificing leisure. On the other hand, when his children have become self-supporting, his estimate of necessary expenditure may fall, and he may decide to work less hard and to take more leisure. To some extent, again, a public authority adjusts expenditure to income. In bad times, when its income falls off, it may practise retrenchment, and in good times, when its income increases, it may embark on policies hitherto considered too expensive.

The adjustment of an individual's income and expenditure need not be exact in any given year. " There is no special sanctity in the period in which the earth revolves round the sun." A year is a convenient accounting period for some purposes, but not for others. If an individual's expenditure exceeds his income, the excess may be met out of savings made in previous years, or from the sale of assets. Or he may run into debt, either by straightforward borrowing, or by leaving bills unpaid, in which case, in effect, he borrows from his creditors. And if his income exceeds his expenditure, the surplus income is available either for investment or for expenditure in the future.

Similarly, the adjustment of a public authority's income and expenditure need not be exact in any given year. When its income exceeds its expenditure, it has a realised surplus, which is available for future uses. Again, when its expenditure exceeds its income, a public authority, like an individual, may draw on its savings, if any, or sell some of its assets, or run into debt. But here a point of difference arises. For a public authority may raise either an internal or an external loan, that is to say, may borrow either from those who are subject to its authority, or from those who are not. Or again it may make ends meet by inflating the currency. But an individual cannot raise an internal loan. The nearest approach he can make to such a transaction is, if he keeps two banking accounts, by borrowing from one for the benefit of the other. Nor can an individual inflate the currency by decreeing that his I.O.U.'s shall be legal tender.[1]

§ 2. In some economic text-books it is said that an individual so distributes his expenditure on various commodities and services, that the marginal utilities of

[1] See Ch. XXVI for a fuller discussion of the questions raised in this paragraph.

all these expenditures are equal, and the total utility of the whole expenditure a maximum. It is one of the chief advantages of a money economy that it makes it possible for this to be done, and for this reason we may anticipate the survival of money even in the socialistic communities which the future may bring forth.[1] In reality most individuals do not thus equalise their marginal utilities with any great exactitude, but in the schemes of expenditure of all except the least intelligent, who have no scheme at all, there is an approach towards such equalisation.

A public authority, not being a person except in a legal sense, cannot estimate the marginal utilities of its various expenditures as an individual can. But the general principle, on which statesmen should attempt to act, is the same. The marginal utility *to the community* of all forms of public expenditure should be equal, and the distribution of a given total of expenditure between different objects is thus theoretically determined.[2]

§ 3. What, however, should determine the total of public expenditure? Here, again, the theoretical answer is clear. Public expenditure in every direction should be carried just so far, that the advantage to the community of a further small increase in any direction is just counterbalanced by the disadvantage of a corresponding small increase in taxation or in receipts from

[1] In the Soviet Union the use of money was soon resumed after a brief and unsatisfactory experiment in "moneyless economy."

[2] It should be noticed, however, that a statesman, in estimating the marginal utility of any form of public expenditure, must follow an objective standard of public welfare, or social advantage. An individual, on the other hand, follows a subjective standard of utility, or private advantage, linked with an objective standard of price.

any other source of public income. This gives the ideal total both of public expenditure and of public income. The ideal distribution of this total public income between different taxes and other sources of income is similarly given by the requirement that the marginal social disadvantages, or disutilities, of raising income from all these sources should be equal.

It is not to be imagined that public authorities, any more than individuals, ever achieve perfect solutions of these complex problems of balancing marginal utilities and disutilities. But some statesmen miss perfection by a longer chalk than others. In practice these problems of public finance are settled by a tug-of-war between rival spending Departments, and between spending Departments and the Treasury, modified by pressure from other influential quarters—elected persons, organised interests, newspaper editors and so forth. And, in practice, neither public authorities nor individuals are often required to rearrange the whole oftheir schemes of expenditure from top to bottom. Certain expenditures are actually going on, and the problem is usually restricted to the desirability of making certain changes, which affect only a small proportion of the whole. Moreover, much expenditure, particularly by public authorities, is commonly based on legal contracts, or on quasi-contractual assurances which cannot, without serious disturbance, be varied at short notice.

§ 4. None the less, for making deliberate changes in its income and expenditure, and particularly for making increases, a public authority is generally in a much better position than an individual. The chief reason for this is obvious; it has the whole wealth of the community on which to draw, in addition to the possibility of raising external loans. But there is another, though less important, reason. In some theoretical discussions it is suggested that individuals go on working, until the marginal utility of more product, or more pay, just falls short of the marginal disutility of more work. But this is only true of those who work independently of others, boys picking blackberries, to take Marshall's familiar example, or artists, or free-lance journalists. But most people have to fit in their hours of work with those of others, and often with collective agreements and sometimes with Acts of Parliament. Some would like to work more and others less than they do, but have to conform with general arrangements. Public authorities are usually free from this disability and can make their own financial arrangements without much regard to what others are doing. Expenditure on armaments is an exception to this general rule.

§ 5. In the pure theory of individual finance, the principle of the equalisation of marginal utilities includes, as a special case, the equalisation of the marginal utilities of present and future expenditure, and hence determines the provision which individuals will make for the future. Most people, however, discount the future to some extent. For its satisfactions, and equally its dissatisfactions, quite apart from any factor of uncertainty, look shrivelled to the normal eye beside equal satisfactions, or dissatisfactions, in the present. Moreover, one's life is, in fact, uncertain and one's descendants, after a certain point, uninteresting. Most individuals, therefore, make less provision for the future than they would do if their power of visualising it were stronger or if they expected their earthly life to last forever, or even for a hundred years. But, since the community outlasts the individual, and since, as was pointed out in the last chapter, the statesman should regard himself as trustee for the future, the latter is not entitled to discount the future at so high a rate as most individuals in their private capacity normally do. Indeed, it is doubtful whether he is entitled to discount it at all. It follows that, in so far as future conditions can be reasonably foreseen, statesmen should sometimes aim at making a more generous provision for the future than would be made by private individuals left to themselves. Important examples of this principle will be given later, when we come to deal with public expenditure. But the task of statesmen will often be rendered difficult by the political pressure of those who repeat the ancient question, "What has posterity done for me, that I should do so much for posterity?"

PART II

PUBLIC INCOME

Chapter IV

SOURCES OF PUBLIC INCOME

§ 1. The income of a public authority may be defined either in a broad or a narrow sense. In the broad sense it includes all "incomings" or "receipts," in the narrow sense only those receipts which are included in the ordinary conception of "revenue." Thus the attentive reader will have noticed that the word was used in the broad sense in Chapter I, § 3, where it was said that public borrowings form part of public income, but in the narrow sense in Chapter III, § 1, where it was pointed out that a public authority's income may fall short of its expenditure in any given year and the deficit be made up by borrowing. As between these two senses, the context is generally a sufficiently good interpreter but, where necessary, ambiguity may be avoided by using the terms "public receipts" and "public revenue" to denote public income in its broad and in its narrow sense respectively. The chief elements included in the conception of public receipts, but excluded from that of public revenue, are receipts from public borrowings and from the sale of public assets, such as war stores, and paper money newly printed and delivered from the public printing press.

§ 2. The classification of the sources of public income is discussed at great length by many writers, but the chief purpose of any such classification should be to throw light on the nature of public income and, judged by this standard, much of the discussion in the textbooks is of small practical utility.

The first and most important practical distinction is between taxation and other sources of income. A tax is a compulsory charge imposed by a public authority and, as Professor Taussig puts it, "the essence of a tax, as distinguished from other charges by Government, is the absence of a direct *quid pro quo* between the taxpayer and the public authority."[1] We have, on the other hand, as an important source of public income, the prices charged by a public authority for specific services and commodities supplied by it, including the prices charged for the use of public property. Generally speaking, these prices are paid voluntarily by private persons, who enter into contracts, express or implied, with public authorities, whereas taxes are paid compulsorily.

Developing the broad distinction between taxes and prices, we have on the one side (1) taxes ordinarily so called; (2) tributes and indemnities, whether arising out of war or otherwise; (3) forced loans, such as old time princes of doubtful credit used often to extract from Jews and others, but which are not much used in modern public finance; and (4) pecuniary penalties for offences, imposed by Courts of Justice. On the other side we have (5) receipts from public property passively held, e.g. public lands leased to tenants, or the British Government's Suez Canal shares; (6) receipts from enterprises carried on by a public authority which does not make use of monopoly power to raise its prices above "the competitive level"; (7)

[1] *Principles of Economics*, II, p. 483.

fees or payments made for services, not in the nature of business services, performed by a public official, such as the registration of births; and (8) receipts from voluntary public loans.

Four other sources of public income may be distinguished which do not fall completely under either of our two main headings, namely, (9) receipts from enterprises carried on by a public authority which does make use of monopoly power to raise its prices above "the competitive level"; (10) receipts from "special assessments"; (11) receipts from the use of the printing press, for the purpose of meeting public expenditure by the issue of paper money; and (12) voluntary gifts. Many enterprises are carried on by public authorities with the primary object of raising revenue by the use of monopoly power. Thus many governments have established State monopolies of matches and tobacco. That part of the price of such commodities, which exceeds their cost of production (including normal profits), is indistinguishable, in principle, from a tax on such commodities.[1] A special assessment is an American invention, defined by Professor Seligman as "a compulsory contribution, levied in proportion to the special benefits derived, to defray the cost of a specific improvement to property undertaken in the public interest."[2] It is a device for securing for the public treasury part of the unearned

[1] In practice, it is not a simple matter to divide, with any degree of precision, the price of a commodity or service monopolised by a public authority into its component parts, competitive price plus tax. For, in the absence of competition, the competitive price can only be roughly estimated. And the cost of production of either a private competitor or a private monopolist might differ widely from that of the public authority.

[2] *Essays in Taxation*, p. 283.

increment in the value of fixed property, which arises, for example, in the neighbourhood of a newly opened thoroughfare. A special assessment resembles a tax in that it is a compulsory payment, but differs from it in that the payer has received a definite and direct *quid pro quo.* In the latter respect it resembles a price, but differs from it in that the payment is not voluntary and does not arise out of a contract with the public authority. In this country such a charge, under the title of "betterment," is imposed by local authorities in connection with public improvement and planning schemes. The issue of new paper money by a public authority is not quite the same thing as the imposition of a tax, though its effect, through reducing the value of money, is similar to that of a general tax upon all commodities and services.[1] Voluntary gifts form, unfortunately, only an infinitesimal part of the income of public authorities. They are exemplified in this country by "conscience money," which, however, is usually only a delayed part-payment of taxes which have already been evaded, and by occasional gifts for the reduction of the national debt.

§ 3. The boundary lines between the various kinds of public incomes just enumerated are not, in most cases, clear cut, but one kind shades gradually into another. Thus taxes shade gradually into prices, since the services rendered by public authorities to taxpayers often stand in a somewhat indefinite relation to the payments made by the latter. Local rates for the supply of water, where no meters are used, illustrate this.

Again, Professor Taussig's description of a tax, quoted above, would cover penalties for offences, the

[1] See Ch. XV for a further discussion of this point.

underlying idea of which is clearly distinct. The distinction between taxes and penalties is one of motive; a public authority imposes taxes mainly to obtain revenue and enacts penalties mainly to deter from certain acts. If motorists were fined £1 for every infraction of the speed limit, and the money were collected periodically, such fines might be regarded as a tax on high speed, comparable to a tax on petrol. But if, at each successive offence by the same motorist, the fine were increased, and the offender finally put in prison or deprived of his license to drive, so that no more fines were obtainable from him, those already collected would clearly be in the nature of penalties and not taxes. Similarly with customs duties, in the language of which, as Swift remarked, two plus two is often less than three. If, as the rate of a particular duty is increased, the revenue yielded increases, the duty is predominantly a tax. But when the rate is increased above the point at which the yield in revenue is a maximum, it is clear that some element of penalty is present, and we finally reach a duty of prohibitive amount, whose yield is very small or even non-existent, and which is closely akin, in the case of an import duty for example, to a simple prohibition of importation, with a penalty for infraction. Intermediate between a tax and a penalty is a duty primarily designed to check consumption, such as the liquor duties, the raising of which in 1909 was said to have caused many Scottish farmers to drink milk instead of whisky, or the increase in railway fares during the war which was defended partly on the ground that people were travelling too much, and hindering the use of rolling stock for military purposes.

Deterrence, again, shades into discrimination, as in schemes of Imperial Preference, in special taxes on land values or on mineral royalties or on war profits, or in lower rates of income tax on "earned" than on "unearned" incomes.

§ 4. It has already been pointed out that the monopoly profits, if any, of a public enterprise are closely akin to a tax. There is no substantial distinction, from this point of view, between the French Government's monopoly profits from the sale of tobacco and the British Government's revenue from tobacco duties imposed on private traders. Public enterprises, which make monopoly profits, shade into those which do not. The test is not whether a public authority has an absolute monopoly of the supply of any commodity or service, for, in the first place, very few monopolies are absolute, when substitutes, actual and potential, are taken into account. A legal Government monopoly of railway transport, for instance, is open to competition from private transport both by water, road and air. And, in the second place, monopoly need not be absolute, in order to permit of the use of monopoly power to raise prices above cost of production. This power is available, as a general rule, wherever a considerable proportion of the total supply of any commodity or service is under a single control. The test is whether such monopoly power is, or is not, actually used. For a public authority conducting an enterprise may have a large degree of monopoly power, but may decide that it is in the public interest that the product of the enterprise shall be sold at, or even below, cost price. The practical difficulty of applying this test lies in the determination of the cost of production of the products of a public enterprise. What allowances for interest, depreciation, etc., should be made? Anyone who doubts the reality of these difficulties should try to determine the cost of production of British postal services.

There is no sharp distinction between fees on the one hand, and taxes and public monopoly profits on the other. For the cost of performing a service is often less than the fee charged for performing it. Nor is there any sharp distinction between fees and receipts from public enterprises generally. For there is no sharp distinction between those services which are "in the nature of business services" and those which are not. Thus some writers have proposed to class all postal receipts as fees. Again, there is no sharp distinction between receipts from public enterprises and receipts from public property passively held, for some supervision and management are required even in the most humdrum administration of public lands and, if schemes of afforestation, irrigation, etc., are undertaken, these constitute an enterprise no less than the delivery of letters and telegrams.

The general conclusion of this discussion is that the sources of public income may indeed be classified, but that many of the distinctions involved are not clear cut and that, here as elsewhere, the search for a classification is more instructive than the classification when found.

CHAPTER V

TAXATION AND SOME DISTINCTIONS BETWEEN TAXES

§ 1. We have seen that a tax is a compulsory contribution imposed by a public authority, irrespective of the exact amount of service rendered to the taxpayer in return, and not imposed as a penalty for any legal offence. Auberon Herbert, who was a philosophic anarchist, thought that taxation was never morally justifiable, but this is a rare and eccentric opinion which may be ignored. Yet taxation, though justifiable, might not be necessary, or might be necessary to only a small extent, if other sources of public income were more prolific, if, for instance, public authorities owned larger quantities of income-yielding property or if it was more the fashion among wealthy people to make large voluntary gifts to the State. If the London County Council were the sole ground landlord within its area, London rates would be very much lower than they are.[1] Again, if voluntary contributions to the Treasury were made to bear the same vague, but perceptible, relation to the conferment of "honours," which contributions to the funds of some political parties do now, the burden of taxation in Great Britain

[1] A Canadian student who attended my lectures told me that the Municipality of Guelph, Ontario, imposes no local taxation, but lives entirely on the rent of municipally owned land leased to the Canadian Pacific Railway.

might be lessened, at any rate until a greatly increased supply had seriously reduced the purchase price of a Viscounty or a Knighthood of the British Empire. Even so, the ingenious invention of new "honours" might keep the tide flowing for a time, but at this stage of the business we should be gathering public income, not from voluntary gifts, but from a skilfully conducted public enterprise. As things are now ordered, however, a large amount of taxation is necessary in all modern communities and, as public expenditure increases, taxation increases also.

§ 2. The classification of taxes in many textbook discussions is even more arid ground than the classification of public income in general, but a few distinctions may be noticed in passing. That most commonly made is between direct and indirect taxes. The idea usually underlying this distinction is that a direct tax is really paid by the person on whom it is legally imposed, while an indirect tax is imposed on one person, but paid partly or wholly by another, *owing to a consequential change in the terms of some contract or bargain between them.* A tax is not held to be indirect merely because it is collected from one person and paid by another. Thus, under Schedule A of the British Income Tax, the so-called "Landlord's Property Tax," which is a tax on the income derived from the ownership of land and buildings, is collected from the occupier who, however, has a statutory right to deduct it from the rent which he pays to the owner, any contract not to deduct it being legally void. Neither the imposition of this tax, therefore, nor any change in its amount causes any change in the terms of the bargain already entered into between the occupier and the owner.

It may be described as a direct tax legally imposed upon the owner, but collected from the occupier.

An indirect tax, in short, is conceived as one which can be shifted or passed on; a direct tax as one which cannot. This distinction is less fundamental and useful than is commonly supposed. The reasons for this will appear more clearly when we come to consider the incidence and effects of taxation. Nor is the distinction always clear in common usage. An income tax is generally regarded as a direct tax; but the United States Supreme Court in 1868 held it to be indirect, when they wished to declare it constitutionally valid. This, however, was only the economics of clever lawyers in a tight place. An inheritance tax is generally regarded as a direct tax and so are other taxes on property. On the other hand, taxes on commodities and transactions are generally regarded as indirect. But doubts begin to arise when we reflect that commodities only differ from most other forms of material property in being less durable, and that an inheritance tax is merely a tax on a particular class of transactions.

The distinction between direct and indirect taxes is made by some writers to turn on whether or not it is intended by the statesmen, who impose it, that a tax shall be shifted. But this is to introduce an additional and needless difficulty. For the intentions of statesmen and the facts of incidence may be at variance. Some statesmen, indeed, do not realise the problem of incidence at all, and think that all taxes are paid by those on whom they are legally imposed. I remember asking a member of the British Government in 1911, whether either the Cabinet or the Treasury had made any estimate of the incidence of the weekly levies imposed on employers and employees under the National Insurance Act of that year. But the Minister could not see that there was anything to estimate. "The men pay 4d.," he said, "and the employers pay 3d. and the State pays 2d., and so the men get 9d. for 4d." It is best in this matter for the economist to ignore the intentions of the statesman.

It is often vaguely supposed to be a sign of financial virtue to "keep a balance" between direct and indirect taxation, an idea encouraged by Gladstone's well-known simile, in which he likened these two sources of revenue to "two attractive sisters," as between whom he was "perfectly impartial," believing that, as Chancellor of the Exchequer, it was "not only allowable, but even an act of duty, to pay my addresses to them both."

This notion of "keeping a balance" is bound up with ideas about the proper distribution of the burden of taxation between persons, which will be discussed later, and with the belief that direct taxes are paid by the rich and indirect by the poor. There are no theoretical, but some practical, grounds for this last belief. Most existing direct taxes in modern communities do, in fact, involve larger contributions from the rich than from the poor, in proportion to their incomes, and the opposite is the case with many existing indirect taxes. But the position would be reversed, if direct taxation were limited to a poll tax of equal amount on every citizen, and indirect taxation to duties on luxuries which only the rich could afford to pay.

§ 3. There are various other distinctions between taxes which, though sometimes discussed at great length, are a good deal less important than they seem at first sight. Consider, for example, the distinction between taxes on income and taxes on capital. It can make no difference whether a given revenue is raised by a flat-rate tax assessed on the annual value or by a similar tax assessed on the capital value of property, so long as the ratio of annual value to capital value is the same in all cases affected by the tax. If, for instance, this ratio is one to twenty, a tax of one and eightpence in the pound on an income, or annual value, of £500 will bring in the same revenue as a tax of a penny in the pound on a capital value of £10,000. If, however, the ratio varies, a tax on capital value will be heavier than a tax on annual value, yielding the same revenue, in those cases where the ratio of capital to annual value is abnormally high, and less heavy where it is abnormally low. For example, owners of undeveloped or " under-developed " land will be hit harder than the owners of fully developed land. This is why those, who wish to compel landowners to " put their land to the fullest use,"[1] advocate a tax based on the capital, rather than the annual, value of the land. Similarly holders of gilt-edged will be hit harder than holders of speculative securities.

The above distinction between taxes *assessed on* income and capital respectively is often confused with the quite separate distinction between taxes *paid out of* income and capital respectively. But there is no reason why a tax assessed on capital should not be paid out of income, nor conversely. A man liable to death

[1] " Fullest use " here means that which, taking account of the tax, is most profitable to the private owner. This is not necessarily identical with the use which brings the maximum social advantage. To secure the latter intelligent geographical planning is required.

duties may pay them out of income; a man may sell securities or borrow from his bank in order to pay income tax. The precept "tax income, not capital," sometimes elevated to the dignity of a maxim of public finance, is, therefore, ambiguous. It may refer to the source of payment, and amount to an injunction that taxation should check the accumulation of capital as little as possible. Or it may refer to the basis of assessment, and indicate a preference for an income, rather than a capital, basis. Both these alternative meanings of the precept will claim attention later.

§ 4. Another distinction sometimes drawn is between taxes assessed on property and taxes assessed on commodities. This distinction, as already remarked, turns on relative durability. Land is evidently property from this point of view, sugar evidently a commodity. Houses and machines are intermediate, being less durable than land, but more durable than sugar. In practice, this distinction often turns largely on whether the tax is imposed periodically or once for all. In the former case the object of the tax may generally be regarded as property, in the latter as a commodity. Nor in the former case need the period be regular. An inheritance tax, though levied at irregular intervals, may reasonably be called a tax on property. British local rates, being a periodic tax on the annual value of land and buildings, treat houses as property, but a tax levied once for all on the value of newly built houses would treat these as commodities.

Taxes on commodities may be either "specific" or *ad valorem*. A specific tax is based upon some physical measurement such as a unit of weight or volume, *e.g.*, a tax of a shilling a pound on tea or fifty shillings a gallon on beer. An *ad valorem* tax is based upon a unit of value, *e.g.*, a tax of a third of their value on imported mouth-organs.

§ 5. A distinction of a different kind is between taxes intended to be only temporary and taxes intended to be comparatively permanent. A special tax, whether assessed on an individual's income, his capital or his war profits, designed to pay off in a short time a large amount of public debt, would be an example of the former. The British income tax, at any rate since Gladstone's death,[1] is an example of the latter, though many taxpayers hope that the present rates of tax will not be permanent. The chief value of this distinction lies in its bearing on the probable conduct of taxpayers, which will vary with their expectations regarding future taxation.[2]

§ 6. A distinction is sometimes suggested between taxes on persons and taxes on things. But this form of words may be used in at least three different senses. In the most natural sense, taxes on persons would include, on the one hand, a poll tax, either equal in amount for all persons or assessed in some quite arbitrary manner and, on the other, all taxes based on purely personal characteristics of the taxpayer, such as his height, weight or religion, or the colour of his eyes or hair, while taxes on things would include all taxes based on criteria external to the taxpayer, such as his income, the rent which he pays for his house, or the amount of tobacco which he smokes. But in this sense the distinction would be without practical

[1] Gladstone always regarded it as temporary and in 1874, on the eve of a general election, promised to repeal it. But he lost the election.

[2] See Ch. X, §§3-8.

value, since all actual taxes, with few and unimportant exceptions, would be on things and not on persons. The tax on the wearing of beards, imposed by Peter the Great with the object of encouraging cleanliness, was, however, a personal tax in this sense.

A second sense, in which the distinction has sometimes been used, implies that some taxes are paid by persons and other by things.[1] But this is a very gross error. It is natural, when thinking of the basis of assessment, to speak of taxes on land, on imports, on industry and trade. But neither inanimate objects, such as plots of land and bundles of imported goods, nor general terms, such as " industry " and " trade," are endowed with pockets or banking accounts, out of which they, as distinct from persons, can pay taxes. It is a platitude that all taxes are paid by persons, not by things.

In a third sense, taxes on persons are sometimes treated as equivalent to direct, and taxes on things to indirect, taxes. But the terms " direct " and " indirect " are here used in what is called by some " an administrative sense." Thus some " practical financiers . . . regard those taxes as direct which are levied on permanent and recurring occasions,

[1] See, for example, Giffen's observations on pp. 93-4, of *Memoranda on the Classification and Incidence of Imperial and Local Taxes* (C. 9258, 1899) :—" rates on real property are for the most part burdens on the property itself, and therefore not taxation in the proper sense of the term ; in other words not contributions to the expense of the State by the individuals who bear the rates in the same way that the Income Tax is a contribution by those who bear it. . . Duties upon the succession to property at death are not taxes upon the dying, because they are not levied till they have ceased to own the property, and not taxes upon the inheritors because they only inherit by the will and permission of the State itself."

while charges on occasional and particular events are placed under the category of indirect taxation."[1] There is no logical connection between this view of the distinction between direct and indirect taxation and the view considered above, which makes the distinction turn on incidence. This tiresome duplication of terms is a further argument for their abandonment. Other writers have drawn a distinction, roughly equivalent to that between direct and indirect taxes in an administrative sense, between " personal " and " specific " taxes, and again between " subjective " and " objective " taxes. But the whole idea is woolly and, so far as the study of first principles is concerned, unprofitable.

§ 7. There are certain taxes, the place of which in tax classifications may at first sight appear doubtful. Stamp duties, taxes on business profits, on sales and on turnover are examples. But a little reflection will make it clear that a stamp duty or stamp tax is not a special kind of tax, but only a special method of collecting taxes. People are required in certain circumstances to buy stamps of a certain value from a public authority and to attach them to certain documents. Many taxes on transactions are collected by this means, and any tax could be so collected. The question is simply one of administrative convenience. Thus some of those, who have advocated a weekly income tax on wage earners, have proposed to collect it by means of additional stamps on health insurance cards. Again, a tax on business profits is only a tax on a particular kind of income, while a tax on sales or on turnover is only a tax on the commodities sold or turned over.

[1] Bastable, *Public Finance*, p. 291.

Chapter VI

SOME CHARACTERISTICS OF A GOOD TAX SYSTEM

§ 1. Any system of public finance must be looked at as a whole, before any final judgment can be passed upon its merits or demerits. So, too, any tax system must be looked at as a whole. For different taxes may, in certain of their effects, correct and balance one another.

Assuming that in a given year a given revenue is to be raised by taxation, alternative tax systems will result in alternative distributions of the total burden of taxation, which will itself be greater under some systems than others, and in other alternative effects upon the economic welfare of the community. These matters will be discussed in the next seven chapters. But in this chapter a few preliminary points will first be noticed.

§ 2. The comparative advantages of single tax and multiple tax systems have been much argued. Various types of single tax have been proposed. The Physiocrats proposed a single tax on the economic rent of land, because they thought that this was where all taxes ultimately fell, and that it would, therefore, save trouble and misunderstanding to put them there straight away. But this idea involved a false theory of incidence. Henry George made a similar proposal, partly because he thought that a tax on rent did not check industry, whereas all other taxes did, in which opinion there is a grain of truth, and partly for reasons of a supposedly ethical character, to which less weight need be attached. There are, however, two grave objections to a single tax of this kind. The first is that it would not, in most modern communities, bring in enough revenue to balance the public accounts. The second is that it would lead to a very bad distribution of the burden of taxation. For a millionaire, who owned no land, would pay no taxes, while a poor man, who had invested all his savings in the purchase of his house, would pay in taxation, in respect of the land on which it stood, a considerable proportion of his income. A single tax on land has no relation to individual "ability to pay."

A much stronger case can be made out for a single tax assessed on income. Such a tax could be made to yield all the tax revenue normally required, and, by means of graduation, differentiation and other devices, could be made to distribute the burden of taxation between individuals in whatever way was thought best. There are, however, in addition to certain arguments against *any* single tax, three objections to exclusive reliance upon an income tax. The first is that such a tax imposed upon small incomes is relatively difficult and expensive to collect.[1] The second is that it secures no special contribution from inheritors of wealth, a pre-eminently taxable class. The third is that it tends to check saving more than certain other taxes do.[2] The first objection might be overcome to some extent by administrative improvements, and indeed would not arise at all, if it were desired to

[1] See Ch. XII, § 1.
[2] See Ch. X.

distribute the burden of taxation in such a way as to exempt small incomes altogether. The second could be overcome by treating wealth acquired by inheritance or gift as taxable income at the time of its acquisition. There is a good deal to be said for doing this and it has sometimes been done, *e.g.*, in the United States income tax of 1861. The third could be overcome by exempting savings from taxable income, and thus imposing a single tax, not upon personal income, but upon personal expenditure. But, in the present state of our administrative technique, this scheme also encounters grave practical difficulties and would involve great expense and leave open large loopholes for undetected fraud. The easiest way of taxing expenditure is to tax commodities or services straightforwardly, and not in a roundabout fashion through personal incomes. But taxes on commodities must necessarily be multiple. No single tax on a particular commodity would bring in sufficient revenue. Moreover, if the attempt were made and the taxed commodity were one for which substitutes were easily available, heavy taxation would drive it out of use, while, if it were a necessity of life for which no substitutes were easily available, a very bad distribution of the burden of taxation would result, the poor paying a much larger proportion of their incomes than the rich.

A variant to a single tax assessed on income is one assessed on the capital value of property. The latter tax, however, has a smaller range than the former, since it does not fall upon incomes from work, but only upon the source of incomes from property. It is also the teaching both of theory and experience that income is a better basis for tax assessment than the capital value of property. For the former, given clear legal definitions, only raises questions of fact. But the latter raises questions not only of fact but of opinion, as regards the valuation of many forms of property which cannot be said to have a market value. Thus the comparative success of the British income tax as a financial instrument may be contrasted with the comparative failure of the general property tax in the United States, according to the testimony of Professor Seligman and other American authorities.[1]

§ 3. The preceding arguments against particular forms of single tax are reinforced by certain general arguments against any form of single tax. For, in the first place, anomalies as between persons, which are liable to arise under a single tax, are liable to be corrected under a multiplicity of taxes and, in the second place, evasions, which may be comparatively easy under a single tax, are more readily detected under the check and counter-check which a multiple tax system may provide. Thus valuations for death duties and the previous income tax returns of the deceased may be checked against one another.[2] Again, the ill-contrived land value duties of the British Budget of 1909, though they never brought in any appreciable revenue, necessitated a land valuation which, though never completed, is said to have more than paid for itself by the additions which it indirectly brought to the death duty revenue.

[1] Though some Americans point with pride to certain of their partial property taxes as powerful revenue raisers.

[2] And in Sweden, where the supply of spirits is limited to a fixed ration per head, a ration card is only issued if the applicant can produce a certificate to show that he has paid his income tax.

Thus the weight of argument against a single tax is heavy. In the case of local authorities, exercising comparatively few functions over a comparatively small area, there is something to be said, on grounds of convenience, for a single tax on "immobilia" or immovable property. Local rates in this country are a tax of this sort, based on the annual value of land plus buildings, though some classes of land and buildings are subject to exemption or abatements by way of "derating." It is often argued that rates would be better based on the capital, or even the annual, value of land only. For local rates are, in great measure, a tax on houses, which are not a good object of taxation. Moreover, heavy rates on business premises sometimes impose a very severe check upon production. But local rates are not, in reality, a single tax, for local authorities derive a considerable part of their revenue from grants-in-aid out of the proceeds of national taxation, and from the ownership of public property and the conduct of public enterprises in their own areas. And local rates are only in part a genuine tax. In part they represent prices paid by ratepayers for specific services rendered to them by local authorities. There is, however, a good deal to be said for giving local authorities power to levy certain local luxury taxes, as in some European cities.

§ 4. But though a multiple tax system is generally preferable to a single tax system, too great a multiplicity of taxes is not desirable. Advocates of "broadening the basis of taxation" are to be distrusted. Of this fellowship was Arthur Young, who said, "if I were to define a good system of taxation, it should be that of bearing lightly on an infinite number of points, heavily on none."[1] But there is not necessarily any less total pressure under such a system, for, as mathematicians at any rate are aware, the sum of an infinitely large number of infinitely small weights may be greater than a single moderate weight. Moreover, a large number of taxes, however small, usually involves a large cost and a large amount of vexation in collection.

The path of wisdom in this matter, for a modern community with a well developed economic life and a reasonably efficient administrative system, is fairly clear. It is best to rely on a few substantial taxes for the bulk of the tax revenue. In so far as it is desired to tax the rich, income and inheritance taxes are the best means; in so far as it is desired to tax the poor, taxes on a few commodities of wide consumption, preferably commodities not necessary to health and efficiency. Some commodities, of which alcohol is the most important example, may indeed be taxed on their merits, or, as some would say, on their demerits, apart from any question of the distribution of the burden of taxation between different sections of the community. Taxes on luxuries have their legitimate place and other taxes with special objects may be added, but it is desirable to keep their number within bounds.

Almost everywhere, and even in Great Britain, whose tax system, even after the adoption of a tariff in 1932, is simpler and more efficient than that of any other important modern community, so-called "historical causes" have led to a needless multiplicity of taxes and to needless complexity in methods of assessment. But, especially where multiplicity is

[1] Quoted by Bastable, *Public Finance*, p. 344.

reduced, particular taxes may need to be somewhat complex,—the British income tax and death duties for example—if the tax system as a whole is to be satisfactory.

§ 5. A further point of occasional controversy may be noticed here. Is it a characteristic of a good tax system that taxes should be "felt" as much, or as little, as possible? The plain man will be inclined to think that the best tax is that which is least felt, that is to say which causes the least inconvenience and conscious sacrifice to those who pay it. But some austere thinkers take the view that mankind can only learn through suffering, and that political responsibility can only be brought home to us through conscious payment of the price of greatness—or of folly, as the case may be. Thus some people believed that, unless the Germans paid, or at least tried to pay, an immense war indemnity, they would light-heartedly make war again in a few years time, and a Scottish Professor of Economics thought that we should be tempted to do the same, if we rashly destroyed, by means of a capital levy, the Great War Debt, which would otherwise be one of the most impressive of our national war memorials. It has also been maintained that, if income tax were resolutely imposed upon all, however poor, all would eagerly co-operate in checking wasteful expenditure, while the poor would also gain in moral stature. Men take sides in this controversy according to opinions not exclusively economic. Personally, I take sides with the plain man. In particular, I believe that, in a modern democratic state, the reaction to a universal income tax, newly imposed, would not be at all that imagined by the austere. The public mind would, I think, be less pre-occupied with checking public expenditure than with throwing out of power those responsible for the austere reform and with redistributing the burden of taxation according to some brusque canon of outraged popular equity. On the other hand, an increase in a well-established tax, such as local rates, undoubtedly creates a popular and somewhat indiscriminating demand for "economy."

§ 6. The practical application of a decision, in either sense, of the main controversy is not, however, wholly clear. Thus it is commonly supposed that an income tax is more keenly felt than taxes which, being levied on commodities, are wrapped up in their prices, as some of the medicines of childhood are wrapped up in jam. (The austere should pass a law requiring grocers to say of their jam, not "this is eighteen-pence a pound," but "this is one and fourpence a pound and the tax on sugar, to pay the interest on the War debt, is two-pence a pound.") But on the other hand, as will be argued later,[1] an income tax hits only marginal expenditure and marginal savings all round, whereas a tax on a particular commodity hits expenditure, including non-marginal expenditure, on that commodity only, and is thus apt to cause a greater loss of satisfaction. Moreover, when income tax is "deducted at the source," that is to say intercepted before his money income actually reaches the taxpayer, it is apt to be less keenly felt, than if he first receives his income in full and then at a later date, when he has already spent most of it, receives a demand note from the tax collector. An inheritance tax, again, is often less keenly felt than might be supposed, since its

[1] See Ch. X.

payment is generally made through the agency of executors, before the inheritors receive the balance of the property, and since the payment coincides both with a positive accretion of personal wealth to the inheritors and with other events, which should generally force considerations of tax payments into the background of their minds.

§ 7. An ingenious formula, of Cambridge origin, is that the rich should pay more taxation than they think, while the poor should think they pay more than they do. This double illusion, it is argued, will keep the rich contented and the poor virtuous, and will tend to maximise work and saving by all classes. But, whatever else may be said of this idea, it is more ingenious than practicable. It would be hard to create, and still harder to maintain, such an unstable equilibrium of errors.

A distinction may, indeed, be drawn between the subjective and the objective burden of taxation.[1] Corresponding to the same objective burden, as viewed by the statesman, there may be a different subjective burden on two different taxpayers, due to differences of taste and temperament, even if their economic situation, as regards income and other factors, is the same. Corresponding to two equal objective burdens, due to two different taxes, there may likewise be different subjective burdens for a particular taxpayer. Corresponding to a given objective burden, taxes which are "much felt" impose a heavier, and taxes which are "little felt" a lighter, subjective burden. But, in general, this distinction is only of secondary importance.

[1] And similarly between the subjective and the objective benefit of public expenditure.

The primary consideration is the objective burden, as measured by a given loss of resources to a taxpayer in a given economic situation. To this there corresponds what may be called a normal subjective burden. Deviations on either side from this normal are mainly due either to personal peculiarities of taxpayers, which cancel out in the average, or to transitory conditions, such as the novelty of a particular tax, which pass with time. The objective burden will vary only with variations in the loss of resources imposed by taxation, or in the economic situation of the taxpayer, as measured by his income, number of dependents, etc.

We may also, if we choose, distinguish between the weight and the burden of taxation; the weight absolute, in terms of commodities surrendered, the burden relative to the taxpayer's power to carry the weight.

CHAPTER VII

THE INCIDENCE OF TAXATION

§ 1. The problem of the incidence of a tax is commonly conceived as the problem of who pays it. More precisely we may say that the incidence is upon those who bear the direct money burden of the tax. Every tax produces a number of economic effects, and it has been questioned whether it is either practicable or desirable to try to separate the special problem of incidence from the more general problem of effects. But clearly the attempt must be made, if anything is to be said on the distribution of the direct money burden of taxation, a subject to which many theorists and nearly all plain men attach importance.

A distinction must be drawn between the direct and the indirect burden of a tax, and also between the money burden and the real burden. The total direct money burden is equal to the total yield of the tax to the public treasury. To every shilling of revenue raised there corresponds a shilling of direct money burden, or incidence, falling upon someone.[1] To part with a shilling in payment of a tax means a greater sacrifice of economic welfare for a poor man than for a rich man. But that is a question, not of the incidence, but of the direct real burden of the tax. Again, when the price

[1] Except in the limiting case of escheat, that form of inheritance tax, under which the property of an intestate, who possesses no discoverable relatives however remote, reverts at his death to the State.

of sugar is raised by taxation, a family may be compelled to consume less sugar, and thereby to make a sacrifice of economic welfare. But that is a question, not of the incidence, but of the indirect real burden, of the tax. Again, when the tax on sugar is collected from the dealer in respect of his stocks and some time elapses between the collection of the tax and the sale of the stocks, the dealer is out of pocket by the amount of the interest, which he could otherwise have obtained during that period on the money paid to the tax collector. But that is a question, not of the incidence, but of the indirect money burden, of the tax.[1]

§ 2. Thus the incidence of a tax on sugar collected from the seller is wholly on the buyer, if, as a direct result of the tax, the price rises by at least the full amount of the tax; wholly on the seller, if the price does not rise at all; partly on the buyer and partly on the seller, if the price rises by an amount less than the full amount of the tax.

We may illustrate at this point the unsatisfactory character of the distinction, based on incidence, between direct and indirect taxes.[2] Before we can decide whether a particular tax is direct or indirect, in this sense, we must know its incidence, and this will often depend, not only on the nature of the tax, but on other circumstances. It is commonly assumed that a tax on a commodity is an indirect tax, which is "passed on," in whole or in part. But if, whether collected from buyers or sellers, it leaves the price unchanged, then it must be classed as a direct tax. For it is not then passed on. And, as will be seen later, such

[1] Compare, however, Ch. VIII, §4.
[2] Compare Ch. V, §2.

circumstances are not impossible. Again, the incidence of a tax on a monopolist varies with the character of the tax and, therefore, to take two examples which will be discussed later in this Chapter, a tax proportionate to output must be classed as indirect, while a tax independent of output will be direct.

It is commonly assumed, on the other hand, that an inheritance tax is a direct tax, though there has been some dispute as to whether its incidence is on the successor or the predecessor. Clearly, however, it is on the successor, for the predecessor must be dead before the tax can be levied and dead men, like other inanimate objects, can pay no taxes. The fact that the predecessor may have insured against the tax beforehand is irrelevant to the question of incidence, though not, of course, to the wider question of effects. The burden of such an insurance policy must be classed, not as a direct, but as an indirect, money burden, due to anticipation of the tax. It is, moreover, balanced by a money benefit to an insurance company.

Again, it is commonly assumed that an income tax is a direct tax. The extent to which income tax payers in general can shift the incidence of the tax is, no doubt, so small, especially in the short run, as to be practically negligible. But exceptional conditions may make even an income tax, or parts of it, indirect, as judged by incidence.[1]

§ 3. So far as taxes on particular commodities or services are concerned, two general propositions may be laid down. The first is that, other things being equal, the more elastic the demand for the object of taxation, the more will the incidence of the tax be upon

[1] This case is further examined in the Note following Ch. VIII.

the seller. And the second is that, other things being equal, the more elastic the supply of the object of taxation, the more will the incidence of the tax be upon the buyer. For, the more elastic the demand, the more will the demand fall off, as a result of a given rise in the price of the object of taxation, and the less, therefore, will it be worth while for sellers to raise the price. And, on the other hand, the more elastic the supply, the more will the supply fall off, as a result of a given rise in the cost of production (including tax) of the object of taxation, and the less, therefore, will it be worth while for buyers to resist the raising of the price. The sellers, in short, try to put the incidence on the buyers by reducing supply, the buyers try to put it on the sellers by reducing demand. The relative ability of the two groups to achieve their aims, with the minimum loss to themselves, determines the result. When either or both of these groups are consolidated into monopolist combinations, the case requires some further discussion, but we may first consider some examples of the working of the two propositions just laid down, when competition prevails both among buyers and sellers.

It makes no essential difference whether the tax is legally imposed on buyers or sellers, though this may affect the length of time which will elapse before the process of shifting the direct money burden, or part of it, from one side to the other is completed. Every tax tends, for a time, to " stick where it falls." . But a tax on an ordinary commodity, such as sugar, causes a more rapid adjustment of price than a tax on houses, for example, where bargains as to rent cannot be altered during the currency of a lease.

Cases of absolutely inelastic demand are seldom, if ever, found in practice. But the demand for luxuries is more elastic than the demand for necessaries and, therefore, other things being equal, a tax on necessaries will raise their price by a larger amount than an equal tax on luxuries. Again, the demand for new durable objects, such as houses, of which a large stock is already in use, is generally more elastic than the demand for commodities which are perishable or quickly consumed.

Cases of absolutely inelastic supply are less remote from reality. Thus the supply of land in well populated districts may be regarded as absolutely inelastic. It follows that a tax on land, as distinct from improvements, will not raise the price of land, and its incidence will be entirely on the owner.

Where, however, the supply of a commodity is at all elastic, it is generally very elastic in the long run, and considerably more elastic than the demand. When, therefore, conditions of production have had time to adjust themselves to changes due to taxation, the greater part of the incidence will generally be upon buyers, and not upon sellers. But, during the period of adjustment, the elasticity of supply may be small and then a large part of the incidence may be upon the sellers. Thus, in the case of commodities produced by means of an expensive plant and much fixed capital, the elasticity of supply may remain small for a considerable time after a tax has been imposed upon them.

Our two general propositions may now be combined into one. The direct money burden of a tax imposed on any object is divided between the buyers and the sellers in the proportion of the elasticity of supply of the object taxed to the elasticity of demand for it. Thus in the particular case when the elasticity of supply is equal to the elasticity of demand, the burden is equally divided, and the price of the object taxed rises by half the amount of the tax.

This is a first approximation, based on the assumption that a tax on a commodity leaves unchanged the conditions of demand for, and supply of, all other commodities. This assumption is seldom completely justified, but often sufficiently nearly justified to be legitimate for rough practical purposes. Clearly, however, part of the incidence of a tax imposed upon the sellers or buyers of a commodity may fall, not upon these sellers or buyers, but upon the sellers of some other commodity, which is necessary to the production of the former, or upon the buyers of some other commodity, to the production of which the taxed commodity is necessary. Thus part of the incidence of a tax on jam may fall upon the sellers of tins or glass jars, in so far as the latter are compelled by the tax to reduce their price to the jam makers.

§ 4. The preceding theory has been stated, so as to apply to the incidence of taxes on the internal trade of a community, but substantially the same theory applies to the incidence of taxes on international trade, in the form of customs duties on imports or exports. In the case of internal trade we have considered the exchange of goods for money, the elasticity of demand of the buyers, who give money for goods, and the elasticity of supply of the sellers, who give goods for money. In the case of international trade it is more convenient to consider the exchange of goods for goods, and the elasticities of demand of the two groups of buyers for the goods respectively furnished by the other group in exchange for their own. Thus in the exchange of Canadian wheat for British woollen goods, assuming that no other goods are exchanged between the two countries, the elasticity of supply of Canadian wheat in Great Britain is the same thing as the elasticity of demand for British woollen goods in Canada.

Taxes on imports and exports may, then, be regarded as obstacles to exchange and, in accordance with the preceding theory, the direct money burden of any such obstacle is divided between the two parties to the exchange in inverse proportion to the elasticities of their respective demands. In other words, it is divided in direct proportion to the urgencies[1] of their respective needs, which are satisfied by the exchange. For, the more urgent the need of either party, the less elastic his demand. Other things being equal, the less elastic the British demand for Canadian wheat, the greater the proportion of the incidence, of a tax either on British woollen goods or Canadian wheat in transit between the two countries, which will fall upon the British party to the exchange. Similarly, the less elastic the Canadian demand for British woollen goods, the greater the proportion which will fall upon the Canadian party to the exchange.

§ 5. It is thought by some to be a practically universal rule that the incidence of customs duties is on consumers of foreign goods in the countries where such duties are imposed, and hence that attempts to "make the foreigner pay" such duties can practically never succeed. The preceding argument does not support this idea in general, but it does support it

[1] Ignoring differences in the wealth of the two parties.

in important particular cases. The inhabitants of a region, in which is produced a large proportion of the world supply of some commodity essential to foreigners, could make foreigners pay a large part of export duties on this commodity, or of import duties on what foreigners offered in exchange for it. The inhabitants of Great Britain were in such a favourable position, when this country was practically the only source of supply of wool to Flanders during the Middle Ages, of machine-made manufactured goods to the continent of Europe in the early nineteenth century, and of steam coal to the world's navies in the later nineteenth century. The inhabitants of oil-producing regions[1] are in a somewhat similar position at the present time. On the other hand, the inhabitants of a region, in which is produced no commodity very essential to foreigners, or only a small proportion of the world supply of essential commodities, are not in a position to throw any appreciable part of any customs duties, which they may impose, upon foreigners, while, if foreign products are essential to them, foreigners are in a position to impose customs duties, a large part of the incidence of which will fall upon the inhabitants of this less fortunate region.

In the present conditions of international trade, the incidence of customs duties imposed in countries whose exports are chiefly manufactured goods and whose imports are chiefly food and raw material, can hardly be, to any appreciable extent, upon the foreigner. For the foreign demand for their manufactures is, in

[1] Assuming, what is often not the case, that the inhabitants, or at least some of them, and not foreigners, control the oil production and are able to deal with it in accordance with their own economic interests.

most cases, much less keen, that is to say much more elastic, than their demand for the foreigners' food and raw material. The inhabitants of Great Britain, in particular, are not now in a position to make the foreigner pay British customs duties, except in rare and unusual cases. It has been suggested that the British import duty on Greek currants is largely paid by the Greeks, but even this exception to the general rule is doubtful.

Moreover, commodities, which have a wide world market, have a very elastic supply to any small part of that market. Thus a tax imposed on the imports of such a commodity into a single "national" market, provided that sales in that market are small relatively to world sales, will generally raise the price *in that market* by about the amount of the tax. Again, the demand of the inhabitants of a country for a commodity from *any particular foreign market* is much more elastic than their demand for that commodity from the outside world as a whole. Thus the inhabitants of a number of important countries acting in combination would have a better chance, than the inhabitants of any one acting alone, of throwing the incidence of their customs duties upon foreigners outside the combination. But such forms of international co-operation are not worthy of encouragement, unless they serve some good international purpose.[1]

§ 6. It remains to consider how far the theory of incidence should be modified in the case of taxes on monopolists. Where a tax is imposed upon a

[1] An international boycott of "sweated goods," designed to persuade a "backward country" to conform to International Labour Conventions, might, under favourable conditions, serve such a purpose.

commodity, whose seller is a monopolist, the effect on the price, and hence the incidence, varies according to the character of the tax. Assuming that the monopolist will fix his price, so as to secure for himself the maximum monopoly profits, the incidence of a tax, whose total amount is proportionate to the volume of his output, or, more generally, whose total amount increases as his output increases, will be similar to that of the taxes discussed in preceding sections of this Chapter. Except in the unlikely event of either the supply being absolutely inelastic or the demand absolutely elastic, the tax will raise the price of the commodity to some extent and, other things being equal, this rise in price will be greater, the less elastic the demand and the more elastic the supply.

If, however, the tax is one, whose total amount is independent of the size of the monopolist's output, it will not raise the price and its incidence will be wholly on the monopolist. Examples of such a tax are a fixed contribution, independent of output, or a sum proportionate to the monopoly profits, assuming that these are discoverable by means of government costing or otherwise.

There is also a third possibility, that of a tax whose total amount diminishes as the monopolist's output increases. Such a tax, if its imposition were practicable, would in some cases[1] cause the monopolist to increase his output and lower his price. An example would be a tax, whose total amount was proportionate to the price of the commodity per unit, or a lump sum

[1] In those cases, namely, in which, as his output increases, his tax payments diminish faster than his monopoly profits, apart from the tax. The object aimed at might be attained by a tax suitably graduated according to the monopolist's rate of profits.

with a rebate proportionate to output. In favourable cases the incidence of such a tax would be entirely on the monopolist who, in addition, would be compelled to transfer part of his monopoly profits to the buyers of his product in the form of lower prices. The chief practical obstacle in the way of carrying out this policy arises from the difficulty of checking the quality of the monopolist's product. For it will obviously pay him, if subjected to such a tax, to sell an inferior product at a lower price.[1]

Where the product of the monopolist is an import from abroad, it will sometimes be possible to make him bear the incidence of an import licence, such a licence being a fixed payment for any given period, with or without a rebate proportionate to his importation during this period.

[1] There is an analogy between the stimulus to lower prices, which such a tax would afford, and the operation of the so-called " gasworks' clause," under which gas companies and other " public utility " concerns are legally forbidden to increase their rate of dividends, unless they lower their selling prices, and must reduce dividends if they raise prices. This plan imposes upon certain monopolists, and semi-monopolists, compulsory profit-sharing with the consumers of their products. But its practical success largely depends on the fact that the quality of gas, electric current, water and other " public utility " products is easily checked.

CHAPTER VIII

THE INCIDENCE OF TAXATION

(Continued)

§ 1. The argument of the last chapter needs to be supplemented by various considerations, some of which blunt the sharp edge of the general theory of incidence as applied to practical problems.

§ 2. The argument that the incidence of a tax on the value of land, as distinct from improvements, falls entirely on the landowner, assumes that the latter is already securing the highest rent that he can from his land. Where he is not doing so, one of the effects of the imposition of a new tax, or the increase of an existing tax, may be to make him " look sharply to his rents and take in the slack." In this case part of the incidence will be upon the occupier. The practical deduction is that, in order to be sure of taxing landowners, it is better to impose a heavy tax than a light one. For a light tax may be less than the amount of " slack " in existing rents, whereas a sufficiently heavy tax will be greater. The practical valuation of land, as distinct from improvements, is often difficult, though many experts consider it to be quite feasible, and taxes in many parts of the world are based upon such valuations. It is not really necessary to separate the value of land from that of all improvements, but only from that of temporary, as distinct from permanent, improvements. But the line of division between temporary and permanent is somewhat arbitrary.

§ 3. The incidence of a tax on buildings presents many complications. Not only the owner and the occupier, but also the builder, may bear part of the incidence. Further, the occupier of a building, if engaged in trade, may be able to shift part of the incidence, which would otherwise fall on him, on to the purchasers of his products. And where these products are not consumable commodities, but machinery, etc., to be used in the production of further commodities, the purchasers of the machinery may, in turn, be able to shift part of any incidence falling on them on to the purchasers of their own products.

The power of shopkeepers to shift their local rates on to their customers is greater when the purchases of the latter are restricted to shops in their own neighbourhood than when they are not. For in the former case the demand of customers for goods sold at shops in their own neighbourhood is less elastic than in the latter. Thus the development of postal communications, the increasing circulation of price lists and the increasing use of motor transport, both for the delivery of goods at a distance and for carrying purchasers further afield, make it less easy for shopkeepers in any particular district to shift their rates on to their customers. But the poorer customers are at a disadvantage in this matter as compared with the richer, in so far as they are less able to make distant purchases.

As between owners and occupiers, it is often argued that the incidence of rates is on the owner. For, it is said, if an occupier has to pay more rates, he will only offer correspondingly less rent. A similar argument could be used to prove that the incidence of a tax on any commodity is wholly on the seller. For example, it might be said that, if a buyer of sugar has to pay a tax on it, he will reduce the price that he will offer, apart from the tax, by a corresponding amount. The argument assumes that the demand for the taxed commodity is perfectly elastic. But this is not true, either of sugar or of houses. The demand for houses is, on the contrary, rather inelastic, since houseroom is a necessity, in which people are less willing to economise than in many other objects of their expenditure. The only other condition, under which the incidence of rates would be wholly on the owner, would be if the supply of houses were perfectly inelastic. But this, again, is obviously not the case, though the supply is less elastic than that of less durable commodities. It is, therefore, reasonable to conclude that occupiers bear a considerable part of the incidence of rates.

§ 4. As regards the effects of a tax on a commodity upon its price certain further points are worth noticing.

It has already been mentioned that, where a tax is collected from the seller in a lump sum in respect of a large quantity of the commodity, he will be out of pocket by the amount of interest, which he would otherwise have obtained, on the sum paid to the tax collector during the period between the payment of the tax and the sale of the goods. He will, therefore, attempt to shift on to the buyers of the commodity, not only the sum paid in taxation, but also the sum lost in interest. How far he will be able to do this, i.e., how far he will be able to raise the price of the commodity, depends, as before, upon the elasticity of the demand for, and of the supply of, the commodity. But, if the former elasticity is small and the latter large, it is possible that the price of the commodity will rise by more than the amount of the tax.

Another case in which a tax on a commodity may raise its price by more than the amount of the tax is that of a commodity produced under conditions of "increasing returns," that is to say under such conditions that the cost of production per unit diminishes, as the amount produced increases. In this case not only does an increased price mean a decreased demand, but a decreased supply means increased cost of production and hence an increased price, apart from the increase directly due to the tax.

Again, the sellers of a commodity, on which a new tax is imposed or an existing tax increased, even though they do not normally act in combination, may agree to raise prices by more than the amount of the tax, for the sake of producing a political effect and creating an agitation among consumers for the repeal or reduction of the tax. But, unless the agitation succeeds quickly, the sellers are likely to lose by such a policy.

Finally, the effect of imposing import duties on commodities, other than gold, may lead to increased imports of gold and reduced imports of the taxed commodities. In so far as this happens, the increased supply of gold will tend to raise the prices of all commodities within the taxing country and the prices of the taxed commodities may, therefore, be increased, for this reason also, by more than the amount of the duties imposed upon them. Similarly, export duties on commodities, other than gold, may lead to increased exports of gold and thus tend to lower all prices within the taxing country, but, unless the country contains gold mines, this process cannot be carried far. An import duty on gold would likewise tend to lower all prices within the taxing country. But it would also have the effect, under a gold standard, of increasing the range of fluctuations in the country's rates of foreign exchange. The above argument pre-supposes a fairly free flow of gold across political frontiers and has no application, when gold movements are severely restricted by governments.

It is doubtful whether the four cases discussed in this section properly belong to the theory of incidence, as distinguished from the more general theory of the effects, of taxation. For when the price of a commodity rises, owing to any of the causes just mentioned, more than it would have risen apart from these causes, the extra rise in price should, perhaps, be described as an indirect, rather than a direct, money burden on the buyer. In conformity with the definition of incidence given in Chapter VII, § 1, the test would appear to be, whether such an extra rise in the price of the taxed commodity leads to an increased revenue, *per unit of commodity*, to the public authority imposing the tax.[1] That is to say, the test is whether the tax is *ad valorem* or specific. In the former case the extra rise in price is partly a question of incidence and partly of other effects; in the latter case it is entirely a question

[1] This is not, of course, the same thing as an increased tax revenue in respect of the commodity. For the total tax revenue may be diminished by a falling off of demand owing to the extra rise in price, though the tax revenue per unit of commodity may increase.

of other effects. The need for introducing such a distinction here illustrates the difficulty of effectively separating incidence from other effects.

§ 5. The argument of the preceding chapter regarding the incidence of taxes on a monopolist must be applied with discretion to practical problems. In reality perfect competition is rare, and perfect monopoly is still rarer. Some element of monopoly enters into the determination of nearly all prices, and fear of competition, actual or potential, actuates nearly all apparent monopolists. Price may be influenced by the exercise of monopoly power, as soon as a single seller, or group of sellers acting in combination, controls a considerable proportion of the commodity to be sold. But where monopoly power exists, though we may assume that it is seldom neglected, yet it is not always fully exercised. Investigations under the British Profiteering Act into the prices of soap, sewing thread and other commodities immediately after the war illustrated this.

It follows that a tax on a monopolist, such that its incidence, according to the argument of the preceding chapter, would be entirely on him, may sometimes be shifted on to his customers by means of a more rigorous exercise than before of monopoly power. A monopolist, in fact, like a landowner, may react to taxation by " taking in the slack." Further, a group of sellers (or buyers), who have previously competed against one another, may react to taxation by acting in combination and thus enabling themselves to exercise monopoly power.

§ 6. Many schemes of social insurance are partly or wholly financed by weekly contributions from employers and workers. The incidence of these contributions may be traced as follows. The employers' contributions, being proportionate to the number of workers employed, are a tax on the number of units of labour employed, or, more shortly, a tax on employment. The workers' contributions are a tax on wages. The incidence of both sets of contributions depends on the relative elasticity of the demand for, and supply of, labour in various occupations. In general, the demand for labour is much more elastic than the supply. In general, therefore, much the greater part of the incidence is on the workers, and much the smaller part on the employers. The workers, therefore, pay by far the greater part both of the employers' contributions and of their own, and the employers pay by far the smaller part. The proportions will vary according to the circumstances of particular industries and localities and in exceptional cases, where the demand for labour is less elastic than the supply, the relative situation of employers and workers will be reversed. An example of such an exceptional case is, perhaps, that of domestic servants.[1]

§ 7. Before leaving the subject of incidence, we may notice a few mistaken ideas, which are sometimes put forward.

It is sometimes argued that the incidence of all taxes on commodities is entirely on consumers, because the effect of imposing a tax on any particular commodity is to reduce the profits obtainable from its production and sale below the " normal level " of profits

[1] Professor Pigou (*Theory of Unemployment*, p. 41) argues that the employers' contributions come out of wages, since the marginal net product of labour equals wages plus employer's contribution. Therefore, an increase in the contribution means an equivalent decrease in wages.

elsewhere, and that its production will, therefore, be restricted, and its price consequently raised, until its producers and sellers are again making "normal profits." When this has come about, it is argued, its producers and sellers will be in the same position as producers and sellers elsewhere and, therefore, they will have shifted the whole incidence on to the consumers.

A preliminary objection to this argument is that the conception of "normal profits" corresponds very imperfectly with the facts of reality. There is, of course, a constant tendency for both workers and capital to move from points where remuneration is low to points where it is high. There are, however, many obstacles to movement, some of which prove insuperable for considerable lengths of time.

But a more fundamental objection is that the argument takes no account of differences in the elasticity of demand for different commodities. Suppose an equal tax per unit to be imposed upon two commodities, for one of which the demand is considerably more elastic than for the other. Then, even when the producers of both are again making "normal profits," the price of the first will have risen, other things being equal, considerably less than the price of the second. Therefore, the consumers of the first will be bearing a smaller part of the incidence of the tax than the consumers of the second. And even the latter will not be bearing the whole incidence, unless, as a direct result of the tax, the price has risen by the full amount of the tax, *i.e.*, unless either their demand is absolutely inelastic, or the supply of the commodity is absolutely elastic.

A corresponding, and equally valid, objection may be raised from the side of supply. If an equal tax per unit is imposed on two commodities, one of which has a more elastic supply than the other, the price of the former will tend to rise more than the price of the latter and, in general, neither price will tend to rise by the full amount of the tax.

§ 8. Again, it is sometimes said that "an old tax is no tax," by which it is intended to imply that a tax, which has been in existence a long time, imposes no present burden on anyone.[1] Thus Mill said of the "old land tax" that "there is not the smallest pretence for looking on this tax as a payment exacted from the existing race of landlords." But this is quite fallacious. The incidence of any tax, however old, is its direct money burden, and falls on those who would derive a direct money benefit, if it were now repealed. If the "old land tax" were now repealed, those members of "the existing race of landlords" who now pay it, would secure a direct money benefit in the form of an increase in income and in the selling value of their land. Its incidence, therefore, is upon them.

Another form of the same fallacy is the so-called "doctrine of capitalisation" of taxes. It is argued that taxes on land and other more or less permanent sources of income, such as government securities, depress the selling value of the object taxed when they are first imposed, but that no burden is transmitted to subsequent purchasers of this object, since they buy knowing that the tax is payable, and reduce accordingly the price which they are willing to pay. But they are willing to pay less, precisely because they

[1] It is true, but comparatively unimportant, that for a while people feel the incidence of a new tax more keenly than that of an equally heavy old tax, to which they have become accustomed. Compare Ch. VI, §7.

realise that they will have to pay the tax. And clearly, if the tax were to be repealed, the holders for the time being of the taxed object would gain through an increase of its selling value, or of their income, or both. And, therefore, the incidence of the tax is on them.

Some writers have enveloped the theory of incidence in a fog of vague words, among which the terms "diffusion" and "absorption" are prominent. The conclusion of their argument is akin to that of those philosophers who maintain that nothing definite can be known except that nothing can be definitely known, but that all is probably for the best. All taxes are "diffused" and "absorbed," until no one's burden can be determined, but probably no one's burden is heavier than that of anyone else. This is thought to be true of all systems of taxation, any of which, therefore, is as good or as bad as any other. This line of argument is very futile, and merely runs away from all the difficulties. It is true that many of the effects of taxes are widely diffused, but it is possible, if the problem is posed with precision, to arrive at certain quite definite conclusions regarding both their incidence and their wider effects.

Finally, it is sometimes argued that the incidence of a tax on a commodity can be determined by a comparison of the price of the commodity at two different dates, before and after the imposition of the tax, in the same country, or at the same date in two different countries, in one of which there is a tax and in the other no tax, or a tax at a different rate. This type of argument is freely used both by Protectionists and Free Traders. Thus some economic historians have tried to prove that the repeal of the Corn Laws in this country had no effect upon the price of bread, except perhaps slightly to raise it. The attempted proof consists of the statement, which is true, that the price of bread rose slightly in the years immediately following the repeal. But all prices were rising at this time, chiefly owing to increasing gold production in California and Australia, and the price of bread rose less than other prices in this country and less than the price of bread in other countries during the same period.

But, in order to determine the incidence of a tax from price statistics, what should be compared with the price of the commodity at one time or place with the tax on, is not the price at a *different* time or place with the tax off, but the price at *the same* time or place with the tax off. And obviously there will be no statistical record of the latter price. For it is not any price which ever actually existed, but a price which would have existed, if certain conditions had been different. Nearly all statistical arguments on incidence are worthless, because a tax is only one of many factors which determine the price of a taxed commodity, and the effect on its price of changes in the tax may be, and often are, small compared with the effect of changes in the other factors. "You can prove anything by figures" to your own satisfaction, provided that neither you, nor those to whom you speak, know how to use them.

Note to Chapters VII and VIII

§ 1. Some parts of the theory of incidence may be conveniently expressed by geometrical or algebraical methods. What follows is not intended to be an exhaustive discussion, but only to illustrate the use of mathematical methods in this field.

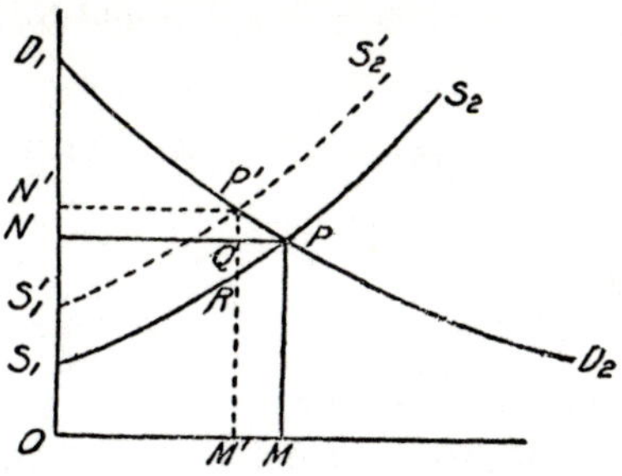

Let D_1D_2 be the demand curve, S_1S_2 the supply curve for a particular commodity (or service), PM the price per unit, and PN the amount sold per unit of time.

Now impose a tax on the commodity and collect it from the sellers. Let $S_1'S_2'$ be the new supply curve, P′M′ the new price, P′N′ the new amount sold, and P′R the tax per unit.

Thus the price rises by P′Q and the sales fall by PQ.

The incidence of the tax, P′R, is divided between buyers and sellers. The buyers bear P′Q, the sellers QR.

Now the elasticity of demand, $e_d=\dfrac{MM'}{OM}\bigg/\dfrac{P'Q}{PM}$

and the elasticity of supply, $e_s=\dfrac{MM'}{OM}\bigg/\dfrac{QR}{PM}$

$$\therefore \frac{P'Q}{QR}=\frac{e_s}{e_d}$$

That is to say, the incidence is divided between buyers and sellers in the ratio of the elasticity of supply to the elasticity of demand.

If the same tax were collected from buyers, instead of sellers, the only difference would be that, instead of a rise in the supply curve, there would be a fall in the demand curve.

If t is the tax per unit, it is obvious that, since $t=P'R=P'Q+QR$,

$$P'Q=\frac{te_s}{e_d+e_s} \quad \text{and} \quad QR=\frac{te_d}{e_d+e_s}$$

The following limiting cases obviously suggest themselves: (*a*) with perfectly elastic demand, D_1D_2 becomes a horizontal straight line, and P′ coincides with Q, so that P′Q vanishes and the price is unchanged by the tax, though sales diminish; (*b*) with perfectly inelastic demand, D_1D_2 becomes a vertical straight line, P coincides with both Q and R, and $P'Q=t$, so that the price rises by the full amount of the tax, and sales are unchanged; (*c*) with perfectly elastic supply, S_1S_2 and $S_1'S_2'$ become horizontal straight lines, Q coincides with R and $P'Q=t$, so that the price rises by the full amount of the tax and sales diminish; (*d*) with perfectly inelastic supply, S_1S_2 becomes a vertical straight line and $S_1'S_2'$ coincides with it, while P, P′, Q and R all coincide with one another, so that P′Q vanishes, the price is unchanged by the tax and sales are likewise unchanged.

§ 2. It is not necessary to assume, so far as the preceding geometrical proof is concerned, that the tax is small relatively to the price or to the amount sold. The proof holds good equally for small taxes and for large. In the former case the elasticities of demand and supply are "point elasticities," in the latter they are

" arc elasticities." But no ambiguity results from this in the present context.[1]

Nor is it necessary to assume that the rate of tax per unit is independent of the price, or of the sales, though this assumption represents the simplest case, that of a " specific tax." The geometrical proof remains unaffected, if we assume that the tax per unit is proportionate to the price per unit (the case of an " *ad valorem* tax "), or if we assume, more generally, that the tax per unit is *any* function of the price, or of the sales. For P′R will still represent the tax per unit, when equilibrium is reached with price P′M′ and sales P′N′. But the position and shape of the new supply curve will, of course, vary in relation to the old according to the nature of the tax.

§ 3. An independent algebraical proof is as follows.

Before the tax is imposed, let y be the price and x the sales, and let $y=D(x)$ represent the demand curve and $y=S(x)$ the supply curve. Then equilibrium is given by $y=D(x)=S(x)$.

If a (specific) tax of t per unit is imposed on the sellers, we have a new supply curve $y=t+S(x)$, but the old demand curve $y=D(x)$.

Therefore the new equilibrium is given by

$$y+\delta y=D(x-\delta x)=t+S(x-\delta x),$$

Where δy, the increase in price, and δx, the decrease in sales, are both measured positively.

Assuming that δx is small, so that its squares and higher powers may be neglected, we have

[1] For a discussion of the distinction between these two conceptions of elasticity, and of the ambiguities which are apt to arise from failure to make this distinction clear, see my *Inequality of Incomes*, pp. 186-90 and pp. 192-97.

$$y+\delta y=D(x)-\delta x\, D'(x)=t+S(x)-\delta x\, S'(x)$$

$$\therefore\ \delta y=-\delta x\, D'(x)=t-\delta x\, S'(x)$$

$$\therefore\ \delta x=\frac{t}{S'(x)-D'(x)} \text{ and } \delta y=-\frac{t\,D'(x)}{S'(x)-D'(x)}$$

$$\text{Now } e_d=-\frac{y}{x\,D'(x)} \text{ and } e_s=\frac{y}{x\,S'(x)}$$

$$\therefore -D'(x)=\frac{y}{x}\,\frac{1}{e_d} \text{ and } S'(x)=\frac{y}{x}\,\frac{1}{e_s}$$

$$\therefore\ \delta y=\frac{t\,\frac{1}{e_d}}{\frac{1}{e_d}+\frac{1}{e_s}}=\frac{te_s}{e_d+e_s}$$

This algebraical treatment can be generalised, though the geometrical treatment cannot, to cover the case of specific taxes at different rates on a number of different sources of supply. If taxes t_1, t_2 . . . . t_n are imposed on n sources of supply, with supplies x_1, x_2 . . . . x_n and elasticities of supply e_1, e_2 . . . . e_n, and if e_d is the elasticity of demand, it is easily shown that the increase in price

$$\delta y=\frac{t_1 e_1 x_1+t_2 e_2 x_2+\ \ldots\ldots+t_n e_n x_n}{e_d\,(x_1+x_2+\ \ldots\ +x_n)+(e_1x_1+e_2x_2+\ldots\ldots+e_nx_n)}$$

A similar formula would represent the effect on price of the differential taxation of a number of sources of demand.

But the algebraical treatment cannot be so easily generalised, as the geometrical, to cover the case of large taxes and arc elasticities, as distinguished from small taxes and point elasticities.

§ 4. The possibility that the price may rise by more than the amount of the tax, owing to loss of interest by the seller, may be thus exhibited.

If a tax t per unit be imposed on the seller, and if, in addition, he suffers a loss of interest i per unit during the interval between the collection of the tax and the sale of the commodity, he will try to pass on i, in addition to t.

Let $t+i=t'$

Then the price will rise by $\dfrac{t'e_s}{e_d+e_s}$

This quantity will be greater than t, if

$$\frac{(t+i)\ e_s}{e_d+e_s} > t$$

that is to say, if

$$\frac{i}{t} > \frac{e_d}{e_s}$$

This result is, therefore, the more likely, (*a*) the less elastic the demand, (*b*) the more elastic the supply, and (*c*) the larger the loss of interest relatively to the tax, or, in other words, the higher the rate of interest and the longer the interval.

It should, however, be remembered that i is, for the most part, an *indirect* money burden and, therefore, outside the realm of incidence. Compare Chapter VIII, § 4.

§ 5. In the case of increasing returns, we have the supply curve sloping downwards and e_s, the elasticity of supply, negative.[1]

The geometrical construction of § 1 must, therefore, be modified accordingly. It is then evident that the increase in price, P′Q, is greater than the tax, P′R.

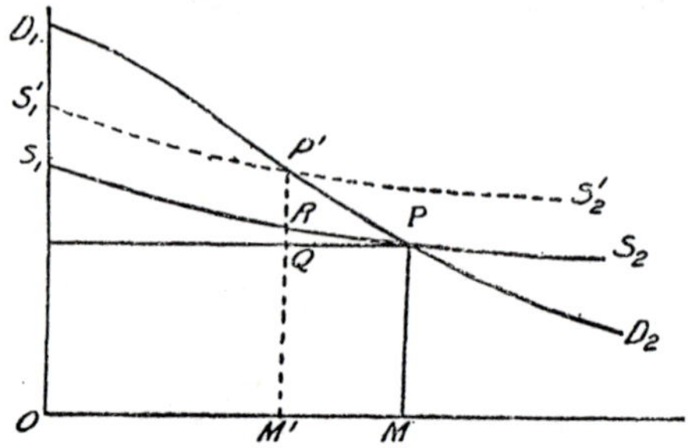

But we still have

$$e_d = \frac{MM'}{OM} \bigg/ \frac{P'Q}{PM} \text{ and } e_s = -\frac{MM'}{OM} \bigg/ \frac{QR}{PM}$$

$$\therefore \frac{P'Q}{QR} = -\frac{e_s}{e_d}$$

Thus the rise in price will be greater, other things being equal, (*a*) the greater the elasticity of demand, and (*b*) the smaller the negative elasticity of supply, or, in other words, the more rapid the rate of increase of returns.

§ 6. The incidence of various types of tax on a monopolised commodity may be treated either geometrically or algebraically.

[1] Much has been written recently concerning the conditions, if any, under which this simple conception is legitimate. But I cannot here explore these byways, interesting though they are.

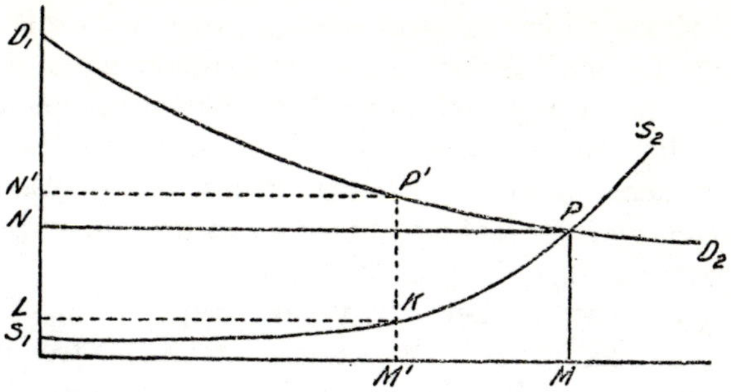

As before let D_1D_2 be the demand curve, and S_1S_2 the supply curve for the commodity, with diminishing returns. Then PM may be called the competitive price and PN the competitive sales. But, since the commodity is monopolised, the price will be P′M′, the sales P′N′, and the restriction of sales (or output) by reason of monopoly MM′. The position of P′ will be determined by the condition that monopoly profits, represented by the rectangle P′KLN′, shall be a maximum.

The extent to which it will pay the monopolist to raise price and restrict sales depends on the shapes of the relevant portions of D_1D_2 and S_1S_2, that is to say on the elasticities of demand and supply. The profits of restriction will evidently be greater, the smaller the elasticity both of demand and of supply. Apart from the possibility of endangering his monopoly, there is no limit to profitable restriction of output, so long as the elasticity of demand at each point of the demand curve, going upwards, is less than unity. For then, with each additional restriction, he will produce a smaller output at less cost and sell it for more money. But, in reality, the demand for any commodity, even if it shows a low degree of elasticity over a considerable range of price variation, becomes much more elastic at comparatively high prices. A point must sooner or later be reached, when the will of consumers to keep their demand for a particular commodity inelastic is broken by their inability to do so, without making still greater sacrifices in other directions.

§ 7. The incidence of various types of tax on a monopolised commodity depends on their effect upon the position of P′. If they have no tendency to alter this position, their incidence is wholly on the monopolist seller. Geometrical constructions may be elaborated to illustrate alternative types of tax and consequential new positions of the supply curve. It is, however, clear, without such elaboration, that a tax which is independent of the amount of sales—either a lump sum tax, or a tax proportionate to monopoly profits—has no tendency to alter the position of P′.

It is clear, on the other hand, that a tax which is a function of the sales, or of the price, has, in general, such a tendency. Geometry can add little here to the verbal argument of Chapter VII, § 6.

Algebraically, if $y=D(x)$ is the demand curve and $y=S(x)$ the supply curve, monopoly profits on sales x are

$$x\ \{D(x)-S(x)\}$$

This is a maximum when

$$D(x)-S(x)+x\{D'(x)-S'(x)\}=0.$$

This equation determines the most profitable level of sales, x, and also the most profitable price, y, since $y=D(x)$.

If a tax of $f(x)$ per unit is imposed on the monopolist, so that the total tax payable on sales x is $xf(x)$, the most profitable level of sales will be given by the equation

$$D(x) - S(x) - f(x) + x\{D'(x) - S'(x) - f'(x)\} = 0.$$

There is scope here also for mathematical manipulation,[1] to examine how various forms of the function $f(x)$ will affect the optimum value of x for the monopolist. But the verbal argument of Chapter VII, § 6 is simpler and more direct.

§ 8. I now put mathematics aside and pass from the incidence of taxes on *particular* commodities and services to that of a tax on income in *general.* This characteristic of generality in any tax has a primary importance in the theory of its incidence. For the incidence of such a tax cannot be shifted by the diversion of resources from taxed to untaxed fields. Precisely because the tax is general, no untaxed fields exist.[2] A tax on income in general is the same thing as a tax on the prices of all commodities and services, which in turn is equivalent to a tax on all those commodities and services themselves.

Most serious economists, though not all business men, agree that the usual incidence of income tax is on the income receiver, who is thus quite accurately described as the "income tax payer." This doctrine, according to an often quoted pronouncement, "is true over practically the whole field and for practically the whole of the time, any exceptions being local or temporary and insufficient to invalidate it."[3] The belief, held by

[1] And for the use of integral, as well as unitary, curves and functions.

[2] I leave out of account here the argument that an income tax differentiates against savings, as to which see Ch. X, §10.

[3] *Report of Colwyn Committee on National Debt and Taxation,* p. 119.

many business men, that income tax imposed on them can be passed on, by way of higher prices, to the purchasers of their goods, is, apart from occasional exceptional cases, simply wrong. But, though economists agree that, in general, and certainly in the short run, income tax cannot be shifted, there has been some dispute as to what arguments establish this conclusion. The following considerations, however, appear decisive.

First, in reply to the business men who assert the contrary, income tax is not, like a tax on raw material or on finished articles, or like local rates, a true "overhead charge" which "enters into cost of production." It is, as applied to business incomes, a tax on net profits, that is to say on the realised surplus of a period's trading. If there is no surplus, there is no income tax, whatever other taxes may still be payable. Income tax is not a cost of production, but a cost of success in business. It no more "enters into costs" or "imposes a burden on industry" than does a business man's expenditure on consumption. As regards other kinds of income, and especially fixed incomes from property, not even business men commonly allege that the recipients of those can, as a rule, pass on their income tax.

Second, some business men may think that they actually add all their taxes, including income tax, to the selling price of their goods. But this is a delusion. They may, indeed, go through the form of doing such an arithmetical sum.[1] But, in fact, they have to quote prices at which it is possible to sell. They may begin

[1] Though, when they price their goods, they do not know what their subsequent liability in income tax (including, in England, surtax) will turn out to be.

by asking what they like; they must end by taking what they can get.

The price which they can get is not affected by the amount of income tax, if any, which they pay. Under perfect competition, a seller has no power at all to alter the market price; under perfect monopoly, he has unlimited power; under imperfect or partial monopoly, he has some power. But in all three cases the price which, allowing for the opportunities open to him, will bring him in the largest profits, is independent of whether he pays income tax or not, or of how much he pays.

Third, and this is the underlying reason for the two previous arguments, and could, therefore, stand alone as a sufficient logical support of the doctrine that income tax cannot be shifted, the elasticity of supply of resources subjected to a general income tax tends, in the short run at any rate, to be so small as to be negligible. For no diversion of resources from one employment to another will, as a result of the tax, be worth while, which would not have been worth while before. And it is the possibility of such diversions, which makes the supply of *particular kinds of resources* elastic in other cases. Moreover, this inelasticity of supply, which is a certainty over a short period, is likely to persist over long periods, especially if the demand for income by those who supply resources is also, in terms of effort and sacrifice, highly inelastic. And there are grounds for believing that this state of things often prevails.[1]

Only on the assumption that the supply of resources, or of some kinds of resources, is relatively elastic in the

[1] Compare Ch. X, §4.

long run, can any plausible case be made for the view that, in the long run, the incidence of income tax can sometimes in part be shifted. But to assert that the incidence of income tax cannot, in the short run, be shifted by the income receivers is not, of course, to deny that the effects of income tax may include some check to work, savings and investment. This possibility will be examined in Chapter X.

§ 9. The argument that a general income tax cannot be shifted, owing to the inelastic supply of the resources on which it falls, is not invalidated by any details of graduation, differentiation between earned and unearned incomes, or abatements and allowances, which the tax may contain. For no such details diminish appreciably its attribute of generality. Substantially it remains neutral as between alternative employments of resources.

It might, at first sight, be argued that differentiation between earned and unearned incomes is a breach of this neutrality. But it is not a relevant breach, so far as incidence is concerned. For the diversion of income from unearned to earned sources, in order to escape the higher rates of tax, is not a practicable operation.

This line of argument, indeed, leads further. Where income receivers fall into " non-competing groups," so that no appreciable diversion can occur between such groups, a special tax on the income of such a group has the same incidence as a general income tax, and cannot, as a rule, be shifted. A tax on wages, for example, such as the workers' contributions to social insurance, tends, for the most part, to be paid by wage-earners, because the supply of labour in general is highly inelastic, and no wage-earner can escape the tax by changing his trade. But a tax on wages in a particular trade can, in some measure, be shifted, since the supply of labour to particular trades is comparatively elastic, and since the demand for labour in some particular trades is comparatively inelastic. It may be added that the argument of some of the classical economists, that a tax on wages could be shifted, assumed that wages were at, or near, subsistence level and that, in consequence, the supply of labour was highly elastic. But, whether this assumption was right or wrong a hundred years ago, it is not tenable to-day, except, perhaps, in very backward and poverty-stricken communities.

Chapter IX

THE DISTRIBUTION OF THE BURDEN OF TAXATION FROM THE POINT OF VIEW OF EQUITY

§ 1. Much has been written on "the distribution of the burden of taxation," but the range of questions usually covered by this title is narrow. Assuming that the incidence of all taxes is known, and that the necessary statistics of income, consumption, etc., are available, it is possible to determine how the direct money burden of any tax system is, in fact, distributed among different individuals and classes. It is also possible to discuss, in general terms, how this direct money burden ought to be distributed. In such discussions it is usual to take account of the direct real burdens, which correspond to tax payments. But the indirect money burdens, and still more the indirect real burdens, of taxation are not, at this stage, brought under review.

§ 2. Assuming that a given revenue is to be raised by taxation, the total direct real burden will be greater under some tax systems than others.[1] It is an obvious idea that the tax system should be so arranged, as to make the total direct real burden as small as possible. This has been called "the principle of minimum sacrifice." It has been suggested that this principle

[1] Also, of course, in so far as foreigners can be made to bear any of the direct money burden of any of the taxes, the total direct real burden on members of the taxing community is reduced.

would be realised by taxing only the largest incomes, cutting down all above a certain level to that level, while exempting all below that level. Thus all incomes above, say, £1,500 a year would be reduced by taxation to that figure, and no one, whose income was less than this, would be taxed at all. We are led to this rough and ready plan by the conception of the diminishing marginal utility of income.[1] The chief objection to it is that, especially if it were introduced suddenly, it would probably check nearly all economic activity, beyond what was required to secure the maximum income not subject to taxation.[2] This is an objection based on grounds of economy, that is to say on the consideration of economic effects. But some people would also object to it on grounds of equity or "fairness," and it will be found that, in most discussions of "the proper distribution of the burden of taxation," arguments based on equity are more prominent than those based on economy.

Different people, however, have very different ideas of what is equitable, and many of these ideas prove to be vague and unhelpful, when it is attempted to apply them to practical problems. "It is equitable that people in the same economic position should be treated in the same way for purposes of taxation." Perhaps; but what differences in treatment are equitable for people in different economic positions? And, moreover, what is meant by the "same economic

[1] Another name for "the principle of minimum sacrifice" is "the principle of equi-marginal sacrifice." But this is clumsier.

[2] As when the Soviet Government in 1918-20 requisitioned from the peasants all their foodstuffs in excess of the immediate requirements of themselves and their families. See Dobb, *Russian Economic Development*, p. 119, and also Ch. V.

position ? " Clearly a bachelor with an income of £1,000 a year is not in the same economic position as a married man with three children and the same income. But by how much must the income of the latter be increased, in order to put him in the same position as the former ?

§ 3. It is, in any case, an error to object, as is sometimes done, to particular taxes, as distinct from the tax system as a whole, as inequitable. For the inequity of one tax, as between different taxpayers, may be cancelled by that of another. There may be inequity in the parts, but equity on the whole. But it is not necessarily an error to approve particular taxes, as distinct from the rest of the tax system, as being in themselves equitable. Thus a plausible case may be made out, on grounds of equity, for taxes on " windfall wealth." This form of wealth, of which war profits and " unearned increment " in the value of land are examples, has two characteristics. The first is " undeservedness," in the sense that such wealth accrues to its possessor without his rendering any, or at any rate any equivalent, service in return, and the second is unexpectedness. The first characteristic is thought by many to justify the taxation of windfall wealth from the point of view of equity, while the second, as will be argued later, justifies its taxation on economic grounds.[1] But it is not obviously equitable to tax some forms of windfall wealth, unless all forms

[1] See Ch. X, §5. But, except in a few glaring cases, the attempt to apply the test of deservedness or undeservedness to economic payments leads to great perplexities and illustrates afresh the difficulties and vagueness of the conception of equity. " If we all got our deserts, who should escape whipping ? " as Shakespeare asks.

are taxed, nor is it obvious at what rates it is equitable to tax such wealth.

§ 4. Returning to the tax system as a whole, three alternative principles for the equitable distribution of its direct money burden have been suggested: first, the cost to the public authority of the services rendered to individual taxpayers; second, the benefit to individual taxpayers of such services; and third, individual "ability to pay" taxation.

"The cost of service principle" can be applied to the supply of postal services, electric light, etc., by public authorities, and the prices of such services can be fixed in accordance with this principle. But it cannot be applied to services rendered out of the proceeds of taxes, as distinguished from prices. For a tax, by definition, is a payment, in return for which no direct and specific *quid pro quo* is rendered to the payer. The services, if any, rendered to individual members of the community by expenditure on the King's Civil List, on armaments, police or public parks cannot, in fact, be determined and, therefore, the cost of rendering these services to different individuals cannot be determined. Thus the "cost of service principle," however equitable it may seem in the abstract, is not capable of wide practical application.

The "benefit of service principle" fails in the same way. Since the services rendered to individuals by many forms of public expenditure cannot be determined, the benefits to individuals from such services cannot be determined. The principle can, indeed, be applied in certain cases. For example, the benefit derived by an old age pensioner from his pension is definite enough, and the benefit of service principle would require him to return it to the public treasury in the form of a special tax.[1] If this is equitable, it would be a simpler way of giving effect to equity to repeal the Old Age Pensions Acts. Those, who think that this would not be equitable, cannot think that the benefit of service principle without qualifications is equitable. And, if qualifications are to be introduced, it is not clear, so far as equity is concerned, on what principle they are to be based, nor how far reaching they are to be.[2]

It has, indeed, been argued[3] that, so far as public expenditure for common benefit, as distinct from individual benefit, is concerned, all citizens benefit in proportion to their incomes, and hence that such expenditure should be paid for by taxation proportional to individual incomes. But the first step in this argument is false. In general, the benefit to individuals is simply unascertainable.

§ 5. The principle that taxation should be distributed between individuals in accordance with their "ability to pay" is, on the face of it, somewhat more practicable. But how is "ability to pay" to be measured? It is usual, in discussions of this question, to consider the "sacrifice" to the taxpayer of paying his taxes, and then to deduce some scheme of distribution of the burden of taxation from some

[1] Under the cost of service principle, he would be required to repay, not only the amount of his pension, but also a small charge to cover the cost of administration of the scheme.

[2] See Ch. XIV, §§5-7, for a discussion of how far, on grounds of economy, the cost of service or benefit of service principles should govern the prices of services supplied by public authorities.

[3] By Professor De Viti De Marco in his *Primi Principii dell' Economia Finanziaria*.

principle concerning sacrifice. The three most common of such principles are those of "equal sacrifice," "proportional sacrifice" and "minimum sacrifice." To these we may add a fourth, which is sometimes expressed by the injunction, "leave them as you find them," or, more precisely, "do not alter the distribution of income by taxation." *Prima facie*, it is not clear, on grounds of equity, which of these four is to be preferred.

According to the principle of equal sacrifice, the direct money burden of taxation should be so distributed that the direct real burden on all taxpayers is equal; according to the principle of proportional sacrifice, so that the direct real burden on every taxpayer is proportionate to the economic welfare, which he derives from his income; according to the principle of minimum sacrifice, already referred to, so that the total direct real burden on the taxpayers as a whole is as small as possible; according to the principle of "leave them as you find them," so that the inequality of incomes should be neither increased nor diminished by taxation.

In order to apply any of these four principles, it is necessary to assume some relation between money income and the economic welfare derived from it. According to the relation assumed, there will result a tax system which may be either proportional, progressive or regressive. Under proportional taxation all taxpayers contribute the same proportion of their incomes; under progressive taxation, the larger a taxpayer's income, the larger the proportion which he contributes; under regressive taxation, the larger a taxpayer's income, the smaller the proportion which he contributes.[1] These terms may be applied, not only to tax systems as a whole, but also to particular taxes. Thus a tax system which is proportional as a whole may contain some taxes which are progressive and others which are regressive, and a tax system which is progressive as a whole may contain some taxes which are regressive, and conversely. Again, a particular tax system may be proportional over a certain range of incomes, progressive over another range and regressive over yet another range, while there are, of course, an infinite number of possible degrees of progression and regression.

Assuming that the relation between income and economic welfare is the same for all taxpayers[2] and that the marginal utility of income diminishes fairly rapidly as income increases, the principle of equal sacrifice leads to progressive taxation, the principle of proportional sacrifice to still steeper progressive taxation, and the principle of minimum sacrifice, as already pointed out, to a relatively high level of exemption and very steeply progressive taxation of those not exempt. The principle of minimum sacrifice, indeed, gives this result, so long as it is assumed that marginal

[1] Another and rather superfluous term sometimes used in these discussions is degressive taxation, which means that all incomes below a certain level are exempt from taxation, and that all incomes above this level are taxed proportionately on the surplus. For the latter class of incomes, therefore, degression is a particular case of progression, but in a very mild form.

[2] Some economists, chiefly in England, of the London individualist school, have emphasised that this is only an assumption—none who have used it have claimed that it was more—and have pronounced it both " unscientific " and untenable. But it is an assumption which, in civilised countries at any rate, equity demands and politicians and administrators, at least, must make. Nor is it so remote from reality as some of its critics suggest. Most of us, at given levels of income, are more like each other in our normal needs and moods, and in our reactions to variations in our income, than some theorists recognise.

utility diminishes at all with increasing income. Both equal sacrifice and proportional sacrifice, rigidly applied, involve making all members of the community however poor (provided that they have *some* economic welfare to sacrifice) contribute something. But minimum sacrifice does not involve this. Further, the more rapidly the marginal utility of income is assumed to diminish with increasing income, the more steeply progressive must the tax system become, in order to give effect to either equal or proportional sacrifice.

Proportional taxation can only be justified, according to the principle of equal sacrifice, on the assumption that the marginal utility of income diminishes very slowly, and can only be justified, according to the principle of proportional sacrifice, on the assumption that the marginal utility of income does not diminish at all, but remains constant, as income increases. On this last assumption, the principle of minimum sacrifice would lead to no one distribution of taxation more than any other, since the total sacrifice would in all cases be proportionate to the total revenue raised by taxation.

Regressive taxation can only be justified, according to the principle of equal sacrifice, on the assumption that the marginal utility of income diminishes even more slowly than was required in order to justify proportional taxation according to the same principle, or on the assumption that marginal utility does not diminish at all, but remains constant or actually increases. Again, regressive taxation can only be justified, according to the principle of proportional sacrifice, on the assumption that marginal utility actually increases and, on this absurd assumption, the principle of minimum sacrifice would lead to exempting from taxation all incomes above a certain level, and taxing all incomes below this level a hundred per cent.

The fourth principle referred to above, that the inequality of incomes should be neither increased nor diminished by taxation, can only be applied when it has been decided how the inequality of incomes should be measured. It is commonly supposed by its adherents to lead to proportional taxation. But there are strong grounds for holding that, on reasonable assumptions as to the relation of income to economic welfare, this principle also leads to progressive taxation.[1]

It, therefore, appears that, on reasonable assumptions, each of our four alternative interpretations of " ability to pay " leads to some degree of progression in the tax system. This practical conclusion is now generally accepted by modern opinion, which responds readily to the suggestion that considerably the heaviest burdens should be placed upon the broadest backs. A few high authorities of the older generation still cling with a curious fondness to the idea of proportional taxation, and it is true that they have the support, for what it is worth in this connection, of Adam Smith, who held that " the subjects of every State ought to contribute towards the support of the government, as nearly as possible, according to their respective abilities, that is to say, in proportion to the revenue, which they respectively enjoy under the protection of the State." But Adam Smith, though a great economist in his day, wrote nearly a hundred and fifty years ago, and before

[1] See my article on *The Measurement of the Inequality of Incomes.* (*Economic Journal*, September, 1920), reprinted as an Appendix to my *Inequality of Incomes*, and also the Note to this Chapter.

the discovery of the law of diminishing marginal utility.[1]

§ 6. It is important to notice that the four principles considered above, in common with all principles of equity in taxation, including the austere principle that "everyone ought to pay something," are only matters of opinion. Failing a clearer and more generally accepted definition of equity than has hitherto been forthcoming, it cannot be proved that they are, in fact, equitable, but only that certain people at certain times think them so. And it is a fact of common observation that opinion on such questions is very liable to change. It has been truly said that current ideas of equity generally amount to little more than "economy tempered by conservatism." Equity often seems to say "No," but hardly ever "Yes," an elusive mistress, whom perhaps it is only worth the while of philosophers to pursue ardently and of politicians to watch warily.

Yet, even on grounds of equity, it may be argued very cogently that "there is at least as good a case for taxation which makes net satisfactions equal as for taxation which makes sacrifices equal. Indeed, there is a better case. For people's economic well-being depends on the whole system of law, including the laws of property, contract and bequest, and not merely on the law about taxes. To hold that the law about taxes ought to affect different people's satisfactions equally,

[1] Proportional taxation has modern adherents also in Italy. In addition to Professor De Viti De Marco, already cited, Professor Einaudi argues in his *Ottima Imposta* that, since, without the aid of the State, there could be no production, every element of income is born owing a debt, and an equal debt, to the State, and that, therefore, every element of income should pay an equal share of taxation. This reasoning seems fanciful and unconvincing.

while allowing that the rest of the legal system may properly affect them very unequally, seems not a little arbitrary."[1] This line of argument discredits proportional sacrifice, along with equal sacrifice. It is neutral towards constant inequality of incomes, and somewhat more benevolently neutral towards minimum sacrifice.

If, however, we look at the problem of the distribution of the burden of taxation from the point of view, not of equity, but of economy, we stand on surer ground, though we may ultimately be led to conclusions less simple in form than those furnished by equity. It has been argued in Chapter II of this book that any system of public finance should be conceived simply with a view to the maximum social advantage in the long run, and it follows that any tax system, as part of this larger system, should be conceived with the same object. But it is a necessary preliminary to the consideration of any tax system from this point of view to consider broadly the economic effects of taxation.

Note to Chapter IX

§ 1. The chief purpose of this Note is to illustrate the use of mathematical methods in determining the correct distribution, on given assumptions, of the burden of taxation. As in the preceding Note to Chapters VII and VIII, the mathematical discussion is designed to be illustrative rather than exhaustive. For, of the making of mathematical formulæ for

[1] Pigou, *Public Finance*, p. 60.

graduating taxation, as of the making of books, there is no end. It may be worth while to point out that there is no logical distinction, as some non-mathematicians seem to suppose, between " theoretical " scales of graduation based on mathematical formulæ and " practical " scales based on " common sense." Every scale, which is explicitly based on a mathematical formula, can readily be translated into the language of " common sense," which here means nothing more than a series of, apparently unconnected, rates of tax payable in various alternative circumstances. On the other hand, a mathematical formula, even if a long and complicated one, can always be found to " fit," and thus give expression to, any " practical " scale which non-mathematicians may invent.

The following argument illustrates some of the problems suggested in Chapter IX, § 5.

§ 2. Given any functional relation between income, x, and economic welfare, w, it is possible to find a formula to give effect either to the principle of equal sacrifice or to that of proportional sacrifice.

Assume, for example, that

$$w = \log x, \text{ so that } \frac{dw}{dx} = \frac{1}{x}$$

(This is Bernouilli's Law, which is based on the proposition that proportionate additions to income make equal additions to welfare. It gives a somewhat slow rate of diminution of marginal utility.)

Let the rate of tax on an income x be t, so that tx is the total tax on an income x.

Let w' be the sacrifice of welfare due to payment of the tax.

Then

$$w - w' = \log (x - tx).$$
$$= \log x + \log (1 - t)$$
$$\therefore w' = -\log (1 - t).$$

To give effect to the principle of equal sacrifice, we must have w' constant. Therefore t must be constant. That is to say, we must have proportional taxation.

To give effect to the principle of proportional sacrifice, we must have

$$\frac{w'}{w} \text{ constant} = k, \text{ say, where } 0 < k < 1.$$

Then $k = -\dfrac{\log (1-t)}{\log x}$

$$\therefore k \log x + \log (1 - t) = 0 = \log 1.$$
$$\therefore x^k (1-t) = 1.$$
$$\therefore t = 1 - \frac{1}{x^k}$$

As x increases, t increases, and we have a formula for progressive taxation. Given the total taxable income and its distribution, k will depend upon the total tax revenue required.

§ 3. Now assume a more rapid rate of diminution of marginal utility than under Bernouilli's Law. Assume, for example, that

$$w = c - \frac{1}{x}$$

where c is a constant, so that $\dfrac{dw}{dx} = \dfrac{1}{x^2}$

(This is a formula which I have suggested elsewhere, in the *Economic Journal*, September, 1920, and in the

Appendix to my *Inequality of Incomes*, as best combining simplicity and plausibility.)

Then if, as before, w' is the sacrifice of welfare due to a tax tx on an income x, we have

$$w - w' = c - \frac{1}{x - tx}$$

$$\therefore w' = \frac{1}{x - tx} - \frac{1}{x}$$

$$\therefore t = 1 - \frac{1}{1 + w'x}$$

For equal sacrifice, w' is constant and, therefore, as x increases, t increases, so that we have progressive taxation.

For proportionate sacrifice, $\frac{w'}{w}$ is constant $= k$, say.

Then

$$k = \frac{\frac{1}{x - tx} - \frac{1}{x}}{c - \frac{1}{x}}$$

$$\therefore t = 1 - \frac{1}{1 - k + ckx}$$

$\therefore$ as x increases, t increases, which again gives progressive taxation.

§ 4. It is, indeed, clear, without the aid of algebra, that if, any functional relation between x and w being given, equal sacrifice leads to progression, proportional sacrifice must lead to still steeper progression. It is a limiting case of this proposition that, if equal sacrifice leads to proportionality, proportional sacrifice must lead to progression. For consider a community consisting of two taxpayers, A and B, of whom A has the larger income. If, by certain specified contributions, they make equal sacrifices, then they will make proportional sacrifices (the sum of their two contributions remaining the same), only if A pays more and B pays less than before. This means that A will part with a larger proportion of his income, and B with a smaller proportion, under proportional sacrifice than under equal sacrifice. And this is only another way of saying that the tax system is more steeply progressive in the one case than in the other.[1] And what is true of this simple community of two persons, is true also of communities which are more populous.

We may, indeed, generalise along another line. The functional relation of income to economic welfare must be such that (over certain ranges of income, if not continuously over the whole range) equal additions to welfare are secured either by proportionate, or by more than proportionate, or by less than proportionate, additions to income. These three alternatives exhaust all the possibilities. (The phrase, "more than proportionate additions" here means "larger proportionate additions for larger than for smaller incomes"; "less than proportionate additions" has a corresponding meaning.) It follows that *equal subtractions from welfare* are secured in these three cases respectively, by proportionate, or by more than proportionate, or by less than proportionate, subtractions from income. And this is only another way of saying that equal sacrifice requires proportional, or progressive, or regressive taxation, according to which class of relationship between income and welfare

[1] For some further remarks on the degree of "progressiveness" of a tax system, see Note to Ch. XI.

is assumed. For the first two classes, proportional sacrifice requires progressive taxation; for the third class it will require either regressive, proportional or progressive taxation, according to the sub-class of relation assumed between income and welfare.

In the limiting case, where marginal utility is constant, whatever the size of income, equal sacrifice is secured by a poll tax, equal for all taxpayers (a special case of regressive taxation), and proportional sacrifice by proportional taxation.

For we have $w=kx$, where k is a constant, and, $w-w'=k\ (x-tx)$.

$\therefore\ w'=ktx.$

If w' is constant (equal sacrifice), then tx is constant.

If $\frac{w'}{w}$ is constant (proportional sacrifice), then $\frac{ktx}{kx}$ is constant, so that t is constant.

Passing to the other side of this limit, and assuming that marginal utility increases with income, proportional sacrifice requires regressive taxation, and equal sacrifice requires taxation more regressive than a poll tax.

But these hypotheses have long since left the real world behind, and have an interest which is purely intellectual.

§ 5. The principle of constant inequality of incomes, which to some minds seems equitable, leads, I have suggested in Chapter IX, § 5, to progressive, and not to proportional, taxation. I have supported this suggestion by a reference to an argument which I have developed at some length elsewhere. I shall not spend time repeating that argument here, but shall only recapitulate, very summarily, seven of the steps in it, which have a special relevance to our present problem.

(1) The objection to great inequality of incomes is the resulting loss of potential economic welfare. (2) It is, therefore, convenient to *define* the "inequality" of any given distribution as the ratio of the total economic welfare attainable under an equal distribution to the total economic welfare attained under the given distribution, the total income to be distributed being assumed to be unchanged. (3) The measure of inequality, so defined, will depend upon the precise functional relation of income to economic welfare. To every such possible relation there will correspond a different measure of inequality. (4) But, further, common to certain wide groups of possible relations, there will be certain general tests, which all measures of inequality within the corresponding group must pass. (5) If, for example, we assume that equal additions to welfare are secured by more than proportionate additions to income (and even if we assume that they are secured by proportionate additions), all permissible measures of inequality must satisfy the condition that proportionate additions to all incomes diminish inequality. And this range of assumptions covers all probable reality, with a fairly wide margin of safety at both ends of the range. (6) But, if proportionate additions to all incomes diminish inequality, proportionate subtractions must increase it. That is to say, the inequality of incomes will be increased by proportional taxation. (7) Therefore, if the inequality of incomes is to be left unchanged by taxation, that taxation must be in some degree progressive. The precise degree of progressiveness required will vary with the precise relation of income to economic welfare.

CHAPTER X

THE EFFECTS OF TAXATION ON PRODUCTION

§ 1. The best system of taxation from the economic point of view is that which has the best, or the least bad, economic effects. In this and the two following chapters these effects will be considered under three heads, (1) effects on production, (2) effects on distribution, (3) other effects.

The effects of taxation on production can likewise be conveniently classified under three heads, (1) effects on ability to work and save, (2) effects on desire to work and save, (3) effects on the distribution of economic resources between different employments and localities.[1]

In this classification, and in the discussion which follows in this chapter, "work" and "saving" are treated on the same footing. This procedure is legitimate, provided that its limitations are clearly recognised. There is a great variety of possible economic institutions. Under all conceivable institutions, work is essentially an individual function and,

[1] An alternative, and substantially equivalent, classification would be (1) direct effects on ability to work and save, (2) direct effects on desire to work and save, (3) indirect effects on ability and desire to work and save. For a diversion of economic resources from one employment or locality to another will produce indirect effects of this kind.

except under institutions partaking of the nature of slavery, it is, in a legal sense, voluntary.[1] But the case of saving, considered as a means of securing additions to capital, is less simple. Under some institutional arrangements, most saving is both individual and voluntary. But other forms of saving, collective or compulsory or both, may co-exist with this and, under other institutional arrangements, may furnish the predominant means of securing additions to capital. Three such forms are (1) the reinvestment of the undistributed profits of private enterprise, (2) a similar reinvestment in respect of public enterprise, and (3) direct capital expenditure out of the proceeds of taxation. In this country in recent years the importance of the savings of wealthy individuals has much diminished, relatively to the factor of undistributed profits in private industry and to the rapid increase in the proportion of new loan funds furnished by insurance companies and building societies and by public and semi-public bodies. But these considerations need not detain us here.[2]

§ 2. Any person's ability to work will be reduced by taxation which reduces his efficiency. There is, therefore, a strong presumption against imposing any taxation upon the poorer members of modern communities, for these are still so poor that a reduction in their incomes will generally mean a reduction both in the present efficiency of adults and the future efficiency of children. This argument clearly applies to direct taxes on small incomes, including deductions

[1] Under "capitalist" institutions, "work" includes, as an important special case, the undertaking of new enterprises by private "entrepreneurs."

[2] See, however, Ch. XVIII.

from wages, and to taxes on necessaries. It applies also to taxes on commodities, which are not strictly necessaries but the consumption of which contributes to efficiency. As regards commodities, the consumption of which does not contribute to efficiency, it may seem at first sight that the argument does not apply. But where these commodities are treated by the workers concerned as " conventional necessaries," where, that is to say, their demand for them is comparatively inelastic, an increase in their price owing to taxation will cause some reduction in their consumption, but an increase in the expenditure upon them. The workers, therefore, will have less to spend upon real necessaries, and thus the same evil effects upon efficiency may be produced, as if real necessaries themselves had been taxed.

It is doubtful at what level of income the line should be drawn, below which taxation is likely to reduce efficiency.[1] But it is clear that, even in the richest modern communities, the incomes of a large section of the population still lie below it. Moreover, the line must be drawn at different levels for different classes of workers.

Ability to save is reduced by all taxes on those who have any margin of income, out of which saving is possible. The only taxes, therefore, which do not to some extent reduce ability to save, are those which fall exclusively on people who are so poor that they have no such margin. It is evident that heavy taxes on the rich, though defensible on

[1] It must, of course, be drawn considerably higher than " subsistence level." For the efficiency of those who have to live at or near this level is obviously less than it would be, if their incomes were larger.

other grounds, substantially reduce their ability to save.[1]

§ 3. Turning from effects upon people's ability, to effects upon their desire, to work and save, we have to take account, not so much of the primary effects of actual taxation in the present, as of the secondary effects of the expectation that such taxation will continue in the future. For it is these secondary effects, which are here by far the most important. A tax which was expected to be short-lived, a special tax, for example, to meet some special emergency, such as war expenditure or the rapid extinction of a war debt, would not produce important secondary effects of this kind.

It is usually assumed that taxation reduces people's desire to work and save, but on closer examination the question is found to be less simple than is commonly imagined. The effects of any particular tax upon desire to work and save depend partly on the nature of the tax and partly on the nature of individual reactions to taxation. The latter point is most conveniently considered first.

[1] The argument of this section illustrates an economic truth, which is specially important in public finance. It is often supposed that, whereas saving makes an addition to capital, spending does not. This is a double fallacy. For " capital," on a broad view, as many modern economists have shown, includes human beings as well as material equipment. Much " spending," especially by, and on behalf of, the poor, makes an addition, through the increase of efficiency, to human capital. Moreover, short of this, much " spending " is required merely in order to maintain human capital at its existing level of efficiency. Much consumption, in short, is really investment. And, on the other hand, much " saving," particularly in times of trade depression, makes no addition to material capital, because it fails to find its way into investment. This point will be elaborated later.

§ 4. Any person's reaction to taxation is largely governed by the elasticity of his demand for income, in terms of the efforts and sacrifices which he makes in order to obtain his income (or, what amounts to much the same thing, in terms of the services which he renders in exchange for his income).[1] His income, for the purpose of the present argument, is his net income after deduction of taxation. Suppose that, as a result of increased taxation, a given effort or sacrifice,—a given amount of work or saving,—produces less income than before. What is the effect upon his desire to work or save? Obviously, to strengthen it, if the elasticity of his demand for income is small, and to weaken it, if this elasticity is large. In the former case it will seem more worth while than before to work and to save, in the latter case less worth while. The practical question, then, is to find out how the elasticity of demand for income varies with different classes of people and with different circumstances. At this point, perhaps, the economist looks hopefully into the eyes of the psychologist, but the latter is apt to return a stony and uncomprehending stare and to talk of other things, such as the inadequate psychological basis of modern economic theory. Thus the economist is thrown back, until more effective help shall be forthcoming from the psychologist, upon his own slender resources.

It is usually assumed that most people's elasticity of demand for income is large. But is it? Many likely cases to the contrary suggest themselves. People

[1] Alternatively, we may speak of the elasticity of his supply of efforts and sacrifices (or services) in terms of the income which he can obtain in return.

who have dependants to maintain, or who are saving in the hope of securing not less than a certain fixed income at a future date, will often feel compelled by the pressure of increased taxation to work harder or to save more. Such situations are common enough among those who desire income in order to satisfy ordinary human needs, or, in other words, who desire merely to be reasonably well-off. But there are many who desire not merely to be well-off, but to be visibly better-off than those whom they regard as their social rivals. Hence springs much of that ostentatious extravagance, which is typified by the story told of Carnegie, who kept four chauffeurs, because Astor, who lived just across the road, kept only three. The desire to work and save, in order to indulge a sense of vainglorious vulgarity, is not likely to be much, if at all, abated by increased taxation. Again, some men, especially some of the leaders in the world of " big business," desire wealth and an ever-increasing income chiefly as a means of power and as evidence of worldly success. The placing of obstacles, such as increased taxation, in the way of their desire to go on accumulating seems only to exhilarate such men. Thus Leverhulme declared that " every raising of the rate at which income tax is levied has been followed by increased efforts, successfully made, to increase incomes out of which to pay the increased tax . . . We are all inclined to say, with the Irishman, ' be jabers to the tax, if you will give me the income,' and having got the income we are all inclined to make increased efforts to make the income sufficiently large to stand the contribution demanded by the Chancellor of the Exchequer, in the form of income tax, without diminishing the balance remaining for the income earner."[1] According to this view of human nature, demand for income has hardly any elasticity at all. It is, indeed, uncertain how far Leverhulme's bracing attitude towards taxation is shared by other business men, to say nothing of other classes in the community. The " psychology of the business world " remains something of a mystery, though it occupies a central position in some economists' theories of the causes of trade cycles. In times of trade depression it is common form in the business world to ascribe most of the economic evils of the day to the " crushing burden of taxation," though an equal, or even a heavier, burden may have been carried without apparent difficulty through the preceding trade boom. We cannot readily accept, in the face of Leverhulme's evidence, the implication that business men's demand for income is so highly elastic as this, though it may well be more elastic in times of depression than in times of boom, and more elastic among the inefficient than among the efficient. Nor, to return to the broader question, can we readily accept the common view that most people's demand for income is so elastic that taxation is bound, on the whole, to reduce their desire to work and save and, therefore, in this respect to check production. More light on this interesting and important problem is required.[2]

[1] *The Six Hour Day and Other Essays*, p. 248.

[2] In a comprehensive study it would be necessary to distinguish between the immediate and the more permanent effects of changes in the ratio of income to effort. It would also be necessary to take account of social habits. It has been suggested, for example, that the growth of hire purchase, or " instalment selling," tends to make the buyers' demand for income less elastic than before under adverse, and more elastic under favourable, conditions. An alternative view is that these devices, by stimulating new desires, simply raise the whole demand curve for income, without necessarily

So much for the desire to save out of individual incomes, where the alternative to saving is individual consumption. Saving out of corporate incomes—whether through undistributed profits, or through such agencies as insurance companies, or building societies, or public or semi-public bodies—is not directly subject to the competing desire for individual consumption. Those responsible for the handling of such corporate resources are inclined to attach primary importance to the continuance of new investment rather than to alternative uses of their funds. In this increasingly important field, therefore, desire to save is apt to be stimulated, rather than checked, by taxation.

§ 5. So far as we have been speaking of taxation in general in relation to the desire to work and save. It is now necessary to distinguish between the effects of different kinds of taxes.

Whatever the taxpayer's elasticity of demand for income, there are some taxes which have hardly any tendency to influence the desire to work and save. Taxes on windfalls, which have already been referred to in Chapter IX, §3, are an example. From the economic, as distinct from the equitable, point of view the essential characteristic of windfall wealth is its unexpectedness. Evidently there can be no expectation of a tax on an accretion of wealth, which is itself unexpected, and, as has already been pointed out, it is chiefly through the expectation of its future continuance that taxation is liable to affect the desire to work and

altering its slope. I have heard it argued by a business man that "if every workman was £100 in debt for furniture and a wireless set and a motor cycle, there would be far better time-keeping and much higher output."

save. In periods of great economic disturbance, or even of rapid economic change, there may be considerable scope for taxes on windfalls. During the war, for instance, the British excess profits duty, which produced a large revenue, was substantially a tax on windfalls, at any rate for the first year or two of its imposition, though with the passage of time it gradually changed its character. Again, during a period of rapid expansion in a new country, windfall taxes on the value of land and other forms of appreciating property might yield large sums. But in more normal and less unsettled conditions it is not generally possible to raise much revenue by means of such taxes. A tax on the site value of land, or on increments of site value, is a windfall tax in some cases, but not in others, since future appreciation of value is often expected. Inherited wealth, again, is sometimes a windfall to the inheritor, though many inheritances are the subject of pleasant expectation.

Another example is a tax on a monopolist, which gives him no inducement to alter his output or selling price. On the other hand, a tax on a monopolist, which makes a larger output and a lower selling price more profitable, will make him desire to work and save more, whatever his elasticity of demand for income.[1]

§ 6. But in the majority of cases the effect of various taxes upon the desire to work and save depends upon the elasticity of taxpayers' demand for income. Let us first make the assumption, which is most unfavourable to production, that this elasticity is generally large, and let us consider, on this basis, the comparative effect of various taxes, or rather of

[1] See Ch. VII, §5.

the expectation of various taxes, upon taxpayers' desire to work and save.

Taxes on particular commodities will reduce this desire very slightly, in so far as the income derived by the taxpayer from a given effort will have less purchasing power. A general tax on income, including saved income, will reduce the desire to save more than taxes on commodities, which fall on expenditure only and not on savings. Hence has arisen much discussion of the possibility, in the interests of production, of exempting savings, wholly or in part, from income tax. With the same object in view, it has been proposed to substitute a sales tax, which is equivalent to a tax on certain sorts of expenditure, for existing income taxes. It is partly administrative difficulties which have hitherto prevented any sweeping exemption of savings from income tax, and these might in time be overcome.[1] But a more fundamental objection, as also to the substitution of a sales tax for an income tax, in countries which are sufficiently civilised to possess the latter, arises from considerations of dis-

[1] Income from government securities is exempt from income tax in France and elsewhere. But in the United States the growth of tax-exempt securities has been described by serious writers as a "menace" and has made hay of the graduated taxation of income. See Lutz, *Public Finance*, pp. 506-11. Further exemptions of savings in Britain could be secured, without administrative difficulty, by exempting the undistributed profits of companies, which are at present liable to income tax at the standard rate. But the action of certain rich men who, in order to escape surtax, have formed themselves into one-man companies, which distribute hardly any of their profits, has raised prejudice against such an exemption, which is also open to criticism on grounds of equity. The present tendency is in the opposite direction, *i.e.*, increased taxation of undistributed profits. See recent British Finance Acts, and, for a very instructive account of modern methods of tax evasion, the speeches of Mr. Winston Churchill and Sir D. Hogg, now Lord Hailsham, in *Hansard*, July 4th, 1927.

tribution.[1] It will be found, when we come to deal with public expenditure, that there are other and equally effective methods of stimulating saving which are not open to these objections.[2]

Where an income tax differentiates in favour of earned income, or, in other words, taxes incomes from work at a lower rate than equal incomes from property, it is reasonable to expect a greater check to the desire to save and a smaller check to the desire to work than if the tax, while yielding the same revenue, made no such differentiation. But, on the average, the desire to save is probably stronger and more persistent among the recipients of incomes from work than among the recipients of equal incomes from property. For the former have the keener incentive to make provision for the future. This is only another way of saying that demand for future income is probably less elastic among the former than among the latter. Probably, therefore, a moderate degree of differentiation in an income tax, far from introducing any additional check to the desire to work and save, acts the other way.

Where, however, an income tax is graduated or, in other words, taxes larger incomes at a higher rate than smaller ones, it is important to realise that a very high rate of tax will almost certainly result in a sharp check to the desire to work and save at the higher levels of income, and that the sharpness of this check will increase more rapidly than the rate of tax.[3]

[1] See Ch. XI, §§3 and 5.

[2] See Ch. XVIII, §9.

[3] For as, in accordance with the graduation, the rate of tax on the income as a whole increases, the rate of tax on additional income increases more rapidly. If, for example, the tax is six shillings in the pound on £3,000 a year and seven shillings in the pound on

§ 7. A tax, which has much to commend it on other grounds, is a tax on inherited wealth. From the point of view also of its effects on production, such a tax has certain advantages over an income tax. It is sometimes imagined that, in proportion to the revenue obtained, an inheritance tax " falls on capital," in the sense of checking the accumulation of capital, to a much greater extent than an income tax. The prevalence of this idea is, no doubt, partly due to the common confusion, noticed in Chapter V, § 3, between a tax *assessed on* capital and a tax *paid out of* capital. But the idea itself is mistaken.

Assuming that the payment of an inheritance tax is not insured against beforehand, an income tax and an inheritance tax of the ordinary type, yielding the same revenue, probably check saving to much the same extent. For, on the one hand, as regards the actual payment of taxation, an inheritance tax will probably be paid by realisation of securities to a greater extent than an income tax will be paid out of money which would otherwise have been saved. But, on the other hand, as regards the effects of the expectation of having to pay in the future, saving is probably more reduced by the prospect of having to pay income tax each year, than by the remoter prospect of one's heirs having to pay inheritance tax at some uncertain future date. But, where the payment of an inheritance tax

£3,500 a year, the tax on the additional £500 a year is £325 and thus the rate of tax on this additional income is over fourteen shillings in the pound. In other words, the marginal rate of tax increases faster than the average rate, and it is the marginal rate which influences the desire of a clear-headed taxpayer to maintain his existing scale of work and saving. But it must not be lightly assumed that all taxpayers are sufficiently clear-headed to make such calculations.

is insured against beforehand,—and this habit is now fairly common—the actual payment is made, not by the realisation of securities, nor even out of current income, but with a sum of money received from an insurance company. In this case, the effects on saving of the actual payment, as distinct from the expectation of future payment, do not essentially differ from those of an income tax. In both cases, saving is only checked, in so far as the annual payments, whether for insurance premiums or income tax, are made with money which would otherwise have been saved. If, therefore, an inheritance tax is generally insured against, it checks saving less than an income tax yielding the same revenue.

The preceding argument applies to an inheritance tax of the ordinary type, whether assessed, with or without graduation, on the total property passing at death or on individual inheritances, and assumes that such a tax checks to some extent the desire of persons accumulating wealth to work and save. But, if the tax were of the type proposed by the Italian economist, Rignano, the desire to work and save would be checked to a much smaller extent, if indeed it were checked at all. This proposal is that the tax on an inherited fortune should be graduated according to what one may call the age of the fortune, or, in other words, according to the number of times it has already changed hands by inheritance. The greater the age of the fortune, the heavier would be the rate of tax. In its simplest form this proposal would amount to a differentiation between what we may call a person's earned wealth and his unearned wealth, or, in other words, between wealth which he had acquired as a result of his own work and saving and wealth which had come to him by inheritance or gift from others. On his death the latter class of wealth would be taxed at a higher rate than the former, thus giving him a stronger inducement to work and save in order to provide for his heirs, and making it less easy for him to rest on his oars and allow the dead hand to propel his boat.[1]

There is a further consideration which tells in favour of inheritance taxes, as against income taxes, from the point of view of their respective effects upon production. This is their effect upon the expectations of prospective inheritors. The latter will evidently be less inclined to work and save, the more substantial the inheritance to which they look forward. They may even be tempted, by a bright and near prospect of unearned wealth, to indulge in negative saving, running into debt or borrowing on their expectations. An inheritance tax, therefore, by reducing these expectations, stimulates work and saving by prospective inheritors and, the heavier the tax, the greater the stimulus. More and larger life insurance policies, for instance, would be taken out, if the inheritance of wealth was more severely limited by taxation, and more sons and daughters of well-to-do parents would be trained to earn their own living.

§ 8. The argument of the two preceding sections has been based on the assumption that taxpayers' demand for income is, on the whole, relatively elastic, and hence that various taxes check, in different degrees,

[1] See my *Inequality of Incomes*, Part IV, Chs. IX-X, for a fuller discussion of Rignano's scheme and of inheritance taxes in general and, for a fuller discussion still, Mr. Wedgwood's admirable book on *The Economics of Inheritance*.

the desire to work and save. But we have seen, in § 4 of this chapter, that this assumption is of doubtful validity. If we assume, on the other hand, that taxpayers' demand for income is, on the whole, relatively inelastic, it will follow that taxes on particular commodities, on income and on inheritances will stimulate the desire to work and save. Without pursuing in further detail the conflicting results of these two assumptions, we may, I think, safely conclude that, whatever may be the case with other taxes, an inheritance tax on the Rignano plan would stimulate, and not check, the productive energies of those affected by it. The practicability of such a tax should, therefore, be carefully considered by modern finance ministers.

A possible variant of the plan, which is specially adapted to debt reduction and appears to present very few administrative difficulties, is the following. Let some proportion of every estate passing at death, in excess of a certain minimum value, be compulsorily exchanged for terminable annuities to be issued by the Treasury. These annuities might either be terminable with the life of the inheritor, or, preferably, might have a fixed term, say, twenty years from the date of issue. During this period they would carry an annual income equal to the annual value of the wealth surrendered in exchange for them. The forms of wealth which would thus be accepted in exchange might conveniently be limited to public securities, other approved securities and cash The public securities would be cancelled on receipt ; the cash would be applied to debt reduction ; the approved securities would either be realised and the proceeds applied to debt reduction, or held and the interest so applied. The Government would thus, in effect, issue terminable annuities in exchange for the cancellation of an amount of debt of equal annual value. The proportion of the debt consisting of such annuities would gradually increase and, after a period of, say, twenty years from the inception of the scheme, a quantity of these annuities would be running off annually. Inheritors would receive these annuities as part of their inheritance. They would be stimulated, by the prospect of the annuities running out, to work and save in order to make good the prospective loss of income.[1]

§ 9. So far in this chapter we have been considering how taxation may affect production through its influence upon ability and desire to work and save. We have now to consider how it may affect production through its effects on the distribution of economic resources between different employments and localities.

The undesirability, in the interests of production, of diverting "trade," or, more generally, economic resources, from their "natural channels" has been a favourite theme with many economists of past generations, who have argued that the resources diverted will be less productive in their new employment (or locality) than they would have been in the old. Most modern authorities argue that, as a general rule, such diversions tend to check production, but that there are a large number of practical instances to which this rule does not apply. The much too absolute doctrine

[1] See my evidence before the Colwyn Committee, and pp. 317-18 of their Report. Compare also H. D. Henderson, *Inheritance and Inequality*, for a similar proposal. This plan might also be adapted, if desired, to reducing the burden of debt on public enterprises, the bonds of which might be accepted in payment and then cancelled.

of the inviolability of "natural channels," as preached by the ancients, expresses only a half-truth. We may say that, in the choice of taxes, there is a presumption in favour of those which cause the minimum of diversion of economic resources. But this presumption is frequently overthrown by special arguments applicable to particular cases. It will, therefore, be convenient to begin by considering what sorts of taxes cause, in fact, the minimum of diversion, and go on to consider certain particular cases of substantial diversion.

§ 10. As between different employments of economic resources, taxes which have been defended on the ground that they cause little or no diversion, include taxes on windfalls, taxes on the site value of land, such taxes on monopolists as offer no inducement to alter output or selling price, and certain taxes which fall with equal weight on all uses of wealth. In general, the way in which diversion is apt to occur is as follows. A person who owns, or himself embodies, economic resources which, in their actual employment, are subject to tax, seeks to escape this tax by diverting these resources to some other employment, in which they will either be untaxed or taxed less heavily. Such a diversion will be profitable to him provided that the loss of income, apart from taxation, due to the change of employment is less than the gain through the payment of lower taxation. Such diversion of existing resources is often difficult, or even impossible, since capital and labour tend to become fixed or specialised in particular employments. But no such difficulty prevents the diversion to other employments of new resources, not yet specialised, which, but for the tax, would have entered the taxed employment. In practice, it is the diversion of these new resources, rather than of existing resources, which is much the more important. The British rating system, for instance, imposes taxation upon houses and other buildings in the form of onerous rates.[1] The effect is a diversion of capital and labour, which would otherwise have been employed in the building trade, to other employments. The supply of houses and other buildings is consequently smaller than it would otherwise have been, and there is a presumption that the capital and labour, which are diverted to other employments, are less productive there than they would have been had they been employed in the building trade. The extent to which a given tax causes a diversion of resources from the taxed employment and a reduction in the supply of its product depends, as was shown in Chapter VII, upon the elasticity of demand for this product and upon its elasticity of supply.

A tax on windfalls, falling unexpectedly, like a bolt from the blue, upon accretions of wealth which are themselves unexpected, obviously gives no inducement to diversion. A tax on the site value of land, irrespective of the employment to which the land is put, causes no diversion, since its incidence is wholly upon the landowner[2] and since the supply of land is fixed by nature and, therefore, no restriction of supply is possible. A tax on a monopolist, which gives him no inducement to alter his output or selling price, gives no inducement to diversion, because, though the monopoly becomes less profitable than it would

[1] See Ch. VI, §3.

[2] Compare, however, Ch. VIII, §2.

otherwise have been, it remains more profitable than the employment of resources in open competition.[1]

It has been suggested that a tax, which falls with equal weight upon all uses of wealth, or, in other words, upon all employments of resources, gives no inducement to diversion, because no diversion would be a source of profit. Some controversy has taken place as to what would constitute a perfect " non-differential " tax of this kind. On the one hand, it has been maintained that a general tax on income is non-differential, while, on the other, it has been argued that such a tax, since it taxes both income when saved and income subsequently derived from savings, differentiates against saving and gives an inducement to diversion from saving to spending. If the latter argument be sound, a perfect non-differential tax would be a tax on expenditure only, or, in other words, an income tax with an exemption for income which was saved. But whether, in fact, a general income tax causes a diversion from saving to spending depends upon the elasticity of the taxpayers' demand for the future income to be derived from savings. If this elasticity is large, relatively to the elasticity of their demand for income for present consumption, such a diversion will take place; if it is small, the diversion will be in the opposite direction, from spending to saving; if it is of some intermediate size, there will be no diversion. Similarly, an expenditure tax may cause

[1] Though not necessarily more profitable than the employment of resources in other monopolies, if these are not correspondingly taxed. But the policy of monopolists, based upon restriction of output, deliberately obstructs the entry of new resources into the monopolised employment.

a diversion in either direction, or no diversion at all, according to the relative size of these two elasticities. Without reference to this factor, it cannot be maintained that either tax is perfectly "non-differential." But either tax, in so far as it falls only on marginal expenditures or marginal savings, regardless of their particular character, is evidently less differential, and tends to less diversion of resources, than taxes on particular employments of resources. For the latter fall also upon "intra-marginal" expenditure or savings. Similarly a general property tax, if accurately assessed, is comparatively "non-differential."

In fact, a perfect non-differential tax would not fall at equal rates on all uses of resources. For equal rates of tax would affect unequally the supply of objects of taxation, when these had unequal elasticities of demand or supply. A tax, non-differential in structure, would be differential in its effects, causing a diversion from objects of large elasticity, whether of demand or supply, to objects of small elasticity. Therefore, to be non-differential in its effects, a tax must be differential in its structure. Its rates must be nicely adjusted to all the relevant elasticities, falling most heavily where elasticities were smallest, least heavily where they were largest. But such a tax is only an amusing intellectual toy, not a practically useful instrument.

§ 11. There is, however, a presumption in favour of those taxes which cause a minimum of diversion. The strength of this presumption in some cases and its weakness in others may be shown by a few illustrations. A tax on whisky, by diminishing its consumption and increasing health and efficiency, may cause a diversion which will increase production.[1] Again, a tax on land used for particular purposes will tend to cause a diversion from these purposes to others, which may be more beneficial to production, or to the social advantage. Again, a tax on a monopolist, which gives him an inducement to increase his output and lower his selling price, is likely to cause a beneficial diversion, since the additional resources which he will employ are likely to be more productive than they would have been in some other competitive employment.

On the other hand, examples of harmful diversion are frequently found in modern tax systems. The case of the taxation of houses under the British rating system has already been mentioned. In view of the shortage of houses and of the reactions of bad housing upon health and efficiency, the diversion of capital and labour from house-building to other employments is clearly harmful.[2] Again, a special tax upon business profits, such as the post-war British corporation profits tax, now repealed, was a bad tax from the present

[1] A diversion of economic resources, though not necessarily a diversion of money expenditure in the same direction. A tax on a commodity, by raising its price, will reduce the demand for it, and hence the economic resources required to meet this demand. If, however, the demand is inelastic, a larger sum of money than before will be spent on purchasing a smaller quantity. But, assuming the displaced resources find employment, other commodities will be produced in larger quantities and sold at lower prices.

[2] It is for this reason that the argument for rating site values, rather than buildings, carries great weight, so far at least as onerous rates are concerned. There are, however, certain objections, due to the complications of British urban land tenure, to making such a change at one fell swoop. Since the chief object of the change is to remove the present hindrance to new building, the way of least resistance and greatest convenience would, perhaps, be to stabilise existing rating assessments and only to vary them in future in accordance with variations in the site value. This would effectively free both new buildings and improvements to existing buildings.

point of view. For it discriminated against a particular class of property-owners, namely the ordinary shareholders in joint stock companies, as compared with all other classes, including debenture holders and the holders of gilt-edged securities. It was, therefore, in effect, a tax on risk-bearing and tended to divert the flow of capital from risky to comparatively safe investments. But, in view of the need that risks should be taken and the reluctance of many investors to take them, this was a harmful diversion.

Consider, finally, the case of a protective tariff, which is the classical example of the deliberate diversion of resources from their " natural channels." The case for such a tariff, in the interests of increased production, is often supported in popular discussion by arguments which are grossly fallacious, but in its classical form, as stated by List, it is logically respectable. It is undoubtedly possible that, in some circumstances, a skilfully devised protective tariff, though diminishing production for a while, may yet increase it in the long run, by developing certain sources of productive power faster than they would otherwise have been developed. But, even when such circumstances are present, the likelihood of such a tariff being skilfully devised from the point of view of the community as a whole, as distinct from that of powerful organised interests, which ought not to be protected, is slight. Further, List's argument assumes that protection should be temporary, whereas one of the most difficult tasks in practical politics is to get rid of a protective tariff once established. And such a tariff, even if originally justifiable, may inflict far greater loss on productive power, if too long maintained, than would have been incurred if it had never been adopted at all. Sidgwick, in his day, said almost the last word on this matter, when he remarked that many people seem to suppose that in theory free trade is the best policy, but that in practice protection will not do much harm, and may do some good, whereas the true situation is the exact reverse of this ; in theory a case may often be made out for protection, but in practice it is wiser to stick to free trade. Since then the situation has changed. This country, having long stuck to free trade in an increasingly protectionist world, has now taken to a tariff like the rest. A return to unilateral free trade, either in this country or elsewhere, seems unlikely. More probable is the further development of planned international exchange through bilateral commercial treaties, quotas and other devices. These involve large diversions of trade from its "natural channels" and raise many issues which lie outside the scope of this book. But, fundamentally, the prevalence of high protective tariffs in the modern world is to be accounted for by the great political power of organised interests, which, aided by certain elementary but widespread confusions of thought on the subject of international trade and by nationalist sentiment in favour of economic "self-sufficiency," benefit by protection at the expense of the unorganised general public. In view of the strength of these forces working towards harmful diversions, it is a counsel of wisdom that the protection of particular industries should be a source, not of public revenue, but of public expenditure. For in this case policy will be more critically watched both by finance ministers and by taxpayers. This points to subsidies in special cases, rather than protective duties. But the discussion of subsidies must be postponed to Part III of this book.

§ 12. In the last two sections we have been considering the diversion of economic resources from one employment to another. But diversion may also take place, as a result of taxation, from one locality to another, and the general presumption against diversions is relevant here also, as regards aggregate production in all the localities concerned. Local diversions are specially apt to take place in comparatively small communities, when persons or capital are driven by the pressure of taxation into neighbouring communities where taxation is less heavy. Thus differences in taxation, and also in strictness of assessment, as between different States in the United States of America, seem to have caused considerable movements of this kind.

In this country the argument is often heard that taxation, and especially our income tax and death duties, " drives capital abroad." It is true, but it is a very partial answer, that no taxation can drive abroad existing fixed capital, such as railways and factories. For the argument refers not to existing, but to future, capital goods, whose location is not yet decided.

Specially heavy British taxation might cause either foreign or British capital to be invested abroad, which would otherwise have been invested here. The former possibility is not important, since very little foreign capital is invested here. As to the latter possibility, British income tax falls equally upon income from capital, whether invested in this country or abroad, provided that the owner resides in this country.

British death duties likewise, with a few unimportant exceptions, fall equally upon property, whether situated in this country or abroad, of persons resident in this country. These British taxes, therefore, will only drive British capital abroad, if the owner is willing to be driven abroad along with it, or if, remaining in this country, he is prepared to perjure himself to the Inland Revenue Officials, and thinks himself less likely to be caught in respect of his foreign investments. Wealthy Englishmen, however, show no signs of emigrating in large numbers, and probably not very many are inclined to substantial perjury, particularly since the increasing efficiency of the tax collectors is constantly diminishing the chance of escaping detection. A tax on the site value of land has, however, these two further arguments in its favour, in addition to those already mentioned, that, since land is incapable either of exportation or concealment, such a tax can neither cause local diversions nor be evaded by dishonest taxpayers.

Variations of local taxation within a country, such as Great Britain, in so far as they correspond to variations in the cost of rendering those local services, which are paid for by beneficial, as distinct from onerous, rates, do not necessarily lead to harmful diversions but may help to prevent an uneconomic territorial distribution of population and capital. In so far, however, as these two sets of variations do not correspond, harmful diversions tend to arise.

They have recently arisen in a marked degree in connection with the problem of the " distressed areas." In these areas exceptionally severe and prolonged unemployment has led to the continuance of exceptionally high onerous rates, chiefly for poor relief. The effect of these high rates, falling upon local industries which are already depressed and upon local shopkeepers and householders who are already impoverished, has been evil and cumulative. Not only has a train of uneconomic diversions been set up, but, in so far as the labour and capital in these areas has lacked mobility, either towards other places or other uses, a mass of localised unemployment, both of men and of machines, has become chronic, while new industries, for a variety of reasons, have gone elsewhere. The solution of this problem extends beyond the scope of public finance, but there is a strong case for a subsidy to suitable new industries setting up in these areas.[1]

§ 13. To sum up the main conclusions of this chapter, it is probably impossible to impose heavy taxation in a modern community without thereby causing some check to production. How severe this check will be, in respect of any given tax revenue, will depend both upon the character of the taxes imposed and upon the character of the taxpayers. The check may be exercised in three ways. The first is through the effects of taxation on ability to work and save; the second is through its effects on desire to work and save; the third is through diversions, due to taxation, of economic resources as between different employments and localities. It is under the first head, and especially as a result of reduced ability to save, that the check is most certain and probably most serious. Under the second, much depends on the character of the taxpayers, or, in technical terms, on the elasticity of their demand for income. A check to production under this

[1] For a further discussion of the effects of local rates on employment see Ch. XII, §3.

head is not inevitable; on the contrary, a stimulus to production is a possibility. Under the third head, much depends on the wise selection of taxes. Here, again, a check to production is not inevitable, and a stimulus is possible.

If all the proceeds of taxation were spent on waste, which contributed nothing to economic welfare, then any check to production as a result of taxation would be a clear economic loss. But, if the proceeds of taxation are wisely spent, the stimulus to production due to this expenditure may be far stronger than the check to production due to taxation. Public finance, viewed as a whole, would then be responsible for increasing production.[1]

[1] It has been well said that "the whole tendency of modern economic reasoning is to lay less stress on the effects of this or that action in stimulating or checking the *motives* for displaying this or that kind of activity, and more stress on its effects in expanding or contracting the *sources* from which that activity emanates. A high income tax, the proceeds of which are devoted partly to debt reduction and partly to measures of public health and education, may well have a beneficial effect on the sources of both savings and business enterprise far outweighing any discouraging effect it may exercise on the incentives to display those activities" (D. H. Robertson, *Economic Journal*, December, 1927, p. 580). In practice, effects upon ability to work and save are likely to be much more important than effects upon willingness to do these things. This applies to the effects, both of taxation and of public expenditure, upon production. (Compare Ch. XVIII.) Ability is mainly determined by fundamental realities; willingness depends largely on superficial conventions.

CHAPTER XI

THE EFFECTS OF TAXATION ON DISTRIBUTION

§ 1. It is generally admitted that we should study the effects of taxation on production, and that, other things being equal, one tax system is preferable to another, if it has less tendency to check production. It is not generally denied that the effects of taxation on distribution are also worthy of study, but it is less commonly admitted that, other things being equal, one tax system is preferable to another, if it has a stronger tendency to check inequality. The German economist Wagner deserves credit as being one of the first to insist that taxation should be used to reduce the inequality of incomes. His so-called " socio-political " view of public finance displeases certain other high authorities, but it is sound in principle, and is increasingly adopted in modern practice. For a less unequal distribution is no less desirable than an increased production of wealth.[1]

[1] The ideal distribution, from an economic point of view, is that which causes a given amount of production to yield the maximum of economic welfare. This ideal is not, therefore, an absolutely equal distribution, but a distribution " according to needs," or, to put the same thought into other words, according to capacity to make a good use of income. In face, however, of the great inequality of incomes, which prevails in most modern communities, we may be reasonably sure that any practicable reduction in inequality will give us a closer approximation to the ideal distribution. And, therefore, it is legitimate to assume, as a first approximation to reality, that the relation between income and economic welfare is the same for all members of the community.

§ 2. It has been remarked above that the measurement of the inequality of incomes raises some difficult problems,—incidentally this is also true of the measurement of production,—and that, until these have been solved, the comparative effects of different tax systems on inequality cannot be precisely determined. But certain broad conclusions readily emerge.

A regressive tax system tends to increase the inequality of incomes. So does a proportional, or even a mildly progressive, tax system.[1] But a more sharply progressive tax system tends to reduce inequality and, the sharper the progression, the stronger this tendency.[2] Considerations of distribution, therefore, lead us towards the most sharply progressive tax system that is practicable. A rough approximation to such a system is that referred to in Chapter IX, § 2 in our discussion of the principle of minimum sacrifice. All incomes above a certain level would be cut down to that level, and no incomes below that level would be taxed at all. From the economic, as distinct from the equitable, point of view, and so far as considerations of distribution only are concerned, this, with certain minor adjustments, would be taxation according to ability to pay. Considerations of production may make so sharp a progression undesirable. But the case for a marked degree of progression may be taken to be firmly established.

It was, however, pointed out in another connection in the last chapter, and may be repeated here, that

[1] See Ch. IX, §5, and Note to Ch. IX, §5.

[2] Yet another tricky problem of measurement, that of the *degree of progressiveness* of a tax system, may be indicated, but will not be pursued here. It is examined in the Note at the end of this Chapter.

public authorities controlling comparatively small areas must face the possibility that their tax policy may drive persons and capital outside their areas. A small community, instituting a tax system much more progressive than those of its neighbours, might well cause such an exodus and suffer by it. The larger the areas over which strongly progressive tax systems operate, and the smaller the mobility of persons and capital across their boundaries, the less serious is this danger.

§ 3. A poll tax, equal in amount for each taxpayer, is the simplest of all taxes. If all incomes were equal, it would be a proportional tax of great practical convenience. But, if incomes are unequal, it becomes a regressive tax and, the greater the inequality, the greater the degree of regression. It is, therefore, unsuitable to the conditions of modern communities.

Taxes on commodities of wide consumption are generally regressive, since, as a rule, the larger a person's income, the smaller the proportion of it which he spends on any one such commodity. Thus taxes on food are generally sharply regressive. So are taxes on tobacco and the cheaper sorts of alcohol. An *ad valorem* tax on a commodity is less regressive than a specific tax, since the former differentiates to some extent against consumers of the more expensive qualities. A proportional tax on individual expenditure (since the ratio of expenditure to income falls as income increases), and a sales tax, which consists, in effect, of a large number of taxes on particular commodities, are similarly regressive. But taxes on luxuries may be progressive, at least broadly, as between rich and poor.

British local rates, on the other hand, in so far as they fall on occupiers, are broadly regressive, both in particular rating areas and, still more, in the country as a whole. For the rateable value of dwelling houses is a diminishing proportion of income, as income increases, and rates in the pound are higher in poor than in rich districts. If a tax system, which includes regressive taxes, is to be progressive on the whole, it must contain other taxes, which are themselves progressive and exercise a stronger influence on the general character of the tax system.

§ 4. Apart from luxury taxes, the most important taxes, which are easily made progressive, are income and inheritance taxes and general taxes on property.

An income tax may be made progressive by means of a graduated scale of rates, larger incomes being taxed at higher rates than smaller ones. This principle may be applied directly, each taxpayer making a return of his total income and being charged on it at the appropriate rate. But, for administrative reasons, it is more convenient to apply it to a large extent indirectly. Thus the British income tax law imposes a standard rate of tax, which is deducted from most taxable income before it reaches its recipient, who may, however, claim some repayment, if his total income is less than a certain amount. This is supplemented by an additional graduated tax, or surtax, on the larger incomes only, and by a system of exemptions and allowances specially affecting the smaller incomes. The tax is progressive as between different sections of income tax payers and thus helps to counter-balance the effect of regressive taxes in the tax system as a whole. But it is not, of course, progressive as between the various sections of those who are exempted, and may leave the tax system regressive as regards the latter, though progressive over the higher ranges of income. Progression in the British income tax is also secured, to a small degree, by limiting differentiation in favour of income from work, as against income from property, to incomes below a certain level.

A further argument in favour of such differentiation is that an income from property will generally yield a larger amount of economic welfare than an equal income from work, since against the economic welfare derived from the latter must be debited the disutility, or subjective cost, of the work itself, the need of the worker to live near his place of work, and his greater need, as compared with the property owner, to make provision for the future.[1] The income from work should, therefore, be taxed at a lower rate than the equal income from property, if each taxpayer is to make a proportional sacrifice of economic welfare and, *a fortiori*, if the total sacrifice of the two, corresponding to a given total tax contribution, is to be a minimum.

An important question, specially arising in connection with income tax, but relevant to the character of the whole tax system, is that of the allowances which should be made for the domestic circumstances of the taxpayer. Under the British income tax law, the incomes of a husband and wife are treated, substantially, as a single taxable income, and allowances from this taxable income are then given in respect of the

[1] Primarily, because all income from work is, in the language of accountancy, income from a wasting (human) asset.

wife and of any children under sixteen years of age. It is sometimes suggested that married women's incomes should be taxed independently of their husbands'. But, if this were done, a progressive income tax would fall more heavily upon a married couple, one of whom had an income of £800 a year and the other nothing, than upon a married couple, each of whom had an income of £400 a year. And there is no good reason, either in equity or economy, for such a difference of treatment. Unless, however, the income tax payable by a man with a given taxable income and no dependants is made greater than that payable out of a family income of equal size, on which two or more persons have to be supported, mere graduation of the rates of tax will not bring any close approach to taxation according to ability to pay.

§ 5. It is a fundamental weakness of a sales tax that it cannot make allowances for domestic circumstances, and indeed that it tends to fall more heavily, as between taxpayers of equal income, on those who have the largest number of dependants. Nor is it possible, except by a very elaborate differentiation of the rates of tax on various commodities, to make a sales tax progressive as between different taxpayers of unequal incomes. It would probably be necessary, for this purpose, to extend the scope of the tax to cover the sale of personal services. And this would greatly increase its administrative difficulties. A practicable sales tax tends almost inevitably to be regressive.

A progressive tax on individual expenditure might, indeed, be obtained by the exemption of savings from a progressive income tax. But since, as a rule, the larger the income, the larger the proportion saved, a very steep rate of progression on incomes, *i.e.*, on expenditure plus savings, might be required in order to produce a tax which should be even mildly progressive on expenditures.[1] It follows that the complete exemption of savings from income tax would make it very difficult to construct a progressive tax system, in which the income tax was a prominent feature. It has already been pointed out that, if it is desired to stimulate saving through the agency of public finance, this can be better done through appropriate public expenditure than through the tax system.

§ 6. An inheritance tax may be assessed and graduated in various ways. It will, as a general rule, be progressive as between inheritors, if, on the occasion of any particular death, it is assessed on a progressive scale on the amounts inherited by different individuals. Mill's proposal to fix a maximum sum, more than which no individual should be allowed to inherit, only implies a specially sharp progression in a tax of this kind. But, if the same individual receives separate inheritances on different occasions, complications arise. Thus a person who receives two legacies of £1,000 each will be less heavily taxed than one who receives a single legacy of £2,000. It would, therefore, be desirable, from the point of view of distribution, to

[1] For example, if A's income is £20,000, of which he saves £10,000, and B's income is £5,000, of which he saves £1,000, then a given rate of expenditure tax on A is arithmetically equivalent to half that rate of income tax, and a given rate of expenditure tax on B to four-fifths of that rate of income tax. It follows that, if the rate of tax on A's expenditure is to exceed, even slightly, the rate on B's, the rate on A's income must be nearly double the rate on B's.

graduate an inheritance tax, not only according to the amounts received by inheritors, but also according to the amounts of wealth which the latter already possess. Attempts were made to apply this principle after the war both in Germany and in Italy, but they were abandoned owing to administrative difficulties. Many inheritance taxes are assessed on other bases. The British estate duty, for instance, is assessed on a progressive scale on the total value of the property passing at death, regardless of its distribution among inheritors, and the British legacy and succession duties are progressive according to the remoteness of the relationship of the inheritor to the deceased. Neither of these principles of progression necessarily leads to progression as between inheritors. In practice, the British estate duty probably does so in the majority of cases, since testators generally leave most of their property to a few fortunate persons. But the duty would fall more heavily, both absolutely and proportionately, upon an estate of £50,000, to be equally divided among five inheritors, than upon an estate of £40,000 passing to a single inheritor. The legacy and succession duties, on the other hand, are often regressive on inheritors, since testators generally leave more to near than to distant relatives, and very little to persons who are not related to them.

The conclusion is that an inheritance tax, in order to contribute most surely to the progressiveness of a tax system, should be assessed on a progressive scale both on individual inheritances and also, if practicable, on the wealth of inheritors.[1] A heavy inheritance tax

[1] Such a tax could be supplemented by another based on Rignano's principle, referred to in the last chapter.

further tends slightly to reduce the inequality of incomes by stimulating gifts *inter vivos* from the old to the young, with the object of avoiding the tax. But this tendency is less powerful than might be supposed, since those who receive such gifts are generally those who would otherwise have inherited a little later, and since, when the tax is successfully avoided, the recipients are richer than they would have been, if they had had to pay it. In principle, gifts from the living should be taxed on the same footing as gifts from the dead. But here again there are administrative difficulties, though they could probably be overcome.

§ 7. A general property tax may obviously be made progressive as between property owners by means of graduated rates, exemptions and allowances. It has been pointed out above that the capital value of property is generally a less satisfactory basis of tax assessment than its annual value, or, in other words, than the income derived from it. But there is sometimes a strong case for a progressive tax on the value of property held by individuals. Such a case arises, for instance, in connection with the huge war debts of to-day, which, as argued below,[1] might with advantage be greatly reduced, if not entirely paid off, by means of a tax of this kind imposed, not annually, but once for all.

It is an argument in favour of a graduated property tax that it strikes, more heavily than an equally progressive income tax, great wealth held passively by

[1] See Ch. XXIII.

elderly people, and strikes the young and middle aged more lightly.[1]

In the United States taxable income is defined so as to include " capital gains," *i.e.*, any increase in the value of the taxpayer's capital during the year of assessment. When security prices are rising, this provision increases the progressiveness of the tax system. But, " capital losses " being treated as a deduction from taxable income, it operates even more strongly in the opposite direction, when prices fall. Thus Mr. Pierpont Morgan was able in 1931-33 to prove to the Federal tax-collectors that he had no " income." His income, in the ordinary sense, was still gigantic. So was the value of his capital, which had, however, suffered some decline from the high levels of previous years.

§ 8. The principle of progression may also be introduced into other taxes. A tax on land values, for example, may be made progressive on the total value of land owned by individuals, with a minimum of exemption. The Australian Commonwealth land tax is of this type. Such a tax tends to produce a more equal distribution of land, though not necessarily of all wealth, in private ownership. For a big landowner, by selling half his land as measured by its value, will escape more than half his tax.

On the other hand, some taxes, which at first sight appear progressive, are disappointing in this respect on a closer examination. Take, for example, a corporation tax, progressive according to the ratio of the profits

[1] In general, capacity to make good use of income, in excess of a moderate amount, rapidly diminishes as old age sets in. I offer this concession to those who challenge the assumption that the relation of income to welfare is the same for all members of the community.

to the capital of a business. Such a tax is not necessarily progressive on individual incomes derived from businesses subject to it. For a dividend of 5 per cent. on an investment of £5,000 in one company would be taxed at a lower rate than a dividend of 10 per cent. on an investment of £1,000 in another. Still less is it necessarily progressive on individual incomes from property, for incomes, however large, from public securities or land would escape it, while incomes, however small, even below the level of income tax exemption, would be taxed, if derived from businesses subject to it.[1] The latter argument applies also to a corporation tax at a flat rate, such as the British corporation profits tax, now repealed.

§ 9. It is sometimes claimed that a protective tariff might succeed, not only in increasing production, but also in improving distribution by reducing the inequality of incomes. Theoretically, it might do this in either of two ways. It might, on the one hand, tax imported commodities competing with those home industries, in which wages were comparatively high, and thus tend to divert production and employment from other industries, in which wages were lower, to these more favoured industries. And it might, on the other hand,—and for this purpose it would not always need to be protective—tax imported commodities mainly consumed by the rich, and thus not only secure some revenue from the latter, but also tend to substitute for such imports others, which would be more useful,

[1] Similarly the taxation of Co-operative Societies is objectionable, from the point of view of distribution, since the majority of their members are comparatively poor.

directly or indirectly, to the majority of the community.

Both these results are theoretically possible, but probably of small practical importance. If it is desired to improve distribution by taxation, more direct and powerful methods, such as have been referred to in earlier sections of this chapter, are available.

§ 10. It is interesting to notice the extent to which the British tax system has, since the beginning of the present century, become progressive. This was well brought out by Sir Herbert Samuel's comparison of the distribution of the direct money burden of taxation in the three years 1903-4, 1913-14 and 1918-19.[1] His estimates exclude local rates, stamp duties and excess profits duty, but treat as a tax the profits of the Post Office. It is assumed, to facilitate the calculation, that death duties are insured against by annual premiums, which are regarded as additional income tax on incomes from property,[2] and it is also assumed that all taxes on commodities are wholly paid by consumers.

He shows that indirect taxes were sharply regressive in each of the three years, but that direct taxes had become more and more progressive. The tax system as a whole shows the following evolution during this period.

[1] See his paper in the *Journal of the Royal Statistical Society*, March, 1919.

[2] This assumption is not legitimate, since, as was pointed out in Ch. VII, §2, the incidence of an inheritance tax is on the successor, and not on the predecessor. But it is difficult to make an allowance here, on a correct basis, for an inheritance tax, since this is paid by the successor at a time when, by reason of his net succession, he is moving into a higher income class.

Percentages of Incomes Paid in Taxes

Taxpayer's Annual Income.	Incomes from work.			Incomes from property.		
£	1903-4	1913-14	1918-19	1903-4	1913-14	1918-19
50	9·1	8·7	—	9·1	8·7	—
100	6·2	6·0	13·8	6·2	6·0	13·8
150	5·0	4·9	11·0	5·0	4·9	11·0
200	5·6	4·8	10·3	7·8	7·0	12·4
500	6·6	5·8	13·1	8·8	9·9	18·1
1,000	7·4	6·6	19·4	10·3	12·2	26·5
2,000	6·6	5·8	25·6	9·8	12·0	33·6
5,000	5·6	6·8	37·2	9·6	12·4	43·5
10,000	5·1	8·1	42·6	9·5	15·1	50·3
20,000	4·9	8·3	47·6	10·0	16·0	58·1
50,000	4·8	8·4	50·6	10·2	18·1	63·9

Taken broadly, these figures show that in the first year the tax system was, on the whole, distinctly regressive on incomes from work, regressive on incomes from property up to between £150 and £200 a year, then slightly progressive up to about £1,000 a year and then roughly proportional.

In the second year it was still regressive on incomes from work up to between £200 and £500 and on incomes from property up to between £150 and £200. On incomes from work between £500 and £5,000 it was roughly proportional, and above £10,000 again roughly proportional, but at a slightly higher rate. On incomes from property above £200 it was, on the whole, mildly progressive, with a proportional patch between £1,000 and £5,000.

In the third year regression was still found on incomes from work up to between £200 and £500 and on incomes from property up to between £150 and £200. Above these points the tax system had become continuously progressive on both sorts of income, and the scale of progression had been steepened to a degree, which would have seemed incredible both to the Chancellors of the Exchequer and to the economists of the Victorian Age. But there was no reason to suppose that we had reached in 1918-19 the limits of practicable or desirable progression. The persistent element of regression among the smaller incomes was largely due to the maintenance of taxes on food, and was a serious blot, from the point of view of distribution, on the tax system as a whole.

§ 11. Sir Herbert Samuel's estimates were revised in 1927 by the Colwyn Committee, which added similar estimates of its own for the years 1923-24 and 1925-26. These are given in the Note which follows this chapter.

They will be seen to indicate that, as regards incomes from work, the rates of taxation on the smaller incomes, up to between £200 and £500, were increased between 1918-19 and 1923-24, while they were decreased on the larger incomes. Between 1923-24 and 1925-26 they were decreased over the whole range of incomes, but remained higher on the smaller incomes, and lower on the larger incomes, in 1925-26 than in 1918-19. The element of regression on the smaller incomes continued and its range actually increased, reaching in the two later years to incomes somewhere between £500 and £1,000.

The Colwyn Committee made no estimate, as Sir Herbert Samuel had done, of taxation on incomes wholly derived from property. They dealt instead with mixed incomes, derived half from work and half from property. Their figures show that the changes, between 1918-19 and 1925-26, in the relative rates of taxation on those mixed incomes were roughly similar to the corresponding changes in the case of incomes from work.

The broad conclusions which emerge are that the British tax system between 1918 and 1926 increased its regressive pressure on the smaller incomes, and diminished its progressive pressure on the larger,[1] and that the range of regression widened, while the range of progression narrowed. From the point of view of distribution, therefore, the British tax system deteriorated during this period.

It should, moreover, be noted that the effects of progressive taxation on distribution may be offset, from the side of public expenditure, by the effects of regressive grants.[2] The growth of the national debt is highly relevant here. Giving evidence in February, 1925, before the Colwyn Committee, I pointed out that " the present annual yield of income tax and super-tax (£326,000,000) is only slightly greater than the present annual interest charge on the debt (£305,000,000), and falls short of the present annual charge for interest and sinking fund combined (£350,000,000). In 1913-14 income tax and super-tax, yielding £47,000,000, covered the total debt charges, £25,000,000, nearly twice over. Now, broadly speaking, it is the income tax payers who

[1] As to changes in the *degrees* of regression and progression see the Note to this Chapter, §3.

[2] A system of regressive grants involves greater proportionate additions to large incomes than to small. See Ch. XVII, §3, and Ch. XIX, §2

themselves receive the interest on the debt. Leaving external debt out of account, the collection of income tax and super-tax and the payment of interest resolve themselves into mere transfers of wealth within a comparatively small section of the community. The present situation, therefore, is that income tax and super-tax payers, as such, have practically ceased to make any contribution to the current expenses of the country, as represented by the Supply Services." The features of the situation, which I then depicted, became more marked in the next few years, owing to reductions in the rates of income tax and super-tax, without a corresponding reduction in the debt charges.[1]

Since 1926 there have been many changes, pointing different ways, but no new comprehensive examination

[1] In confirmation of my argument on this point, I quote the following passage from Professor Pigou's *Public Finance* (p. 244). It will be observed that he is dealing with the situation more than a year later than the date of my evidence before the Colwyn Committee, after the rates of income tax and super-tax had already been reduced by the Finance Act of 1925, that he credits the wealthier classes with their contribution to the death duties, and that he excludes from the balance sheet the interest and sinking fund on the external debt. "In 1925-26," he writes, "the net produce of income tax and super-tax was £295,000,000 and of death duties £50,000,000 making £345,000,000 in all, while the interest on the internal debt amounted to £273,000,000. When to this is added management expenses, and, say—to make allowance for foreign debt—six-sevenths of a £50,000,000 sinking fund, it appears that practically the whole of the contribution to the national revenue made by the income tax paying class was absorbed in financing a debt in the main held by members of that class, nothing being left over for general government services. It is certain that, had the war been financed out of taxes, so that no aftermath of internal debt remained, the income tax paying class would have been called upon for a very substantial contribution towards those general services. Thus resort to the method of loans has enabled them to escape, at the expense of poorer persons, from a heavy burden of charges, which, had the tax method been more largely employed, they must inevitably have borne."

of their effects. Probably, on balance, there has been a further deterioration, to which the adoption of a protective tariff has contributed. As against this, conversion operations have reduced the debt charge.

NOTE TO CHAPTER XI

§ 1. The purpose of this Note is twofold, first to reproduce, in summary form, the statistical conclusions of the Colwyn Committee on the distribution of the burden of taxation and, second, to examine more closely the conception, and measurement, of "progressiveness" in a tax system.

The Colwyn Committee revised Sir Herbert Samuel's figures on the basis of alternative estimates of the consumption in past years, at various income levels, of taxed commodities. Their estimates of such consumption, and hence of rates of tax on typical incomes, are generally lower than his. But I doubt whether they are likely to be much more accurate. They exclude Post Office profits, which he had included, but otherwise retain his framework, including his assumption that the taxpayer has a wife and three dependent children. They add comparable estimates for the years 1923-24 and 1925-26. The estimates for 1923-24 show, as compared with 1918-19, the effect of the first four British post-war Finance Acts. Those for 1925-26 show, as compared with 1923-24, the effect of the Finance Acts of 1924 and 1925. The chief feature of the Act of 1924 was Mr. Snowden's reduction of food taxes, the chief feature of that of 1925 was Mr. Churchill's reduction of income tax and super-tax, partially balanced by his increase of the estate duty. The chief effect of the Act of 1924 was to reduce taxation on the smaller incomes, that of the Act of 1925 to reduce it on the larger.

The estimates of the Colwyn Committee are summarised in the following table.[1] I have already commented, in the last chapter, upon the main changes which they indicate.

PERCENTAGES OF INCOMES PAID IN TAXES.

Taxpayers' Annual Income.	Incomes wholly from work.				
£	1903-4	1913-14	1918-19	1923-24	1925-26
50	8·7	8·0	—	—	—
100	5·6	5·4	9·9	14·1	11·9
150	4·5	4·4	9·0	13·5	11·6
200	4·8	4·0	7·9	11·8	10·2
500	5·3	4·4	10·2	8·0	6·2
1,000	6·1	5·2	16·9	14·1	11·0
2,000	5·7	4·9	24·0	17·9	15·2
5,000	5·5	6·7	36·6	28·5	23·2
10,000	5·0	8·0	42·5	37·1	31·2
20,000	4·9	8·3	47·6	42·3	37·5
50,000	4·8	8·4	50·6	48·0	44·4

[1] See *Report*, pp. 94-5.

Taxpayers' Annual Income.	Incomes half from work and half from property.				
£	1903-4	1913-14	1918-19	1923-24	1925-26
50	9·5	8·8	—	—	—
100	6·8	6·6	11·1	15·3	13·0
150	5·7	5·6	10·2	14·7	12·7
200	6·0	5·3	9·1	12·9	11·3
500	6·5	7·1	13·5	9·9	8·4
1,000	7·8	8·3	20·6	16·9	14·4
2,000	7·4	8·4	28·1	21·5	19·3
5,000	7·5	9·6	39·2	32·6	29·5
10,000	7·6	11·8	46·3	43·0	40·1
20,000	7·7	13·0	52·3	51·4	48·7
50,000	8·0	13·6	58·2	60·7	57·7

§ 2. Turning from statistics to theory, it is a simple idea, with which some economists have rested content, that, if a rate of tax t falls upon an income x, the progression, or "degree of progressiveness," of taxation may be measured by $\frac{dt}{dx}$. According as this is positive, zero or negative, we have progressive, proportional and regressive taxation respectively. If it is both large and positive, we shall naturally speak, thinking in terms of a graph, of "steeply" progressive taxation.

But this idea, though useful as a starting point, does not carry us far. It only relates to progression *at a particular point* on the tax scale. It throws no light on the degree of progression of the tax scale *as a whole.*

This more general conception may be approached from several alternative angles. The first is as follows.

Begin, as in the Note to Chapter IX, § 4, with a community consisting of two taxpayers only, A and B, of whom A has the larger income. Let the rates of tax falling upon their incomes be t_1 and t_2 respectively. Then the degree of progression of this elementary tax system may be conveniently measured either by

$p=k\ (t_1-t_2)$, or by $p=k\ \dfrac{t_1-t_2}{t_1+t_2}$, when k is a constant.

The second of these two formulæ is to be preferred, in accordance with the rule that relative are better than absolute measures of dispersion. Here again, if $p>0$, we have progression; if $p=0$, we have proportionality; if $p<0$, we have regression.

We have now to generalise this formula for a more populous community. Of what more general measure of dispersion is it a particular case? Obviously of several. The two simplest are the relative mean deviation and the relative mean difference. (The former, for n quantities, is the average of their deviations, all taken positively, from the arithmetic mean, divided by the arithmetic mean itself. The latter is the average of the differences, all taken positively, between all possible pairs selected from these n quantities, divided by the arithmetic mean.)

If, then, we have n incomes, $x_1, x_2, \ldots x_n$, arranged in descending order of magnitude, and if the respective rates of tax are $t_1, t_2, \ldots t_n$, it would seem that the degree of progression of the tax system may plausibly be measured either by the relative mean deviation, or by the relative mean difference, of $t_1, t_2, \ldots t_n$. Between these two alternative measures, there is *prima facie* nothing to choose. In general, though not always, they will corroborate each other's evidence.

But a further condition must be added. These measures are only directly applicable, if $t_1, t_2, \ldots t_n$ likewise fall either into a continuously descending, or into a continuously ascending, order of magnitude. In the former case we have continuous progression in the tax scale, in the latter case continuous regression.[1] In both cases a simple measure, either positive or negative, of the degree of progression of the tax scale as a whole can be obtained. For regression is only negative progression. But, if the tax scale contains one or more ranges both of progression and of regression, no such simple measure can be applied. The progression or regression of each range must then be measured separately.

Here again we may rest content with a series of such separate measures over defined ranges of income, or we may seek to combine them into one single measure for the tax scale as a whole. This raises a further question. What formula for combination will be appropriate?

This question invites a lengthy mathematical discussion, on which I shall not here embark. But obviously the answer depends upon the relative weight to be attached, in formulating a single measure, to the component measures for the separate ranges. And this suggests a further distinction.

When we speak of the degree of progression of a tax system, we may mean either of two things. We may mean, on the one hand, the degree of progression of the *tax scale itself*, regardless of the distribution of incomes along the scale. Or, on the other hand, we

[1] And, of course, if $t_1 = t_2 = \ldots = t_n$, we have continuous proportionality.

may mean the degree of progression of the *incidence of the tax scale*, taking account of the distribution of incomes along it. This distinction is a particular case of that between an unweighted and a weighted index-number. Evidently the second meaning is the more significant, for parts of the tax scale will be more densely populated by taxpayers than other parts, and some parts may be wholly unpopulated, so that the scale is, to that extent, inoperative and merely hypothetical. But evidently, also, the first meaning is often the only one which it is practicable to adopt, owing to inadequate knowledge of the distribution of taxable incomes.

If $x_1, x_2, \ldots x_n$ are actual individual incomes, our measure of progression bears the second meaning; if they are only representative income levels, it bears the first. In fact, the enquiries of Sir Herbert Samuel and the Colwyn Committee do not reach beyond representative income levels; they take no account of the number of dwellers at each level. Provisionally, therefore, we will accept this first meaning of progression.

§ 3. A few easy sums in arithmetic will illustrate concretely the preceding argument. Take the five tax scales of the Colwyn Committee set out above, affecting mixed incomes, half from work and half from property, and calculate the corresponding measures of regression and progression. Let the measure applied be the relative mean deviation.

The first scale, for 1903-4, divides into no fewer than four ranges, regressive below £150, progressive between £150 and £1,000, regressive between £1,000 and £2,000, progressive above £2,000. The measures of progression for these four ranges are −·2, + ·1, −·03 and + ·002 respectively. The scale as a whole is not far from proportionality, with regression on the smallest incomes as the most marked departure from this general feature.

The second, third, fourth and fifth scales all divide into two ranges, regressive below, and progressive above, a certain dividing line. This dividing line is at £200 for the second and third, and at £500 for the fourth and fifth. The measures of progression for these two ranges respectively work out as follows:

Second scale (1913-14)	−·17 and +·28
Third scale (1918-19)	−·07 and +·47
Fourth scale (1923-24)	−·14 and +·46
Fifth scale (1925-26)	−·13 and +·48

These are rough and ready calculations applied to a mere handful of tax rates. They illustrate method rather than establish secure conclusions. They must be regarded very tentatively. They illustrate also the distinction between changes in the *general level* of a tax scale and changes in its *shape*. Thus there were substantial reductions, between 1923-24 and 1925-26, in the general level of the tax scale. But there was no substantial change in its shape. The element of regression was only fractionally diminished, while the element of progression was even fractionally increased.

How should these pairs of measures be combined to give a single measure of the progressiveness of the tax scale as a whole at the different dates? Combining on an "unweighted" basis, we shall simply set the progressive plus against the regressive minus. This makes each of these four scales progressive on balance, their respective measures of progression being +·11,

+·40, +·32 and +·35. The first scale, that of 1903-4, is, however, regressive on balance, its measure of progression being −·13. If, on the other hand, we aim at combination on a properly "weighted" basis, how shall we weight? The fact that many more individual incomes fall within the regressive, than within the progressive, range points to a heavier weight for the former. The fact that much more taxation is collected within the progressive range points in the opposite direction.

§ 4. The problem suggested by such conflicting claims admits of more than one solution, according to the shade of meaning which we choose to assign to the word "progressive." But there is one particular shade of meaning, which itself suggests another line of approach to the general conception of the degree of progression of a tax scale as a whole. Since the interest of this conception is purely distributional, it is not unreasonable to measure the intensity of progression directly, by its effect on distribution, that is to say by its effect on the inequality of incomes. The degree of progression of a tax system might then be measured by some such formula as

$$p=\delta-\delta'+k,$$

where δ is the inequality of incomes before, and δ' the inequality of net incomes after, the payment of taxation, and k is a positive constant, so chosen as to allow for the fact that inequality is increased, not only by regression and proportionality, but even by the milder degrees of progression.[1] Inequality, in other words, will only be diminished, if p is positive *and greater than* k.

[1] See Note to Ch. IX, §5.

But a given "tax-system," in the sense of an unweighted tax scale, may affect differently the inequality of two different distributions. It may even increase the inequality of the one and diminish that of the other. Therefore p must be a function, not only of the scale of tax rates, but of the distribution to which they are to apply. In other words, it must be a function of a *weighted* tax scale. The line of approach, through effects on inequality, leads back, therefore, to the necessity for weighting.

§ 5. There is, indeed, a third line of approach to the general conception. This is the simplest of all and the most empirical. This line of approach is through the drawing of graphs. Draw comparable graphs of two tax scales and look at them. Sometimes, though not always, it will be possible to judge, from mere inspection, that the general slope of one is "steeper," that is to say more progressive,[1] than the other. And sometimes, though not always, this will be all that need be said, so that no reference to the ambiguities which we have been considering will be necessary. This simple procedure is only applicable to the unweighted tax scale, but it may, if desired, be made more precise by measuring "progressiveness" by the area lying between the graph of the tax scale and two axial straight lines at right angles to one another.

It will be evident from this discussion that "progressiveness" in a tax system is a conception which admits of more than one definition and means of measurement. Our choice, in relation to any particular problem, must depend upon the material in hand and the purpose in view.

[1] Or more regressive, if the slope is reversed.

Chapter XII

SOME OTHER EFFECTS OF TAXATION

§ 1. To complete our study of the economic effects of taxation, there is a little more to say.

Connected with effects on production are considerations of the cost of collection of taxes. For unnecessarily high cost of collection involves a waste of labour and materials, which is equivalent to a diminution of production. Other things being equal, the best tax system is that in which the cost of collection, in proportion to the revenue collected, is a minimum.[1]

As a rule, the cost of collecting a tax on a commodity is the same, per unit of commodity, whether the rate of tax is high or low.[2] Provided, therefore, that the rate of tax is not so high, as to reduce the revenue yield below the maximum, the cost of collection, in proportion to the revenue yield, is less for a heavy tax than for a light one. This is an argument for a small number of fairly heavy taxes on commodities rather than a large number of lighter ones. Again, cost of collection is

[1] One of the beauties of raising revenue by currency inflation, which is discussed in Ch. XV, is that there is practically no cost of collection, the cost of printing even very large supplies of paper money being quite small.

[2] Unless the rate of tax is so high as seriously to stimulate attempts at evasion. Thus high import duties may encourage attempts at smuggling, the prevention of which will be an expensive matter. The increasing use of aircraft in the future is likely to facilitate smuggling, especially of commodities whose bulk is small in proportion to their value.

generally greater for *ad valorem* than for specific duties, and specially heavy for elaborate duties, which differentiate between commodities from different sources of supply.

Similarly, as a rule, the cost of collecting an income tax, or an inheritance tax, at a flat rate is the same, per taxpayer, whether the rate of tax is high or low. It is, therefore, cheaper to collect a given revenue at a high flat rate from a small number of taxpayers than at a low flat rate from a larger number. In practice, an additional cost of collection is involved in the administration of exemptions, allowances and graduated rates and in the taxation of small incomes. An income tax on small incomes from wages must either be paid in one or two annual payments, which inflict great hardship on the taxpayer and are difficult to assess owing to weekly variations in wages, or in a larger number of instalments during the year, an arrangement which greatly increases the cost and trouble of collection, while not altogether avoiding the difficulty of wage variations. Probably the cheapest way to collect an income tax on wages would be to require employers to deduct the tax weekly in the same way as they now deduct the workers' contributions under the Health and Unemployment Insurance Acts. But even under such a system the cost of collection, including checking and supervision, in proportion to the revenue collected, would be large. British experience shows that, in proportion to the revenue collected, cost of collection is smaller for income and inheritance taxes on the relatively rich than for taxes on commodities, and smaller for the latter than for income tax on the relatively poor. Income tax on wages, based on quarterly assessments, is specially expensive to collect.[1] This experience supports the view that it is best to tax the rich principally through their incomes and inheritances, and the poor, in so far as they are taxed at all, through a few commodities of wide consumption, such as alcohol and tobacco. This applies to all communities which are highly developed industrially and fairly thickly populated. But in communities which are more primitive industrially, such as India, or more thinly populated, such as Canada, the cost of collection of income tax may be relatively higher as compared with taxes on commodities, and especially as compared with customs duties. For it is often cheaper and more convenient to tax commodities as they cross political frontiers, than as they are produced or sold within these frontiers. Thus the cost of collection of import and export duties is generally lower than that of a sales tax, or turnover tax, yielding the same revenue.

[1] Thus, in 1920-21, the cost of collecting £754,000,000 of inland revenue, chiefly income tax and death duties on the relatively rich, was £8,500,000, or 1·13 per cent. of the yield. (*Report of Inland Revenue Commissioners*, 1920-21, p. 4.) With the reductions in the rates of tax in subsequent years, the total cost of collection also fell, but the cost per cent. of the yield steadily rose, and reached 1·61 per cent. in 1926-27 (*Report*, 1926-27, p. 10). On the other hand, in 1920-21 it cost £800,000 to collect £5,000,000 of income tax from wage-earners, or 16 per cent. of the yield. (Answer by Sir Hilton Young to a Parliamentary question on February 14th, 1922.) By 1928, Mr. Churchill informed me in answer to a Parliamentary question, the cost had risen to about 33 per cent. of the yield. We may infer from the *Finance Accounts* 1921-22, pp. 6-7, that the cost of collecting £324,000,000 of customs and excise in 1921-22 could not have exceeded £6,750,000 or 2·08 per cent. of the yield. The corresponding figures for 1927-28 (*F.A.*, 1927-28, pp. 6-7) were £250,000,000, costing £4,850,000, or 1·94 per cent. of the yield. For 1934-35 the cost of collecting £667,000,000 of revenue of all kinds was £12,500,000, or 1·89 per cent. (*Financial Statement*, 1934-35, p. 19.)

The British method of collecting a large part of the income tax at the source is cheap and efficient and makes evasion difficult. It is capable of further extension in this country and other governments, which have been less successful in checking evasion, would be wise to adopt it.

§ 2. It is also important to keep the cost of collection to the persons from whom the taxes are collected as low as possible. The olive growers in Turkey, who were legally forbidden to dispose of their olives, even though these should go bad through keeping, until the tax collector had called and counted them, would have appreciated this precept. Even in Western countries taxpayers are often subjected to needless trouble in filling up a number of different forms, where one would be sufficient, and in replying to the demands of a number of different tax collectors, whose activities are not properly co-ordinated. It has been said that, just as a prudent man visits his dentist once a year, so a prudent and honest taxpayer should pay an annual visit to his Surveyor of Taxes, so that his affairs shall be kept in good order with a minimum of inconvenience. Again, some taxes necessarily involve much cost and trouble to those from whom they are collected, even though the latter may be able to pass the tax on to others. So far as it goes, this is an argument against such taxes. An example is the Italian tax on visitors' hotel bills, which compels hotel keepers to keep meticulously careful accounts in duplicate, on prescribed forms, for every visitor, to plaster these with stamps, to make periodical returns and to submit their books to frequent and prolonged examination by inspectors. The cost of collection of this tax to the Italian Treasury must also be considerable.

§ 3. The effects of taxation upon the steadiness of employment are often misunderstood. It is sometimes suggested that taxation, especially of the rich, increases unemployment. But many of those, who entertain this idea, seem to suppose that the money collected in taxation is put into a stocking or thrown into the sea. In fact, of course, it is spent by the public authorities concerned. A transfer of purchasing power takes place from the taxpayer to the public authority, and therewith a transfer of the power to "give employment." As a result of this transfer, there may be a change in the character, but there is not likely to be any appreciable change in the total volume, of the demand for labour. Taxation, therefore, considered jointly with the corresponding public expenditure, has no general tendency to cause unemployment. There is, indeed, a possibility that large and sudden changes in taxation may increase unemployment, through large and sudden displacements of labour. But this applies equally to taxation of the poor and taxation of the rich. Further, it applies to large reductions, no less than to large increases, in taxation.

Certain taxes, however, tend, by their very nature, to diminish employment. An obvious example is a tax imposed on employers, in proportion to the number of workers they employ, a common feature in the finance of "contributory" social insurance. For this is simply a tax on employment. Similarly, any tax imposed on employers, regardless of the amount of business they may be doing, or of the amount of profit or loss they may be making, tends to diminish employment in marginal businesses. The heavier the tax, the wider the margin affected. Local rates, as distinguished from income tax,—and especially heavy local rates—operate in this fashion, being insensitive to variations in employers' "ability to pay." For this reason it is legitimate to regard local rates, and also employers' contributions to social insurance, as a "burden on industry," in a sense in which income tax is not. It might, perhaps, be thought that exceptionally heavy local rates in certain small areas would tend, not so much to reduce employment, as to redistribute it between firms, industries and areas. But this is a "long run" view and assumes mobility. Unemployment, however, is to a large extent a "short run" phenomenon, due to absence of mobility. Hence the urgent problem of the "distressed areas" in this country.[1]

It might be possible to reduce unemployment, almost to vanishing point, by giving a sufficient subsidy to employment through the medium of changes in the income tax.[2] Employers might be given, in respect of each of their employees, an allowance in relief of income tax, and the loss in revenue might be made good by an increase in the standard rate of tax. This would redistribute income tax in favour of those who employed much labour at the expense of those who employed little, and would redistribute industry in favour of concerns employing a high proportion of labour to capital at the expense of those employing a low proportion. From the point of view of employers it

[1] Compare Ch. X, §12.

[2] I owe this interesting suggestion to Mr. N. Kaldor of the London School of Economics.

would be equivalent to a reduction of wages, though wages would not, in fact, be reduced. There would be an increase in profits and a saving, both to the Budget and the Insurance Fund, on unemployment relief. The effect on unemployment of a given subsidy would depend on the elasticity of demand for labour. With ten million working and two million unemployed,—approximately the situation in this country in 1935,—a relief to employers equivalent to a 10 per cent. reduction in wages would absorb one million unemployed if this elasticity was equal to one, and the whole two million if it was equal to two. Owing to the lack of mobility, both geographical and occupational, of many of the unemployed, this ingenious plan, though it might greatly reduce, could not, in fact, within the limits of practical possibilities, abolish unemployment.

Unemployment, within the institutional framework of capitalism, is not so simple nor so static a problem as this line of approach suggests. It is, in part, a consequence of fluctuation in new investment and in other forms of economic activity. But it can be much diminished by wise public action, including wise public expenditure, as will be argued later in Chapter XX.

§ 4. The habit of concentrating attention on the effects of taxation, to the complete exclusion of the effects of the corresponding public expenditure, has led many eminent persons into error.

Thus Mr. McKenna, speaking with the double authority of a Bank Chairman and an ex-Chancellor of the Exchequer, once estimated the "taxable capacity" of the country on the assumption that no money, which is taken in taxation, is available for investment in industry.[1] But what of taxation devoted to the reduction of public debt? If A is taxed £100 in order to pay off £100 of B's War Loan, B will almost certainly reinvest a larger proportion of this amount, than A would have invested, if it had not been taken from him.[2]

Again, it has been argued by Mr. Amery that the Health Insurance Act imposes a tax on British industry, which affords a new and striking reason for "countervailing" import duties on foreign manufactured goods. But, in so far as public expenditure on health succeeds in its object of increasing the efficiency of British workers, it may be said to give a bounty to British industry and the "countervailing" argument might with equal plausibility be used by an ingenious foreigner in search of new excuses for protection in a less healthy land.

Finally, for these instances must not be unduly multiplied, the *Daily Mail*, in discussing, soon after the war, the "taxable capacity" of Germany for the purpose of paying reparations, objected to a certain estimate as too low by comparison with the total of British taxation. But "taxable capacity," however defined, for the purpose of paying a war indemnity to another country is obviously less than taxable capacity for the purpose of paying for public expenditure in one's own country. For, in the former case, part of the product of industry is exported without any corresponding import and the community is to that extent

[1] In a speech at the Annual Dinner of the National Union of Manufacturers on June 14th, 1920. See Note at the end of this Chapter.

[2] For an elaboration of this proposition, which leads to important practical conclusions, see Ch. XVIII, §8.

poorer, while, in the latter case, no such one-sided export is caused and the community is not necessarily any poorer, but may even be richer, if its public finance is wisely conducted.

Note to Chapter XII

§ 1. "Taxable capacity" is a common phrase, but a dim and confused conception. The purpose of this Note is more closely to examine this conception, which has already flitted across the stage of our discussion in Chapter II, § 4, and Chapter XII, § 4. We shall notice in the course of our examination Sir Josiah Stamp's remarks in Chapter IV of his *Wealth and Taxable Capacity*, the paper on *Taxable Capacity and the Burden of Taxation and Public Debt*, read by Mr. Findlay Shirras to the Royal Statistical Society in 1925 (published, with the subsequent discussion, in the *Journal of the Royal Statistical Society*, July, 1925), and the Report of a Committee of the British Association, published in 1921, on the *Effects of the War on Credit, Currency, Finance and Foreign Exchanges*. This last report is, in fact, not a report at all, but a symposium, containing the conflicting answers of a number of economists and others to the questions, "How is the taxable capacity of a nation ascertained? Has it been reached and passed, as Mr. McKenna suggests, in the case of Great Britain?"

We may begin by distinguishing two possible senses in which the phrase may be used: (1) the absolute taxable capacity of a single community, and

(2) the relative taxable capacity of two or more communities. Thus we may ask (1) how much can a particular community be taxed, without producing various unpleasant effects? When these unpleasant effects result from the operation of the tax system, it is possible to say that "taxable capacity has been exceeded" in an absolute sense. Or we may ask (2) in what proportions should two or more communities contribute, by taxation, to a common expenditure? If one of these communities is contributing more than its due proportion, it is possible to say that its "taxable capacity has been exceeded" in a relative sense. But, though it is *possible* to use these forms of words, they seldom promote clear thinking. Some of the problems, in connection with which they have been used, are quite unreal, while others, though real and important, can be better handled in other terms.

§ 2. Let us first examine the conception of absolute taxable capacity. I have deliberately begun by stating it vaguely in terms of "unpleasant effects" which follow, if it is "exceeded." But exactly what "unpleasant effects" shall be taken into account? All taxation has the unpleasant effect of reducing the taxpayers' income in the first instance, though it may sometimes stimulate him to make good the loss, and though his loss through taxation may be outweighed by his gain through the corresponding public expenditure. Much ambiguity has resulted from confusion between two extreme ideas, namely capacity to pay without suffering and capacity to pay regardless of suffering. In the one case taxable capacity is nil, except for the very rich, in the other it is only limited by the taxpayers' total resources. It is evident that the path of practical wisdom lies somewhere between these two extremes, but it is not evident that this path can be illuminated by any more precise definition of this elusive conception.

If we go back to first principles, we may define the unpleasant effects of "exceeding taxable capacity" merely as a diminution of economic welfare. But, as was pointed out in Chapter II, § 4, it is futile to look only at taxation and to ignore the corresponding public expenditure, or to assume that this expenditure brings no benefit to anyone, but represents simply a subtraction from wealth, which is destroyed or thrown into the sea. Yet this seems to be the view of Mr. McKenna in the speech which has already been quoted, for otherwise it is impossible to make any sense of his remarks. Sir Josiah Stamp, commenting upon this speech, says that Mr. McKenna was "doubtless fully alive to" other considerations, but "it would be quite unfair to expect, in an after-dinner statement, on a hot evening in June, any exact review of all the issues involved."[1] This is a good example of the polite art of charitable interpretation!

How much public expenditure we can "afford," and hence how much taxation we can advantageously pay, obviously depends upon the character of the public expenditure. Further, the character of the public expenditure being given, we could, perhaps, "afford" it, if the taxation was raised in one way, but not if it was raised in another. For the effects of tax-systems, on production, on distribution and in other directions, vary, and the gain from a given expenditure might be greater than the loss from one

[1] *Wealth and Taxable Capacity*, p. 125.

tax-system, but less than the loss from an alternative tax-system which raised the same revenue. These considerations are elementary and have already been set out in earlier chapters of this book. But they lead to a very simple and important negative conclusion. It is quite impossible to fix any definite sum, or any definite proportion of a community's income, which could be said to represent the limits of its taxable capacity at any particular time. For any such estimate would necessarily leave out of account almost every factor relevant to a practical decision on policy.

§ 3. In the light of this conclusion, let us now pass in review some of the opinions which have been expressed in the publications mentioned above. The British Association asked in 1921 " How is the taxable capacity of a nation ascertained ? Has it been reached and passed in the case of Great Britain ? " The best and shortest answer to the first question was given by Edwin Cannan, who replied " Nohow." Mr. Ellinger thought that the limit was reached " when so much is taken out of the taxpayers' pockets that the incentive to produce is reduced, and when insufficient remains to provide the necessary capital to make up for wastage and to set to work new workers in an increasing population." He did not think that the limit had been reached. This is a bad answer, (1) because it takes no account of public expenditure, (2) because it assumes that, the limit not having been reached, taxation has no tendency to " reduce the incentive to produce," whereas, in fact, much taxation obviously has such a tendency, and (3) because " necessary capital " is a vague phrase and it is not a mere quantity of capital which determines the available quantity of employment. Sir Hilton Young answered : " Directly, by a census of production only ; indirectly, according to the fancy of the payer, as to what he likes to call a fair measure of it." The second part of this answer, which indicates a certain scepticism, is better than the first, which seems to suggest that excessive taxation is the only possible cause of a decline in production, and that, so long as production is not declining, taxation cannot be excessive. Mr. Mason thought that the limit was passed when taxation " affects production unduly." But what is " unduly " ? Mr. Hoare thought that " taxable capacity can only be ascertained by experimenting with taxes." But how are the experiments to be conducted, and in what form are their results expected to appear ? Sir Drummond Fraser exclaims that " the taxable capacity of a nation is surely reached when taxpayers are forced to borrow from the banks to pay their taxes." But what about those taxpayers who have no banking accounts ? On this criterion, there would be no limit to the taxable capacity of most wage-earners. The British Association was not very successful, on this occasion, in the pursuit either of truth or of general agreement.

I turn to Sir Josiah Stamp's discussion. The first approximation, he thinks, to taxable capacity is total production minus the amount required to maintain the population at subsistence level. But he points out that, if all this margin were taken away, for example from Germany for the payment of reparations, future production and, hence, future taxable capacity according to his definition, would be diminished.[1] This is certainly true. He then argues that taxable capacity

[1] *Loc cit.*, p. 113.

depends also on distribution and will be greater, the greater the inequality of incomes. For this argument I can find no justification. If total production and population are given, and if subsistence level is fixed, and if none are below it, distribution is irrelevant to taxable capacity as defined above. But on the next page Sir Josiah defines it differently, as the margin of total production over total consumption. This means that taxable capacity is measured by the amount of saving, and cannot be exceeded so long as any saving at all is taking place. On this criterion, taxable capacity has very seldom been exceeded in any community. Then, shifting his ground again, he considers the effects of taxation on work and saving and finds two alternative " limits to taxable capacity " in (1) the check to total production, and (2) the check to the total revenue yield, as a result of increasing taxation. Finally he gives five good reasons why the " limit of taxable capacity " is not an absolute or fixed amount. This last conclusion is admirable, but it seems to make nonsense of nearly everything which precedes it.

I turn next to Mr. Shirras' paper, which was highly praised by several speakers when it was read before the Royal Statistical Society. But there is grave confusion throughout this paper between relative and absolute taxable capacity, and a mass of statistics is introduced, dealing with production, distribution, debt and taxation in various countries, which is mere miscellaneous second-hand information, with no direct bearing on what purports to be the central argument. " Taxable capacity," says Mr. Shirras dogmatically, " is the total surplus of production over the minimum consumption required to produce that volume of production, the standard of living remaining unchanged." But of what practical use is this definition? It has the same weaknesses as those of Sir Josiah Stamp. And why should the existing standard of living be assumed to be unchanged? This assumption, indeed, does not endure very long, for Mr. Shirras, like Sir Josiah Stamp, hops gaily from one definition to another on successive pages. With reduced consumption, he thinks, "people could, without living a really down-trodden life, exist" on about three-quarters of their present food and clothing in Great Britain, and on about two-thirds in the United States. We must, however, "define taxable capacity as implying that the standard of living should not be lowered to any serious extent," and that we must not "dislocate industry." But what does "dislocate" mean? Such catastrophic terms are inapplicable to most phases of public finance. Then follows, as in Sir Josiah Stamp's treatment, a series of ruinous admissions. Taxable capacity, says Mr. Shirras, varies according to the nature of tax-systems, according to "the stability of income," according to "the nature of the expenditure for which the taxation was raised," according to the distribution of wealth, according to taxpayers' willingness to pay, and so forth. What residue is left at the end of all this? Nothing but a slipshod muddle. But the muddle, though it might have been less slipshod, is inherent in all such elaborate enquiries into the absolute taxable capacity of a community. The thing is an illusion. Cannan's "Nohow" is the last word.

§ 4. Relative taxable capacity, on the other hand, may be given an intelligible meaning. Principles, as we have seen, may be laid down to govern the distribution of a given burden between two or more persons according to some criterion of "ability to pay." Similar principles may be applied to two or more communities sharing a common expenditure. "Ability to pay" may, if we choose, be renamed "taxable capacity," but the substance of the problem remains unchanged. If the common expenditure increases, the proportions paid by the richer contributors should increase and those paid by the poorer should diminish. Conversely, if the common expenditure diminishes. And so forth. Examples of this general problem are furnished by the financial relations between Great Britain and Ireland, before the birth of the Irish Free State, and between Great Britain and Northern Ireland after this event. Likewise, the problem of distributing the cost of the League of Nations between the Member States, though in this case the cost is so trivial that States have been known to take offence at a proposal to diminish their relative contribution, which they regarded as a measure of their international importance. Problems of Reparations and Inter-Allied Debts fall into the same broad category, though they present special features.[1] In particular, there are strong disharmonies between the interests of different communities and further disharmonies between immediate and more remote interests. Thus one type of settlement may benefit Germany more than France, or the United States more than Great Britain. Again, one type of settlement may secure larger transfers of wealth from debtors to creditors over a short period than another type, but smaller total transfers over a long period.

[1] See Ch. XXV.

§ 5. It is important, however, to recognise that there is no logical connection between relative and absolute taxable capacity. A community may be contributing, in excess of its relative taxable capacity, towards some common expenditure with other communities. But it does not follow that its absolute taxable capacity, according to any of the definitions which we have examined, is being exceeded. Similarly, its absolute taxable capacity, according to some definition or other, may be exceeded, but it does not follow that its relative taxable capacity is being exceeded in any of its common expenditures with other communities. My general conclusion is that relative taxable capacity is a reality, which can, however, be equally well expressed in other terms, while absolute taxable capacity is a myth, which is apt to engender grave errors. In the interests of clear thinking, it would be well that the phrase "taxable capacity" should be banished from all serious discussions of public finance.

Chapter XIII

THE TAX SYSTEM FROM THE POINT OF VIEW OF ECONOMY

§ 1. The last three chapters have been devoted to a discussion of the economic effects of taxation. It is upon the balance, or aggregate, of such effects that tax systems must be judged from the point of view of economy. How far taxation should be carried, and how great use should be made of particular taxes, can only be decided, as was argued in Chapter II, by considerations of the maximum social advantage to be derived from the operations of public finance as a whole. There is no desirable limit to the increase of any particular tax, except that the social loss, if any, from such an increase should not be greater than the social loss from an equivalent increase in any other practicable tax. There are no desirable limits to the increase of taxation in general, except that the social loss from such an increase should not be greater than the social loss of raising further public income by some other methods than that of taxation.[1] The chief of such other methods, apart from borrowing which is discussed in Part IV, will be considered in the next two chapters.

§ 2. As to the ideal distribution of the direct money burden of taxation, considerations of economy lead us

[1] Nor, of course, greater than the social gain from the corresponding increase of public expenditure.

to no such simple solution, as the exponents of equitable formulæ so glibly provide. Nor can we ignore the indirect burdens and other more remote effects of taxation. We may, indeed, still say that taxation should be distributed according to "ability to pay." But we must now interpret this last phrase more broadly. We must measure the relative ability of individuals to pay by the relative effects of their payments, not only upon distribution, but upon production and, indeed, upon the whole economic welfare of the community. Thus A's ability, as compared with B's, to pay a given sum under a given tax system, depends upon the relative economic loss resulting from payment in the two cases, account being taken, not only of the direct loss of economic welfare to A and B respectively, but also of any indirect loss, or gain, to others. Taxation according to ability to pay means, therefore, taxation with the minimum of economic loss to the community as a whole.

But one important practical conclusion, which emerges clearly from the argument of the preceding chapters, is that there is no reason, on grounds of economy, why all, or even the majority of, the members of a community, in which great inequality of incomes prevails, should contribute to taxation. No equitable doctrine, such as equal or proportional sacrifice, which presupposes some contribution, however small, from all who have any economic welfare to sacrifice, finds any strong support in considerations of economy.[1]

[1] The plausible argument that everyone ought to pay something, in order that a sense of political responsibility shall be widely diffused and a check imposed on public extravagance, does not seem to me to be a strong one. For (1) much taxation, especially taxes on commodities, which are the most convenient method of securing

We are rather drawn towards the doctrine of minimum sacrifice, with its widespread exemptions for the poorer sections of the community, and steep progression for the richer. But this doctrine, as we have seen, must be interpreted more broadly by economy than by equity, so as to mean minimum sacrifice in the long run, when all economic effects, including effects on production, are taken into account. And this is much the same thing as maximum social advantage on a long view, so that we come back again to the general principle from which we started. It cannot be claimed that the last three chapters have amplified the principle itself, for its very simplicity and comprehensiveness make this impossible. But they should have thrown light upon its practical application.

a contribution from the poor, is not clearly realised by the taxpayer; (2) a sense of political responsibility is often found, independently of the consciousness of paying taxes, and, where it is absent, such a consciousness will seldom be sufficient to create it; and (3) where a dislike of taxation is keenly developed, especially if its development is provoked by the undiscriminating irritant of a press campaign, false economy, rather than true, is likely to result. Compare Ch. VI, §5.

Chapter XIV

INCOME FROM PUBLIC PROPERTY AND PUBLIC ENTERPRISES

§ 1. All public authorities, in varying degrees, own property and conduct economic enterprises. Net money income derived by a public authority from its property or enterprises is an addition to its net income, and the receipt of such income makes marginal taxation less, and marginal expenditure more, desirable than would otherwise be the case. Thus the receipt of such income justifies a public authority in taxing rather less and spending rather more than it should otherwise do. Often, however, a public authority's property and enterprises are burdened by debts to private persons incurred in respect of their acquisition or development. In such cases debt charges, both for interest and sinking fund, must be deducted from receipts, before the public authority's net money income from these sources can be estimated.

§ 2. Political considerations require that public authorities should undertake certain functions, which necessitate the ownership of property and the conduct of enterprises. The ownership of its armaments and the enterprise of maintaining and training its armed forces and, to some extent at least, of actually producing armaments, are obvious examples. But a public authority cannot hope to obtain any net money income from the performance of these functions. Again, the enterprise of issuing legal tender money, sometimes, as will be explained in the next chapter, an important source of income to a public authority, is governed partly by political and partly by economic considerations.

But it is predominantly the latter, which in most cases bear upon the desirability of a public authority owning property and conducting enterprises. We have here to consider the effects of such arrangements upon production and distribution.

§ 3. Mere passive ownership by a public authority, as compared with passive private ownership, will generally not much affect production. If the terms of his tenancy are the same, it makes no substantial difference to a tenant whether his landlord is a public authority or a private person. In some cases it may be argued that the development of natural resources would have been more effective, and productive methods less wasteful, under public than under private ownership, especially when the latter is much subdivided among proprietors, whose co-operation is essential to efficient production, but in practice is not forthcoming. Passivity may degenerate into stupid obstruction. As regards private ownership of minerals this argument has been forcibly presented before successive Commissions of Enquiry into the British Coal Industry. And, as regards the private ownership of land, it is one of the principal defences of the Town and Country Planning Act and similar legislation, not only that the individual self-interest of private owners is often in conflict with the public interest, but that, even in its own field, it is often short-sighted and sluggish. In other cases it may be maintained that private, rather than public, ownership gives the greater stimulus to development.

Active ownership, on the other hand, which soon merges into actual conduct of enterprises by a public authority, may have very great effects on production. A public authority may be either more or less efficient in the present than a private individual or corporation ; it may make better or worse provision for the future ; it may make greater or less use of monopoly power to restrict output and raise prices. To discuss this question further here would involve too lengthy a digression. It would be necessary to consider various devices, such as semi-independent public boards, by means of which public authorities can organise production, and also the principles and methods of planning and co-ordinating a wide range of public enterprises in a Socialist or semi-Socialist state.[1]

§ 4. As regards effects on distribution, public ownership of property, provided that the latter is free, or at least partly free, from private mortgage, will generally be better than private ownership. For, the larger the proportion of property which is publicly owned in any community, the less unequal is distribution likely to be.[2] The reason for this is that the benefits from public property are likely to be more equally distributed than the benefits from private property. The same argument favours the conduct of enterprises by public authorities. But effects on distribution are partly dependent on the price policy which a public authority pursues.

[1] See, however, my *Practical Socialism for Britain*, Parts III, IV and V.

[2] See my *Inequality of Incomes*, pp. 276-8, and my *Practical Socialism for Britain*, Part VI.

§ 5. The most appropriate price policy will vary with circumstances. Payment may be made for services rendered by a public authority according to any of three alternative principles, or according to various combinations of these.

Payment may be made, in the first place, out of general taxation, collected from individuals without reference to the cost of the service rendered to them. This is the principle adopted as regards the cost of the military forces, the civil service, free education and poor relief. We may call it the general taxation principle.

Payment may be made, in the second place, by compulsory charges, collected from individuals in proportion to the cost of the services rendered, or presumed to be rendered, to them. This is the principle usually adopted as regards the supply of water by local authorities, as regards the cost of road repair, in so far as it is debited to owners of motor vehicles by means of a tax based on their weight or horse-power, and as regards such services as street cleaning and dust collection, paid for out of local rates. We may call it the compulsory cost of service principle.

Payment may be made, in the third place, by voluntary purchases by individuals at prices fixed by the public authority. This is the principle usually adopted as regards the cost of postal services and publicly operated transport agencies. We may call it the voluntary price principle.

§ 6. In this third case the further question arises whether prices should be so fixed, as to result in a profit or a loss to the public authorities, and, in either case, how much. Where a price is charged, but a loss is incurred and made good out of general taxation, we have a combination of the voluntary price principle and the general taxation principle.

Taking, first, passive ownership of property by a public authority, no appreciable public costs being involved, it is reasonable, as a general rule, to make the same charges to private users of such property as a private proprietor, not possessed of monopoly power, would make. There is, for instance, no general reason for making a gift of any of the economic rent of publicly owned land to the tenants for the time being.[1]

Turning to the conduct of public enterprises, or in other words to the supply of services which involve the public authority in appreciable costs, three cases may be distinguished.

Where considerations of social advantage do not require that the services in question should be either specially stimulated or specially discouraged, these should be supplied at a price which will agree, as closely as possible, with that charged for similar services by private traders without monopoly power. Thus surplus stores, or timber from publicly owned forests, should as a rule be sold on the open market at competitive prices, though excessive fluctuations in such prices may properly be eliminated by appropriate marketing arrangements. Unless management is very inefficient or unless prices are falling rapidly, such competitive prices should at least cover cost. They may also prove a useful weapon for restraining the power of private monopolists to keep prices unduly high.

[1] Though in Canada much public land was handed over free to settlers, as an inducement to, and on condition of, its speedy development.

Where, however, considerations of social advantage require that the use of the services in question should be specially discouraged—the supply of alcohol for example—higher prices should be charged, which, as has been pointed out above, must be regarded as containing an element of tax.

The less elastic the demand for such services, the greater the profit which a public authority can obtain by raising their price. The motive to raise prices may be a desire to obtain revenue, and not a desire to check consumption. But a check to consumption is a necessary effect of such a policy. If it is desired to make a publicly supplied service or commodity a large source of revenue, it is practically necessary to establish a legal public monopoly, as various European governments have done with tobacco, matches and other commodities. For otherwise private traders will undersell the public authority and steal away the revenue. Thus the French government has not only established a State match monopoly, but legally prohibits the sale of mechanical lighters and other substitutes for matches.

Where, on the other hand, considerations of social advantage require that the use of the services in question should be specially encouraged, lower prices, or even no price at all, may reasonably be charged and the resulting loss made good out of taxation. This policy involves public expenditure and the circumstances, in which it should be adopted, will be discussed later.[1] Sometimes, however, it is adopted, not with the motive of stimulating consumption, but simply because it is the most convenient arrangement. This

[1] See Ch. XVIII, §8 and Ch. XIX, §2.

explains, for example, the free use of roads, turnpike gates being inconvenient, and the free postage allowed to the British army during the war, where the practical difficulty of selling stamps in the trenches reinforced sentimental considerations. In all such cases of free supply the voluntary price principle disappears and the general taxation principle takes its place.

The general effect upon distribution of these alternative methods of securing payment, according to the voluntary price principle, for services supplied by a public authority is fairly clear. If a service is supplied at a loss, those persons benefit who make most use of it; if it is supplied at a large profit, based on high prices, those persons lose who make most use of it. Thus the supply of a particular service at a loss will make for a more equal distribution, if it is chiefly used by the poor than if it is chiefly used by the rich.[1] And the reverse is true of a service supplied at a large profit. Distribution may also be slightly affected, if the same service or commodity is supplied at different prices to different persons according to their wealth. But price discrimination of this kind is not often practicable.

§ 7. As between the general taxation principle, the compulsory cost of service principle and the voluntary price principle, the choice often depends, as has already been pointed out, largely upon practical convenience. But there are some cases in which, the voluntary price principle being ruled out as too inconvenient, the compulsory cost of service principle is preferable to the general taxation principle, from the

[1] Obviously also, in considering the effect upon distribution of supplying a service at a loss, account must be taken of the general character of the tax system, which will make good the loss.

point of view of effects on production. An example is the cost of road repair, in so far as this is necessitated by damage done to road surfaces by motor vehicles, or the cost of new road construction, or road widening, necessitated by the excessive congestion of traffic on existing roads. If such costs are wholly covered by general taxation, there will be a tendency to an excessive diversion of economic resources from other channels into the development of motor road transport, which will, in effect, be receiving a large subsidy from the general taxpayer and, incidentally, from other transport agencies. For reasons discussed in Chapter X, § 9, there is a presumption that such a diversion will reduce production, and there is, therefore, a case for a special tax on motor vehicles, sufficient to cover at least part of the special costs which they would otherwise occasion to the public. On the other hand, this presumption is weakened by the fact that better transport facilities bring many indirect social gains.

§ 8. Returning to public property and enterprises as a source of public income, we may repeat that such income is of two kinds, first, the equivalent of taxation, where a public authority deliberately charges monopoly prices for its services and, second, the equivalent of profits from ordinary competitive prices, such as a private proprietor or business firm might charge, under competitive conditions, for the use of property or the supply of services. A large public income of the second kind is easily obtainable, without any serious risk of economic loss to the community, by public authorities which retain the ownership of minerals and other natural resources and, subject if necessary to long private leases, of land, both agricultural and urban. If such obvious opportunities, not to speak of others which are more debateable, had been taken in the past, modern communities would be able both to spend more freely on desirable public objects, and to escape part of their present heavy burden of taxation.

Chapter XV

INCOME FROM THE PUBLIC PRINTING PRESS

§ 1. A special form of enterprise, which can be made to yield a large income to a public authority, is the use of the printing press to manufacture legal tender paper money. The printing press may be used for this purpose either directly or indirectly; directly when a public authority pays its creditors with new paper money specially printed for the purpose; indirectly when a public authority pays its creditors out of loans to itself from the central bank and issues new paper money to the bank, in exchange for a deposit of securities, in order, as it is sometimes put, "to support the additional credit thus created," or in other words, in order to save the bank from having to face the alternatives of raising its rates of interest to inconvenient heights or seeing its reserves dangerously depleted. For, if the bank were not thus protected, it would be unwilling to furnish the public authority with loans on the scale required. The indirect method was employed in this country between 1914 and 1921, and both methods have been freely employed, during and since the war, on the continent of Europe. There is no essential difference between the economic effects of the two methods, except that the indirect method, besides mystifying simple minds, involves the public authority in the additional expense of paying interest on its loans from the bank.

If, therefore, either method is to be adopted, the direct method is to be preferred on the ground both of economy and of intelligibility to the public.

§ 2. But either method, if used to excess, causes an undesirable currency inflation. As to the measure of excess, and even as to the proper definitions of "inflation" and "deflation," there is much dispute among economists. These disputes are bound up with controversies over monetary policy. Is a gold standard currency or some alternative form of managed currency preferable ? Is it better that the internal price level should remain stable, or that, with increasing productivity, it should fall, or that it should rise ? These controversies lie outside the field of public finance, though they have repercussions within that field. But if the printing press is so freely used as to cause a substantial fall in the purchasing power of money, this result, at least, may properly be called inflation. The purchasing power of any country's money has two aspects, internal and external. A fall in internal purchasing power means a rise in the internal price level. A fall in external purchasing power means a movement, adverse to the country in question, in the rates of foreign exchange with all those countries which are either abstaining from inflation, or indulging in it only in a more moderate degree. Such movements in prices and exchange rates, on a large scale and predominantly due to inflation, were the sensational commonplaces of economic experience in Europe in the early post-war years. Then Europe seemed to have emerged from this chaos and to have entered upon a new phase of stabilised exchange rates under the gold standard. This might have been a prelude to the stabilisation, by international action, of the value of gold, and hence also of the internal values of the paper currencies related to it. There followed, instead, another phase of monetary chaos, marked by deflation, steeply falling prices and widespread abandonment of the gold standard; also by unprecedented unemployment in many countries. Here, for the moment, history halts.

§ 3. It is sometimes said that the issue of a given amount of new paper money by a public authority is equivalent to the levying of a forced loan, free of interest, to that amount. It is simpler and more correct to say that it is equivalent to the levying of taxation to that amount—a sort of turnover tax on the use of money. But the purchasing power, in the hands of the public authority, of successive equal additions to the supply of paper money decreases as the value (per unit) of the money falls. If all internal prices, including the prices of services and interest on loans, rose equally, this taxation would fall upon individuals exactly in proportion to their incomes. But, in fact, all prices do not rise equally. Wages lag behind the prices of commodities during an upward movement, while investors in gilt-edged securities and other recipients of fixed money incomes, including old age pensioners and the recipients of all similar statutory money benefits, suffer the full force of the fall in the value of money. Inflation, therefore, causes a redistribution of income in favour of business men, who secure large windfall profits, at the expense of wage-earners and, still more, at the expense of the recipients of fixed money incomes.[1] On balance, inflation is likely to increase the inequality of incomes and to operate, on the whole, not as a proportional, but as a regressive tax, supplemented by a subsidy to business men, ordinary shareholders and many classes of speculators. On the other hand, in so far as great fortunes are held predominantly in forms yielding fixed money incomes, inflation eats them away. But, on the whole, from the point of view of distribution, it is a bad means of raising revenue.

§ 4. The effect of inflation upon production is sometimes thought to be stimulating, since business men are encouraged by unwonted gains to undertake new enterprises. But, as recent economic history shows, this is only a temporary and unhealthy stimulus, carrying within itself the seeds of subsequent severe relapse. In a world of super-men, coolly and accurately calculating the future, this would not be so. But most of the business men of reality are not of this kind. Doped by artificial prosperity, they become first light-hearted and then light-headed, miscalculate prospects, misdirect resources, and launch enterprises which are economically unsound. The mere cessation, sometimes

[1] Writing in July, 1922, Mr. Keynes estimated that, as regards "medium fortunes" invested in gilt-edged securities, "the monetary events which have accompanied and have followed the war have taken from them about one-half of their real value in England, six-sevenths in France, eleven-twelfths in Italy, and ninety-nine-hundredths in Germany. This is apart from the increased burden of taxation" (*Manchester Guardian, Commercial Reconstruction in Europe*, Section Five, p. 324). In particular, an internal public debt, bearing a fixed rate of interest, is gradually wiped out by continuous inflation. It is a nice point of dialectics, whether or not this process amounts to "repudiation." See Ch. XXIII, § 2. It may be added that, in so far as depreciating paper is bought and held by foreigners, the latter contribute to the revenue of the public authority which is practising inflation.

even a mere slackening in the rate, of inflation is enough, without any positive deflation, to break the illusion, to destroy " business confidence," to disappoint anticipations of demand, and to put out of action, sometimes for considerable periods, a large part of the productive power which these business men control. On the other hand, the continuance of inflation, and the expansion, even at a constant rate, of the paper currency, sooner or later destroys the confidence, not only of business men, but of the whole community, in the future value of this currency. Then comes the stage, which journalists call " the flight " from the currency, everyone trying to get rid of it, in exchange for goods and services, as quickly as he can, and to conduct transactions, as far as possible, without making use of it at all. In other words, there is a sharp fall in the demand for this discredited money, and an increase, more than in proportion to the increase in the total supply, in that part of the supply which is offered for exchange at any given moment. Hence the fall in its value, both internal and external, is sharply and continuously accelerated. Under such hectic conditions, which prevailed soon after the war in a number of European countries, organised production becomes impossible and all economic transactions, other than by primitive barter, are reduced to a wild gamble. Economic chaos, political upheavals and, perhaps, violent revolution are then not far away.

§ 5. From the revenue point of view, resort to the printing press is often the line of least resistance for an embarrassed government, which dare not cut down expenditure nor take the steps necessary to pay its way by taxing straightforwardly or offering sufficiently high rates of interest to attract an adequate supply of new savings. The comparative acquiescence of public opinion in taxation by inflation is a measure of public ignorance of economic principles and of the inability of wage-earners, and still more of the recipients of fixed money incomes, to safeguard their economic interests.[1]

Further, even from the point of view of raising revenue, the yield of inflation, if pushed beyond a certain point, rapidly dries up. For, as has already been pointed out, not only does the value of paper currency fall as its supply increases, but, after a certain point, when the flight from the currency begins and becomes gradually more and more precipitate, the value per unit falls much faster than the supply increases. Hence, in order to obtain from inflation a given purchasing power, or "command of real resources," a government must work the printing press ever faster and faster, and, by this very process, accelerates the flight, the effects of which it is seeking to counteract.

§ 6. Deflation cannot be, like inflation, a source of public revenue. It leads, indeed, to a shrinkage of public revenue, and so tends to unbalance the budget. Its effects upon production are most adverse. For rapidly falling prices, combined with the increasing pressure of fixed money charges, bring losses and even ruin to producers, and thus not only check production but lay resources, both human and material, idle.

The effects of deflation on distribution do not merely cancel out those of inflation, though they tend to enrich

[1] Thus persons, who would certainly vote against a government which added one shilling in the pound to their income tax, have been found to tolerate a government which, by doubling the price level through inflation, has, in effect, imposed upon them an additional income tax of ten shillings in the pound!

the recipients of fixed money incomes at the expense of other classes. But these fixed money incomes themselves may, under extreme pressure on the budget, be reduced by law, or through the insolvency of debtors, public or private, may even cease to be paid at all. Moreover, by causing heavy unemployment, deflation brings extreme poverty to many. And just as inflation, ruthlessly pursued, may precipitate political upheavals and violent revolutions, so may deflation. In Germany, indeed, in 1933 it did so.

§ 7. In the preceding paragraphs I have used the terms " inflation " and " deflation " to signify *large and rapid changes*, in either direction, due to governmental action, in the value of money. Both theory and recent experience teach that each is, in a different way, disastrous. But, though large and rapid changes are disastrous, moderate and gradual changes may be tolerable, and even sometimes advantageous. Hence, for example, the argument for a moderate measure of " reflation " after a period of severe deflationary damage. But such arguments belong more to monetary policy than to public finance.

§ 8. It is a fallacy, widely held in 1931 in this country, that an unbalanced budget necessarily leads to inflation and thus threatens currency stability. When budget deficits are met by loans, other than bank loans supported by new issues of paper money, there is no threat to the currency, except very remotely and indirectly.

Any government, which issues paper money at all, either itself or through the agency of the Central Bank, may properly obtain an annual revenue, as the British Government regularly does, from the profits of the currency note issue. And any government, which reduces the value of its currency in terms of gold, may properly credit itself with the resulting increased value, in terms of currency, of stocks of gold held by the Treasury or the banks, as the United States Government did in 1934. But this should be treated as a capital asset, not as current revenue.

PART III

PUBLIC EXPENDITURE

14

Chapter XVI

OBJECTS AND CLASSIFICATION OF PUBLIC EXPENDITURE

§ 1. English economists as a body have had surprisingly little to say concerning the principles of public expenditure. As an American critic observes, "the older English writers did not need a theory of expenditures, because the theory of government which they held implied a fixed limit to governmental functions."[1] Typical of such writers is Sir H. Parnell, an early nineteenth century pundit, who maintained that "every particle of expenditure beyond what necessity absolutely requires for the preservation of social order and for protection against foreign attack is waste and an unjust and oppressive imposition on the public."[2] On this pronouncement the comment has been made that, if so, we must give up growing crocuses in the public parks, unless it can be proved that they preserve social order, for they are certainly no protection against foreign attack. This barren and negative view of the proper economic activities of the State still finds some support. It is still true that, in some influential circles, "the dull and drab extravagance of private living is accompanied by a severe scrutiny of any kind of public expenditure,"[3] and that "publice

[1] Adams, *Science of Finance*, p. 53.
[2] Quoted by Adams, *ibid.*, p. 50.
[3] Masterman, *The Condition of England*, p. 23.

egestas, privatim opulentia" is not much less apt a motto for modern Britain than for ancient Rome. Modern economists, especially in this country, have been slow to correct vulgar prejudices on this matter and to place the whole question, from the point of view of principles, upon a proper footing.

One fortunate result of this lack of theoretical discussion is that the path of economic wisdom in public expenditure is practically unencumbered by doctrines of equity. The "passive resistance," in the early years of this century, of Mr. Lloyd George and other Nonconformists to the support of Anglican schools out of local rates was based on considerations of equity as between different religious denominations. But this was transitory and trivial. Again, when non-contributory old age pensions were first instituted in this country, they were sometimes spoken of as "doles," a disparaging term which carried some faint suggestion of inequity. Unemployment benefit is now similarly described. But it is characteristic of the sensitiveness of conceptions of equity to changes in public opinion that, when new forms of social expenditure become familiar, they are generally taken for granted and no longer thought to be inequitable.

Clear thinking is sometimes hindered by the doctrine that "the State has needs of its own," which can only be satisfied through public expenditure. Taken literally, this is a piece of Hegelian nonsense; taken metaphorically, it is a woolly phrase which leads us nowhere. The truth is, of course, that only individuals have needs, but that some of these needs can be most effectively satisfied through the agency of the State and by means of public expenditure.

§ 2. But what needs are these? How shall they be classified, and distinguished from those needs which can be most effectively satisfied by means of private expenditure? A full answer to this question would be long. It cannot, consistently with the scope of this book, be attempted here. The lack of such an answer, in the writings of economists and political scientists alike, is one of the most serious gaps in the modern theory of public finance. I must content myself, in this place, with a few simple propositions and references.[1]

Wagner's "law of increasing State activities" is as nearly universally true in modern times as any inductive generalisation of this type can hope to be. Wagner maintained that there is a persistent tendency both towards an "extensive" and an "intensive" increase in the functions of the State. New functions are continually being undertaken, and old functions are being performed more efficiently and on a larger scale. The evidence of facts supports both these statements. They are true, even if we leave out of account the functions of preparing for war, waging war, and paying for war long after it is over. They are still more obviously true, if these grim functions are included. "Economy campaigns," in spite of the influential forces behind them, produce only temporary fluctuations in the growth of State activities. They do not reverse the continuous upward trend.

It is a fallacy to explain Wagner's law, as some have done, simply in terms of increasing division of labour. It is true that the individual tends to satisfy fewer and fewer of his own needs without the assistance of others.

[1] But see also Ch. XVIII, §§ 7-9.

But the alternative to unassisted individual action is not only collective action through the agency of the State. There is also the alternative of collective action through the agency of private association. Given the increasing division of labour, we have still to explain the fact that the State continually undertakes new functions and strengthens its grip upon old functions, when both might conceivably have been performed by private enterprise.

An alternative explanation, advanced by pessimists, is that the modern growth of State activities is a vast miscalculation of the public interest, due to the lack of wisdom of democracies, to the blindness or lack of courage of their leaders, or to the egoism of dictators. I believe that, as regards armaments and other war expenditure, this explanation is correct, but that, as regards most other modern State activities, it is incorrect.

The wider truth is that modern developments have tended, in many fields, to increase the efficiency of public authorities, relatively to that of those private associations which are the alternative instruments of action. The choice of public, rather than private, agencies is often, therefore, wise to-day, though it might have been foolish yesterday.[1] In other cases, a like

[1] "There are many things," said Edwin Cannan in 1908, "which we can trust Edward VII to do for us, which we should not have expected from Edward VI. There is no reason to suppose that the process of improvement (in the efficiency of public enterprise) will not continue, and we may even hope to accelerate it greatly if we take in hand the education of officials, and perhaps even of legislators. While great things may thus be expected of corporate management in the future, there does not seem the same reason for expecting improvement in private enterprise." (*Economic Journal*, September, 1908, p. 417.) Since 1908 this argument has been justified and has grown stronger.

choice may be wise to-morrow, though still foolish to-day.

Modern developments, moreover, in other fields, have made it necessary for public authorities to assume new functions, which could not, in fact, have been assumed by private enterprise at all. Functions of public health in modern cities are, perhaps, the clearest illustration of this. The hygienic conditions of life in London, for example, and hence the risks of disease and ill-health, are in large measure common both to rich and poor. "When the rich man dies, his lungs will be as black from London smoke as those of any other city dweller."[1] Protection against contagious disease, as against external attack, typifies indivisible benefits, which it would not pay private enterprise to provide, since it could not charge individuals separately for services which all, or none, must take.

Public expenditure, again, particularly under modern conditions, can provide a communal and inclusive use of many goods, where private expenditure tends only to provide an individual and exclusive use.[2] Parks and open spaces, museums, art galleries and public libraries are cases in point. The National Parks in the United States and Canada, and in the Alps and Carpathians, are immense aids to welfare, and specially necessary safeguards against private appropriation, when both population and facilities for travel are increasing. In

[1] Robson, *The Relation of Wealth to Welfare*, p. 39. This book contains an admirable discussion of the superiority of public over private expenditure, as a means of securing many of the chief gains of modern civilisation.

[2] Though private expenditure, if impelled by a sense of public duty, both could, and sometimes does, achieve results comparable here to those of public expenditure. See Smart's essay on *The Socialising of Consumption* in his *Studies in Economics*.

this country we have, as yet, no National Parks and our National Trust is a very small affair and has appeared very late in the day. But it is gathering strength, as is opinion in support of geographical planning and "the preservation of amenities."[1] Yet we have already permitted the private appropriation and "development" of many areas, which should have been kept open for public enjoyment and could, even now, be re-opened at a price worth paying. "Unbuilding," as a *Times* leading article has declared, will in the future be nearly as important as building. On the other hand, the transformation of the country mansions of the vanished aristocracy into rest and recreation homes for urban workers is one of the most striking achievements of the Russian Revolution.

§ 3. Returning, after this digression, to the main line of our analysis, we may recall the principle, stated in Chapter III, §§ 2-3, that public expenditure should be carried just so far that the marginal social advantages of expenditure in all directions are equal, and just balance the marginal social disadvantages of all methods of raising additional public income; that this is a difficult calculus, but that statesmen must handle it as best they can, since there is no practical alternative.[2] Many

[1] On all this see my *Practical Socialism for Britain*, Chs. XXVI and XXVII.

[2] Dr. Benham in an article on *The Pure Theory of Public Finance* (*Economica*, November, 1934), makes a brave attempt to construct an alternative, based on a conception of "neutrality" in a system of public finance. This would "translate into effect the voluntary judgments and preferences of the citizens." Each would pay as much as he felt disposed for whatever public expenditure he fancied. But the practical difficulties of such a system are insuperable. Nor, even if they were not, would such a system commend itself to anyone who regarded great inequality of incomes as an evil, which public finance can help to remedy.

objects of public expenditure are not exclusively, or even mainly, economic, though most have economic effects and all have economic costs.

A broad distinction may be drawn between public expenditure designed, on the one hand, to preserve the social life of the community against violent attack, whether internal or external, and, on the other, to improve the quality of that social life. In other words, the object may be either to keep social life secure and ordered, or to make that secure and ordered life better worth living, whether from an economic or a non-economic point of view.

§ 4. Turning to the actual expenditure of modern public authorities, the following is an obvious catalogue:

(1) the maintenance and equipment of armed forces, including police, (*a*) in peace, (*b*) in war;

(2) the administration of justice;

(3) the maintenance of the ceremonial head of the State, including, in monarchical countries, the Royal Family and Court, and of diplomatic representatives abroad;

(4) the maintenance of the machinery of civil government, including ministers, legislators and civil servants;

(5) public debt charges, including interest, repayment of principal and cost of management;

(6) expenditure directly devoted to "fostering industry and commerce," such as the maintenance of consuls abroad and the performance of industrial and commercial functions, such as the supply of currency, conduct of postal services, transport services, etc.;

(7) "social expenditure" on health, education, old age pensions, poor relief, provision for unemployment, etc.

This is an empirical catalogue rather than a scientific classification. It is convenient rather than strictly logical. For example, the salaries of the Minister of Education and his staff come under (4), whereas they should, perhaps, come under (7). But such points are unimportant. Net expenditures, and not gross, are significant. For example, postal services are only an object of net expenditure, if the gross expenditure exceeds the receipts, and the administration of justice should be credited with the court fees paid by litigants. Broadly speaking, we may say that (1), (2) and (3) are expenditures designed, at least ostensibly, to keep social life secure and ordered. So is part of (4). So, if we look to its origin, is most of (5), for the great bulk of outstanding public debts have been incurred for purposes of war. On the other hand, (6) and (7) together with part of (4)—the salaries of factory inspectors, for example—and that part of (5) which covers debts incurred for purposes of economic development, are designed to make that secure and ordered life better worth living. Within this latter group of expenditures, however, the motives to economic and non-economic improvement are often mixed. Expenditure on health and education are examples. It is not the only, or indeed the chief, advantage of being healthy or educated, that one is thereby enabled to produce more wealth or make more money.

§ 5. Classifications, as distinct from catalogues, of public expenditure may follow several alternative principles. Thus we may construct, if we please, a "functional classification" of expenditure, based on a classification of the various functions actually performed by public authorities. Or, if we prefer, we may adopt a "departmental classification," based upon the expenditure of the actual administrative departments of government. Even where the range of functions is given, these two methods may yield different results. For the distribution of functions between departments is neither invariable, nor logically predetermined. It is often due to historical accident, or to the desires of influential politicians wishing to magnify their office, or to the mutual jealousy or vested interests of officials. But to pursue this matter further, even by way of illustration, would be to drift too far into mere descriptive detail.

We may, however, notice some further distinctions which throw occasional light on particular problems. Thus we may distinguish between optional expenditure, which the public authority is free to increase or diminish at its pleasure, and obligatory expenditure, in respect of which, owing to past contracts and other legal commitments, it is not free. But this distinction, though valid in a limited way, is only one of degree. For, on the one hand, contracts and other legal arrangements may be revised—this has been a common practice with governments embarrassed by unbalanced budgets—and, on the other, expenditure, which is optional from a legal point of view, may be obligatory from the point of view of political expediency.

Again, we may distinguish between real, or "exhaustive," expenditure on the one hand, and mere transfer expenditure on the other. Real expenditure implies the actual using-up of commodities and services, which would otherwise have been available for some other purpose.[1] Transfer expenditure implies, in itself, no such using-up, but only a transfer, from one person to another, of command over commodities and services. Expenditure on armaments and on education are examples of real expenditure ; expenditure on debt interest and on pensions are examples of transfer expenditure.[2] Real expenditure determines, so far as it goes, both the amount and the character of production. Transfer expenditure does not directly influence either, though it has direct effects on distribution and indirect effects upon production.

Again, a classification, which is adopted in many text-books, divides expenditures according as they confer special benefits on particular members of the community, or common benefits on all members, or benefits which are partly common and partly special.[3] To this division, which is relevant to a discussion of the effects of public expenditure upon distribution, we shall refer again in Chapter XIX. There is, however, another distinction which it is convenient to consider first. This is the distinction between grants and purchase prices.

[1] The nature of the distinction, and the need for it, is well illustrated by Smart's observation (*Studies in Economics*, pp. 269-70), that "society involves in the same condemnation the man who spends his income in gambling or speculation and the man who wastes it in foolish eating and drinking, although the world as a whole loses nothing by the former and loses everything by the latter."

[2] Assuming that the recipients of debt interest and of pensions are members of the same community as the taxpayers who provide the funds for those payments. If, however, the recipients belong to one community and the taxpayers to another, the payments are real expenditure from the point of view of the second community.

[3] The distinction between special and common is the same as that between divisible and indivisible benefits.

CHAPTER XVII

GRANTS AND PURCHASE PRICES

§ 1. The division of public expenditure into grants and purchase prices, corresponds to that of public income into taxes and selling prices.[1] An individual, who receives public money or money's worth, may or may not render in return a direct *quid pro quo* to the public authority. In the former case the public authority makes a purchase from him; in the latter case it makes him a grant. This grant may consist either of money, or of services, such as medical treatment or education or the security presumed to be derived from armaments or police. Thus payments by a public authority to any of its employees, by way of salaries and wages, or to contractors, are purchase prices. On the other hand, payments of old age pensions, poor relief, or contributions out of general revenue to schemes of health and unemployment insurance, are grants.

Just as there are costs of collection of taxes, so there are costs of administration of grants. These are, from the public authority's point of view, purchases incidental to grants. Thus a teacher's salary is a purchase incidental to the grant of free education, and a policeman's pay is a purchase incidental to the grant of security.

Payments of interest on public debts, if we look to their origin in the past, may be represented to be

[1] Compare Ch. IV, §2.

purchase prices, paid for the investment of money in public securities. But, if we look to their character in the present, they are grants. For the receivers of interest are not rendering any present *quid pro quo* to the public authority.[1] It is proper, therefore, in a study of things as they are, to treat these interest payments as grants. But sinking fund payments, to buy and cancel public securities, are purchases. Pensions of all kinds, paid from public revenue, are best classed as grants, though in some cases they may be regarded as deferred payments for past services rendered by the recipients.

§ 2. The parallel between taxes and grants on the one hand, and purchase and selling prices on the other, may be carried a good deal further. Just as a selling price may include an element of tax, when a public authority is selling above the price which a non-monopolist private seller would charge, so a purchase price may include an element of grant, when a public authority is buying above the price which a non-monopolist private buyer would offer. This principle applies, in some cases, to the payment of higher salaries or wages in public than in comparable private employment. Where, however, the higher pay results in proportionately better work, the element of grant disappears and the whole payment is a purchase price. Again, a public enterprise run at a loss covered

[1] This proposition is repugnant to those who hold that all interest is a price paid for "the service of waiting," no matter how long. I, therefore, think it worth while to quote here the joint dictum of Professor Bowley and Sir Josiah Stamp (*The National Income*, 1924, p. 41) that "the most important transfers of purchasing power, for which the recipient renders no current economic services, are interest on war debt and pensions."

by taxation makes grants, in proportion to their purchases, to all its customers.

The distinction between grants and purchase prices may be compared with that between transfer expenditure and real expenditure, which was noticed in the last chapter. All grants of money are transfer expenditure and, in general, purchase prices represent real expenditure. But, where a purchase price includes an element of money grant, it includes a corresponding element of transfer expenditure. Moreover, grants of particular services or commodities presuppose a real expenditure in these particular directions.

§ 3. Grants, like taxes, may be classified as direct and indirect.[1] A grant may be said to be direct, if the whole benefit accrues to the person to whom the grant is made. It may be said to be indirect, if the benefit is passed on, in whole or in part, from the person to whom the grant is made to some other person, owing to a consequential change in the terms of some contract or bargain between them. Thus an old age pension is a direct grant.[2] But a subsidy to private enterprise is an indirect grant, in so far as part of the benefit is passed on to consumers through lower prices or to workers through higher wages.

The incidence of grants is similar to that of the incidence of taxes.[3] The incidence of a (money) grant

[1] Compare Ch. V, §2. A grant is a negative tax and, therefore, to every proposition regarding taxes, there corresponds a proposition regarding grants.

[2] Relatives or friends, who are supporting an old person, will benefit through his receipt of a pension, in so far as they reduce the amount of assistance which they were previously giving. But this benefit is best classified as indirect and not as part of the incidence of the grant of the pension.

[3] Compare Ch. VII, and especially §2.

is upon those who receive the direct money benefit of the grant. The incidence of a direct grant is, by definition, wholly on the person to whom the grant is made. The incidence of an indirect grant, or subsidy, in respect of any commodity is divided between the buyer and the seller in the ratio of the elasticity of supply of the commodity to the elasticity of demand for it. For, the more elastic the supply, the more will the supply increase, as a result of a given fall in the cost of production, allowing for the subsidy, and the greater, therefore, will be the fall of price corresponding to any given elasticity of demand. The greater, therefore, will be the proportion of the incidence which will be on the buyer. On the other hand, the more elastic the demand, the more will the demand increase, as a result of a given fall in the price of the subsidised commodity, and the less, therefore, will be the fall in price corresponding to any given elasticity of supply. The greater, therefore, will be the proportion of the incidence which will be on the seller.

The freeing of new houses from onerous rates, as proposed in Chapter X, § 11, would be equivalent in effect to a grant from public funds to the builders of new houses.

§ 4. Just as the proper distribution of the burden of taxation is a possible subject of discussion,[1] so is the proper distribution of the benefit of grants.

Take, for instance, the conception of "ability to pay" taxation. Corresponding to this we may formulate a conception of "ability to receive" grants. But, just as "ability to pay" must be interpreted to mean

[1] Compare Ch. IX.

ability to pay *with a minimum of economic loss*,[1] so "ability to receive" must mean ability to receive *with a maximum of economic gain*. From the three alternative applications of the principle of ability to pay, namely minimum sacrifice, proportional sacrifice and equal sacrifice, we may derive three alternative applications of the principle of ability to receive, namely maximum benefit, proportional benefit, and equal benefit. Maximum benefit would be attained, as a first approximation, by making no grants to anyone whose income was above a certain level, and by raising all smaller incomes, by means of grants, to exactly this level. This plan, as it stands, is too crude for practice, but, in a modified form, it gives effect to the excellent principle of a national minimum standard of economic conditions below which no member of a civilised community should be allowed to fall. There is, however, nothing to be said for adopting the principles of either proportional or equal benefit in the distribution of grants. Again, corresponding to the precept that the inequality of incomes should not be altered by taxation, is the precept that this inequality should not be altered by grants. From the latter precept, which is no more acceptable than its mate, it will follow that, other things being equal, the richer of two old men should always receive the larger old age pension.

Just as a particular tax, or a tax system as a whole, may be either proportional, progressive or regressive, so may a particular grant, or a grant system as a whole. Under a progressive grant system, the larger the recipient's income, the smaller the proportion which is

[1] See Ch. XIII, §2.

added to it by grants, while under a regressive grant system, the larger the income, the larger the proportion which is added by grants.[1]

§ 5. Finally, just as, with taxation, incidence is only part of the wider question of effects, so it is with grants. The next three chapters, therefore, will be devoted to a discussion of the economic effects of grants, and of public expenditure generally. As in the corresponding case of taxation, more light is thrown upon the practical desirability of various policies by such a study in economy than by considerations of equity.

[1] We might, if we preferred, reverse these meanings of the terms "progressive" and "regressive," as applied to grants. But it seems better to use the same terms to describe both taxes and grants, which tend to diminish the inequality of incomes, or to increase it, as the case may be.

Chapter XVIII

THE EFFECTS OF PUBLIC EXPENDITURE ON PRODUCTION

§ 1. The distinction between grants and purchase prices is less prominent in this chapter, which is concerned with the effects of public expenditure on production, than in the discussion, which occupies the next chapter, of the corresponding effects on distribution. In this chapter the essential fact is that public expenditure, combined with taxation and other methods of raising public income, causes large diversions of economic resources from the channels, into which they would otherwise have flowed, into channels determined by public policy, and may consequently cause large changes both in the character and in the total volume of production.

Just as taxation, other things being equal, should reduce production as little as possible, so public expenditure should increase it as much as possible.

§ 2. Many people do not seem to realise that public expenditure can ever increase production. Consider, for example, the following pronouncement. "The proportion of government expenditure to national income is several times as great as it was before the war, which means that a far smaller proportion of that income is available for provision for old age, for saving and business enterprise."[1] It is here apparently assumed that "government expenditure" may be simply subtracted from "the national income," and that the result of this subtraction represents what "is available for provision for old age, for saving and business enterprise." In this view of the matter two essential facts are completely ignored. The first is that much public expenditure involves mere transfers of purchasing power within the community. As we have already seen, payment of interest on internal public debt and payment of old age pensions are obvious examples of such transfers. The authors of the pronouncement just quoted seem to suggest that none of the dividends on War Loan are ever saved, and that old age pensions are not a provision for old age. The second essential fact which is ignored is that much public expenditure, on education and public health for example, directly increases the productive power of the community, and hence the fund available for the purposes to which the authors refer. Public "expenditure," in short, includes public savings, and may promote much investment in human, as well as in material, capital.

A correct view of the effects of public expenditure on production can only be reached by following a line of enquiry parallel to that of Chapter X on the effects of taxation on production. It is necessary to consider successively (1) effects upon ability to work and save,

[1] From a letter on "Prodigal Public Expenditure" (*Manchester Guardian*, July 16th, 1920), bearing the following signatures: "Askwith, Chalmers, Cowdray, A. Herbert Dixon, R. A. Hadfield, Inchcape, Islington, Godfrey Locker-Lampson, Walter Leaf, Midleton, John Denison Pender, W. Peter Rylands, Salisbury, Selborne, Arthur Steel-Maitland, Richard V. Vassar-Smith."

(2) effects upon desire to work and save, and (3) effects of diversions of economic resources as between different employments and localities. And " work " includes, as an important special case, the undertaking of new enterprises.

§ 3. Before taking up these lines of thought, we shall make a digression. A large part of modern public expenditure is devoted to purposes which make no direct contribution to economic welfare. Expenditure on armaments and armed forces is the most striking example of this, and it is often said that such expenditure is economic waste. For men cannot eat guns or high explosives. And the multiplication of battleships is not an economical solution of the housing problem.

The economic waste and destruction of modern warfare need no emphasis, though many of the most overwhelming evils which war brings with it—pain and terror, anxiety and bereavement, hatred and moral degradation, especially among non-combatants—lie outside the economic sphere. But it is undeniable that war expenditure, which results in preventing or limiting invasion or in securing military victory, diminishes the economic loss which invasion or defeat would otherwise have caused. It is even possible that, in exceptional circumstances, a short and successful war may bring to a community as a whole a balance of economic gain, and nearly every war brings gain to a favoured few, even among the vanquished. But, if the speeches of statesmen are the key to history, such possibilities of economic plunder play no part in the diplomacy, which from time to time launches a multitude of lives upon a sea of death. It is, rather, to the non-economic tunes of " national honour," " the defence of liberty " and

" the sanctity of treaties " that the young men, on both sides, march away. Economic considerations enter, perhaps, only as an afterthought, when the time at last arrives to commemorate the glorious dead and to draft new treaties of peace to replace the old.

But the simple economist, unversed in these diplomatic mysteries, cannot deny that the services of soldiers, sailors and airmen, and even of armament manufacturers, may, under favourable conditions, contribute to his security and are thus in principle entitled, no less than the services of plumbers, scavengers and fire brigades, to a place in the aggregate of national " production," in its widest sense. Here, however, as elsewhere, there is need for true economy, and a danger that the diversion of resources into such channels may be either too great or too small. In time of peace, national expenditure on armed forces has the peculiarity that it is almost wholly determined by relative standards. What each nation aims at is to be strong, not absolutely, but relatively to other nations. Much talk, at international conferences and elsewhere, of armament " ratios " and of " parity " illustrates this. A fifty per cent. reduction in the armed forces of all nations would leave them all in much the same apparent state of security or insecurity as before. And the same is true of a fifty per cent. increase. But an all-round increase in armed forces, while adding nothing to apparent relative security, subtracts economic resources from other uses in which they would have made a direct contribution to economic welfare. It subtracts, in particular, the services of a picked body of men, distinctly above the average in physical powers and not below it in mental powers, and also large quantities of important commodities, such as iron, coal and oil. The communities concerned have less economic welfare and no greater security. In fact, they will have less security. For this depends, not only on the relative strength of armed forces, but on the state of men's minds and the extent to which they meditate on the possibility of war with their neighbours. It depends also on the effectiveness of arrangements for collective security through mutual assistance. Security, in other words, is not only material but psychological. And the greater the part which armed forces and armed habits of thought play in the life of a nation, the smaller is the psychological security against war. The era of competitive European armaments, which filled the statesmen of each country with an ever-growing fear of their neighbours and ended in the blundering outbreak of 1914, is sufficient proof of this. There is a like competition and a like fear throughout the world to-day. It is, indeed, very obvious that the cutting down of armed forces, all the world over, to the level of an international police force would be a condition both of maximum security and of maximum economic welfare. What is required here is an international agreement for the limitation of output.[1]

Armed forces for defence, or aggression, against external foes, fall into the same class as domestic police, courts of justice, factory inspectors, and much else, expenditure on which would be largely unnecessary, if only men were a little wiser, or more imaginative, or more honest, than they are. It is to be sharply

[1] I have discussed this and kindred problems at some length in my book *Towards the Peace of Nations*, especially Chs. VII-IX, and in my *Practical Socialism for Britain*, Chs. XXXIV-XXXV.

distinguished from that other class of expenditure, on education for instance, which will always be necessary, either from public or from private funds, whatever changes may take place in average human conduct or outlook.

§ 4. We may now return to the effects of public expenditure upon people's ability to work and save.

Just as taxation will reduce a man's ability to work, if it diminishes his efficiency, so public expenditure will increase it, if it increases his efficiency. This opens a wide field for socially desirable expenditure, which will be further considered below under the head of diversion of economic resources. But it may be pointed out here that grants in money may increase the efficiency, not so much of the direct recipients, as of their children in the future. This is an important part of the case for widows' pensions, for family allowances and similar proposals. Further, certain grants in kind, such as educational and medical services and house accommodation, even at "uneconomic rents," will do more to increase efficiency than equivalent grants in money, which would often be spent to less good purpose. Such reactions of grants upon efficiency are one measure of the recipients' "ability to receive," which is analogous to taxpayers' "ability to pay."

Again, just as all taxation will reduce the victim's ability to save, if he has any margin out of which saving is possible, so all public expenditure will increase the beneficiary's ability to save, in so far as it gives him any additional margin of this kind. If £100 is taken from A by taxation and handed over to B—it matters not whether as dividends on War Loan, or in payment of a civil servant's salary, or on any other pretext—the increase in B's ability to save exactly offsets the decrease in A's ability.

§ 5. Turning from effects upon ability, to effects upon desire, to work and save, it was argued in Chapter X, § 3, that in this respect the expectation of future taxation is more important than the fact of present taxation. The expectation of future benefits from public expenditure has, likewise, an important influence. In many cases the amount of these future benefits, by way of grants, is independent of the amount of the recipient's future work and saving. War pensions and interest on War Loan are examples. The expectation of such fixed, periodical and, so far as the future is concerned, unconditional receipts is seldom[1] likely to increase desire to work or save, and, where demand for income in terms of effort is very inelastic, it is likely to decrease this desire so much that the effort put forth will produce an income smaller by nearly the full amount of the grant. But not all grants are thus fixed and unconditional. The prospect of a conditional grant, which will be paid only in the event of sickness or involuntary unemployment, will not decrease present desire to work. In some circumstances it may even increase it. Again, the prospect of a grant, which is not fixed but increases with the future efforts of the recipient, such as a bounty on his earnings or savings, would, unless demand for income was very inelastic, increase his desire to work or save. But grants of this kind are not often feasible in practice. On the other hand, the prospect of a grant, which diminishes with

[1] Though sometimes the expectation of a small fixed minimum income in the future will, by creating a foundation of security, make it seem more worth while to build on this foundation than it would have been to start building without it.

the future efforts of the recipient, will certainly check his desire to work and save. Similarly a grant which diminishes in proportion to his past efforts, as when, under a "means test," an unemployed man with savings gets less than one without. Thus "thrift is penalised."

§ 6. We may now go on to consider the effects on production of diversions, due to public expenditure, of economic resources as between different employment and localities. Taking first diversions as between different employments, the special case of expenditure on armed forces has already been discussed. Akin to this are all other cases of expenditure designed, according to the classification adopted in Chapter XVI, § 2, to keep the social life of the community secure and ordered. All that can be said of such expenditure, in this connection, is that it should be governed by the principle of economy. The advantage of a little more security and order must be balanced against the disadvantage of doing without those other commodities and services, which would otherwise have been produced.

When, however, we turn to that other category of expenditure, which is designed to make the secure and ordered life of the community better worth living, there is something more to be said. It has been pointed out in Chapter X, § 11, that grants, or subsidies, to particular industries may sometimes be beneficial to production. In more general terms, the diversion, through public expenditure, of economic resources into particular employments will sometimes increase production. Such diversions may be brought about either by subsidies to private enterprises, or by running public enterprises at a loss, which is made good out of general taxation,[1] or by embarking on public enterprises which will cover their own costs. Again, such diversions may either promote the production of particular consumable commodities and services, or may take the form of a diversion of resources from provision for the present to provision for the future, and thus to the building up of future productive power.

§ 7. It is in order to secure a more effective economic provision for the future that the most far-reaching diversions may be justified. The economic institutions of capitalism are such that, apart from the intervention of public authorities, too little provision of this kind is made, and that which is made is badly composed. Too little provision is made, because there are very few people who do not to some extent discount the future, and especially the more distant future.[2] Most people prefer to spend £100 now rather than to have £105 to spend a year hence. And they prefer £100 for themselves now rather than, say, £1,000 for themselves, or, in the event of their death, for some other person, thirty years hence. Again, what provision is made is badly composed, in the sense that too large a proportion takes the form of material capital and too small a proportion takes the form of human capital and of knowledge. For the return obtainable by an individual from a wise investment in human capital or in knowledge is generally smaller than that obtainable from an equally wise investment

[1] See Ch. XIV, §§5-6.

[2] See Ch. III, §5. "Posterity was a chilly thing to work for, no matter how much a man happened to love his own, or other people's already-produced children." (T. E. Lawrence, *Seven Pillars of Wisdom*, p. 191.)

in material capital. But, for this very reason, the return to the community as a whole is generally greater from an increase in the former type of investment than from an increase in the latter.[1]

It follows that there is a large field for the intervention of public authorities to increase economic provision for the future and to secure a better balance between its component elements. These two objects furnish the key to nearly all public expenditure designed to increase productive power.

From the point of view of production, those forms of public expenditure are socially desirable, which will increase productive power more than it would be increased, if the funds required were left in private hands. To this category belongs expenditure on (1) debt redemption, where the bulk of the money repaid will generally be reinvested[2]; (2) objects such as railway development in new countries, irrigation and afforestation, which may be expected to yield large returns in the long run, but not in the immediate future, and which do not, therefore, attract the private investor; (3) the increase of knowledge, by the encouragement of research and invention, and, as regards opportunities of employment, by the maintenance of employment exchanges; (4) education and training; (5) public health; and (6) expenditure in aid of insurance against unemployment and certain other risks outside the control of the insured person.

[1] For a fuller discussion of these important points see Pigou, *Economics of Welfare*, pp. 24-7 and 773-81; Cannan, *Wealth*, pp. 138 and 199-201; and my own *Inequality of Incomes*, pp. 264-8. Compare also Marshall, *Principles of Economics*, p. 661.

[2] For further discussion of the problem of debt redemption see Ch. XXIII, and also §9 of the present chapter.

There are, of course, limits to the amount that can be advantageously spent by public authorities on these objects, but there are strong grounds for believing that these limits lie well ahead of most actual expenditures. Hence increased public expenditure in these directions is desirable with a view to bringing about that distribution of the community's resources between different uses, which will give the maximum future productivity.

This principle is already admitted in this country in the case of free education paid for out of the rates and taxes, in housing subsidies from public funds, and in many other cases. There is much to be said for the extension of the principle to cover the further extension of free education and free medical services, of free milk and free meals at school, and of the cheapening by subsidy of selected foodstuffs, in the interests of health and the development of human efficiency. A subsidy to private savings is also, at first sight, defensible, with the object of stimulating saving. But, as will be argued later, this object can be better secured by other means. Many other extensions of the principle may be defended, but not all of these are simultaneously practicable on a large scale, and it is necessary to balance their beneficial effects, in each case, against the effects on production of raising the necessary funds by taxation or otherwise.

Further, it is a matter for consideration, in each particular case, whether the object in view can be best attained by public enterprise or by a subsidy to private enterprise. Moreover, it is sometimes possible to bring about the desired results more satisfactorily by changes in taxation than by subsidies from public expenditure.

It might be better, for example, to exempt new houses from local rates than to subsidise them.

§ 8. The employment of public expenditure to encourage the use of selected commodities and services may thus greatly increase productivity. But this policy, when it takes the form of the supply of such commodities and services free, or much below cost price, raises some further questions. Since a lowering of price leads to an increase of demand, a public authority must be prepared either to increase correspondingly the supply of the commodities and services concerned, or to ration the supply, if the increased demand exceeds it. But a very large increase of supply would sometimes mean an excessive and wasteful diversion of economic resources. On the other hand, rationing, though often a sound and popular policy in war time, is seldom appropriate to the conditions of peace. The policy of free, or very cheap, supply is, therefore, better suited to commodities and services with an inelastic, than for those with an elastic, demand at low prices. Thus free medical services are, in this sense, more economical than free railway travel or free clothing. Rationing, on the other hand, though generally inadvisable, can be applied to some exceptional cases, such as the number of free places in institutions providing higher education.

Considerations of practical convenience, as has already been pointed out,[1] sometimes turn the scale in favour of free supply, as in the case of roads. But in all such cases " practical convenience " will be found, on closer examination, to imply a power in the public authority to prevent demand from outrunning supply.

[1] See Ch. XIV, §6.

§ 9. It follows from the preceding argument that to promote the growth of material capital, at the expense either of human capital or of knowledge, is a mistaken policy which will tend to diminish, and not to increase, production. But to promote the growth of material capital, at the expense of consumption which does not add appreciably to human efficiency, is a policy which will increase production. Broadly, such a policy will substitute saving, either by public authorities or private persons, for spending. There are very large possibilities here, which modern governments have hardly yet begun to explore. The Government of the Soviet Union is an exception. Under its successive Five Year Plans provision for the future has been made, by means of public investment, on an enormous, possibly even on an excessive, scale.

The operation of a sinking fund for debt reduction, fed from taxation, increases saving. For, whereas only a part of the funds raised by taxation would otherwise have been saved, practically the whole of the funds liberated by debt redemption will be reinvested. A vigorous sinking fund policy will, therefore, give a strong stimulus to saving, even if it necessitates heavy taxation. This proposition may, however, be generalised in a much wider policy.

Three alternative forms of such a policy may be distinguished. In the first place, public expenditure may be directed to the repayment of deadweight public debt, which has no public assets behind it. This is the ordinary policy of the sinking fund. It eliminates what has been called " imaginary capital " and liberates funds invested in public securities for investment in the creation of new capital goods in private ownership.

In the second place, public expenditure may be directed to the purchase by public authorities of existing real capital in private ownership. This policy transfers existing capital from private to public ownership and liberates funds invested in the existing capital goods for investment in the creation of new capital goods in private ownership. In the third place, public expenditure may be directed to the creation of new capital goods in public ownership. This policy invests funds directly in new public assets.

Provided that sufficient opportunities for new investment are available—an important proviso to which I shall return—each of these policies leads to new capital expenditure. The first and second stimulate saving by private individuals; the third takes the form of new savings by public authorities; both the second and third result in the creation of new public assets, while the first diminishes public debt. A policy intermediate between the first and the second consists of the repayment of private mortgages on publicly owned undertakings, such as national railways or electric plants or municipal tramways or gasworks.

The stimulus to saving and to the creation of new capital, which these policies render possible, can be made just as effective as, and is more in accord with modern ideas than, a stimulus secured through increased exemption of savings from taxation.[1] But the undue concentration of the thought of economists on the revenue, as distinct from the expenditure, side of public finance has hitherto left these alternatives in shadow.

[1] Compare Ch. X, §6.

It is not less important to provide new enterprise to absorb new savings than to provide new savings to sustain new enterprise. The volume of new investment, in any given period, does not necessarily coincide with the volume of new savings. The lack of this coincidence is one of the causes of instability in the price level, of industrial fluctuations and of unemployment. To create and maintain such a coincidence public intervention is often required, partly through programmes of public works financed by loan, partly through the organisation and control of new investment in private enterprise.[1] But public works can also be financed otherwise than by loan. A large programme of public capital development along selected lines, financed from taxation, may become one of the most fruitful developments of financial policy in modern communities. This method has been used by many governments in Europe since the war.[2] The magnitude and speed of achievement of such a programme is limited, not by the obstacle of the rate of interest, as with programmes of public or private capital development by loan, but by the obstacle of the rate of taxation which, if it were raised above a certain point, or if it were raised too rapidly, would arouse effective opposition.

The effects of financing public works by loan and by taxation differ in several respects. Finance by taxation causes only a transfer, and changed use, of purchasing power, not an addition to it. But finance by loan may increase purchasing power through an expansion of credit. And sometimes such an increase

[1] See my *Practical Socialism for Britain*, Chs. XXII and XXV.
[2] For details see *Unbalanced Budgets* by myself and other authors.

is desirable, in order to stimulate production. On the other hand, just because it makes no addition to purchasing power, but only transfers it and changes its use, finance by taxation may have an advantage over finance by loan in checking an unhealthy boom. This point is dealt with in Chapter XX. The effects of the two methods on distribution also differ, as is explained in Chapter XIX. Even when funds for public works are raised by taxation, they may, of course, be lent, and interest charged, to public enterprises. For this purpose a public loan fund for development, fed by taxation, may be created.

§ 10. Diversions, through public expenditure, of economic resources as between different localities will sometimes increase productive power. A distribution of grants from a central exchequer to local authorities, in such a way as to stimulate the latter in the efficient performance of their functions, will do this. Further, special grants in aid of public services in the poorer localities—sometimes spoken of as " necessitous area grants "—will enable the public authorities concerned to make a better provision for these services than could have been made, if a given total of grants had been less unequally distributed. Moreover, the deliberate guidance, by geographical planning or financial inducement, of new industries, public or private, into " depressed areas " may make for a fuller utilisation of immobile and unemployed resources and thus lead, even at some initial cost, to increased aggregate production later.

§ 11. The preceding argument has assumed a framework of private property and private enterprise, within which we have studied the diversion of economic resources in consequence of public expenditure, and in an earlier chapter in consequence of taxation, from that distribution between employments and localities which would otherwise have come about. This method of study is most appropriate when the range of public authorities' economic activities is narrow. It becomes less and less appropriate as this range extends, since the basis of comparison becomes more and more remote and unreal. In the Soviet Union, for example, Public Finance merges into Public Economy in a wide sense, and is dominated by a central planned direction of all the economic activities of the community towards certain deliberately chosen ends. Thus in the first Five Year Plan light industry was stiffly taxed to promote the growth of heavy industry and electrification. With the abolition of private property in the means of production, and with the disappearance of nearly all large incomes and of all large inherited fortunes, private saving becomes of small importance and the individual taxpayer fades into the background, the public enterprise becoming the chief taxable subject. The form of any useful discussion of public finance must be adapted to the current economic institutions.

§ 12. To sum up the main conclusions of this chapter,[1] whereas taxation, taken alone, probably checks production, public expenditure, taken alone, should almost certainly increase it. Expenditure on police and armed forces, if not overdone, and on the other apparatus of order and security, creates the conditions under which alone organised production can take place at all. Expenditure of other kinds acts on production in three ways, first, through its effects on

[1] Compare the last section of Ch. X.

ability to work and save ; second, through its effects on desire to work and save ; third, through diversions of economic resources as between different employments and localities. Under the first head, the stimulus to production is clear, just as the corresponding check due to taxation is clear. Under the second head, much depends, as in the case of taxation, upon the character both of persons and of policy. On balance, however, some slight check to production is probable as a result of the expectation of grants. Under the third head, there are very great possibilities, hitherto largely neglected, of stimulating production, more especially through wise expenditure on public health, education and the increase of knowledge, and through a stimulus to saving, both public and private, provided adequate opportunities for investment are created. Such expenditure, in turn, will indirectly increase ability, and perhaps also desire, to work and save.

Striking a balance between the two sides of the account, there can be no doubt that the stimulus to production afforded by a wise system of public expenditure will far outweigh the check, if any, resulting from the taxation and other devices required to finance it, provided that these also are well contrived from this point of view. But the actual public expenditure of many modern communities, predominantly on armed forces and war debts, is a melancholy spectacle, on which the shrill and undiscriminating clamour of "economists," in the vulgar sense of the word, is an inadequate commentary.

Chapter XIX

THE EFFECTS OF PUBLIC EXPENDITURE ON DISTRIBUTION

§ 1. A study of the effects of public expenditure on distribution involves a discussion, on parallel lines to that of Chapter XI, of the effects of taxation on distribution. The parallelism is complete so far as that part of public expenditure, which consists of grants conferring special benefit on individuals, is concerned. We may, therefore, begin with public expenditure of this sort.

Those who find Wagner's "socio-political" view of taxation hard to swallow, will find it a still harder saying that, other things being equal, that system of public expenditure is most desirable, which has the strongest tendency to reduce the inequality of incomes. Yet this follows logically from the view that a less unequal distribution is desirable.

§ 2. As was pointed out in Chapter XVII, § 4, a particular grant, like a particular tax, may be regressive, proportional or progressive. A grant is regressive if, the smaller the recipient's income, the smaller the proportionate addition made by the grant; progressive if, the smaller the recipient's income, the larger the proportionate addition; proportional if, whatever the size of the recipient's income, the proportionate addition is the same. Thus a universal and uniform old age pension payable to all who attain a certain age would be progressive as between the recipients, while interest on public debt is, on the whole, regressive as between the recipients.[1] More generally, a system of grants, like a system of taxes, may be regressive, proportional or progressive either over the whole body of citizens, or over particular groups of grant recipients.

A progressive grant system tends to reduce the inequality of incomes. So does a proportional, or even a mildly regressive, grant system. But a more sharply regressive grant system tends to increase inequality. On the other hand, the sharper the progression, the stronger the tendency to reduction.[2] Considerations of distribution, therefore, lead us toward the most sharply progressive grant system that is practicable. The principle of minimum sacrifice in the distribution of taxation runs parallel to the principle of maximum benefit in the distribution of grants. As pointed out above, a rough approximation to the latter principle would be a grant system, which brought all incomes below a certain level up to that level, and added nothing to any income above that level. But, whereas the policy of the National Minimum embodies the first part of this idea, the second part is not practically attainable, at any rate while large public debts remain. Moreover, considerations of production limit the height at which national minimum standards can advantageously be set. But the case for a considerable degree of progression may be taken to be firmly established.

[1] Most obviously with holdings by individuals, but also, on the whole, when the benefit of corporate holdings, *e.g.*, by banks or insurance companies, are traced through to individual shareholders.

[2] Compare Ch. XI, §2, and Note to Ch. IX, §5.

When grants take the form, not of money payments, but of particular services or commodities, such as free medical treatment or education, it is difficult to assess these at their money value to the recipients. But, as was pointed out in the last chapter, such grants will often increase the economic welfare of their recipients, and also the productive power of the community, much more than equivalent money grants would do.

The question of subsidies, referred to in the last chapter from the point of view of production, may also be looked at from the point of view of distribution. Thus a bread or a milk subsidy which lowered prices would operate as a progressive grant, while a subsidy on private savings would be regressive. Given a great inequality of incomes, the case for progressive subsidies is strengthened.

§ 3. The effect of grants upon distribution may be modified by their reactions on individual incomes. If the prospect of a grant causes a person to work or save less than he would otherwise have done, the effect of the grant in increasing his income will be diminished, and in the opposite case its effect will be increased. But this class of problem is covered by the discussion in the last chapter.

Again, distribution would be indirectly affected, and the inequality of incomes reduced, by educational expenditure on a scale sufficient to enable the younger generation to move in large numbers from the worse paid to the better paid occupations and thereby to reduce considerably the differences between the higher and the lower rates of pay.[1]

[1] See my *Inequality of Incomes*, pp. 264-7.

§ 4. So far we have been considering effects upon distribution, in the sense of effects upon the inequality of incomes. Grants may improve distribution simply by diminishing this inequality. But they may also improve it by adjusting individual incomes more closely to individual, or family, needs during different periods. The latter sort of improvement is the aim of much modern legislation, as, for example, the provision, wholly or partly out of public funds, of old age pensions, sick benefit, unemployment benefit, maternity benefit, widows' pensions, family allowances, and so forth. There is some parallelism here with the adjustment of taxation to the domestic circumstances of the taxpayer.

From the point of view of distribution, expenditure according to ability to receive, the correlative of taxation according to ability to pay, is achieved, when, corresponding to a given expenditure, the maximum addition is made to economic welfare.

§ 5. We may now turn from grants conferring special benefit on particular persons to grants conferring common benefit on all members of a particular class. The effects of the latter upon distribution are difficult to trace, and the dividing line between the two sorts of grants is not clear cut. But common benefit is sometimes clearly traceable to particular groups, as, for example, when grants-in-aid from the central exchequer benefit local ratepayers, when local expenditure increases the value of fixed property and thus benefits local landowners, when expenditure on roads benefits motorists, or when expenditure on a public park confers a common benefit on all who use it.

Again, the benefit of security is common to all members of the community, except a few criminals.

But this benefit cannot be accurately allocated as between different people. It is, indeed, clear that, the greater a man's wealth, the greater the benefit which he derives from security of possession. But the relative advantage, which accrues to people of different degrees of wealth, from the protection of life and property and the prevention of military invasion, cannot, in fact, be estimated.

§ 6. In the last chapter we compared the effects of financing public works by taxation and by loan. From the point of view of distribution finance by taxation has the advantage that it creates no new private investment income. New publicly owned capital assets are created, free from any interest charge in favour of private persons. But if public works are financed by loans from publicly owned banks, so that no interest on the loans is paid to private persons, there is little difference, in respect of distribution, between the two methods.

CHAPTER XX

SOME OTHER EFFECTS OF PUBLIC EXPENDITURE

§ 1. In this chapter we shall conclude our study of the economic effects of public expenditure.

Just as the cost of collection of taxes is an important criterion of the efficiency of a tax system, so the cost of administration of policies involving public expenditure is an important criterion of the success of such policies. If the cost of administration is greater than it need be in order to obtain a given result, this is equivalent to a diminution of production, through the waste of labour and materials. Many popular accusations of waste and inefficiency made against public departments are based on ignorance and prejudiced exaggeration. But there is no doubt that the cost of public administration is sometimes excessive in relation to the results obtained. This opens up large questions, which cannot be pursued here, of the organisation of public departments, and of how far they might adopt the business methods appropriate to private firms. But it is very desirable that public departments should cultivate to the full what may be described as a marginal sense, and, with the aid of cost accounting in suitable cases, should balance the advantage of a small increase in their activities against its cost. Sometimes such considerations will point to the need for an increase, rather than a decrease, of expenditure. The policy embodied in the Factory and Trade Board Acts, for example, cannot be properly carried out without an increase in the inspectorate of the Home Office and the Ministry of Labour. And again, according to the official evidence given before the Royal Commission on Income Tax, a comparatively small increase in the staff of the Inland Revenue Department would enable a large additional revenue to be collected.

§ 2. On the relation of public expenditure to unemployment something further may be said here, not so much from the point of view of increasing production, which was considered in Chapter XVII, as from that of steadying employment by diminishing fluctuations in the demand for labour.

A policy having this object may take various forms. The least ambitious of these requires only that a public authority shall keep its own demand for various kinds of labour as steady as possible, and not allow it to fluctuate in the same direction as private demand for the same kinds of labour. There is not much in this, and public authorities could easily succeed in going thus far.

Carrying the policy a stage further, a public authority, without undertaking any special enterprises in periods of trade depression, may so arrange its ordinary expenditure, as between different years or between different seasons of the same year, that the public demand for various kinds of labour fluctuates in the opposite direction to the private demand for the same kinds of labour. This does not involve any greater public expenditure over a period of years, but only a change in the distribution of this expenditure through time. It may even involve a smaller expenditure, in so far as prices of stores and other materials and wages of labour are lower when trade is bad than when it is good.

Carrying the policy a stage further still, a public authority may, when trade is bad, itself undertake special enterprises, in the form of public works, or may make grants in aid of enterprises undertaken by subordinate authorities or even by private firms. The increased demand for labour thus created, whether financed by taxation or by loans, may be partly offset by a decreased demand from other sources for the same or other kinds of labour. If finance is by taxation, it will be nearly all offset, since there is only a transfer of, and no addition to, purchasing power.[1] But, even so, this fixed quantity of purchasing power may now create a greater demand for labour, and a smaller demand for other factors of production, than it would otherwise have done. If, on the other hand, finance is by loan, the possibilities of an increased demand for labour are much greater, since purchasing power may be increased through an expansion of credit, and opportunities provided, which might otherwise be lacking, for the full use of new savings in new investment. Putting the argument in another form, there will be a net increase in the demand for labour, and hence a net reduction in unemployment, in so far as accumulated stocks of goods are drawn upon, which would otherwise have lain idle. And in a trade depression, large stocks of this kind are generally available.

[1] Except in so far as the velocity of circulation of money may be increased, as a result of the transfer.

Further, the unemployed and their dependants are in any case maintained out of the proceeds of taxes, public loans or other sources of public or private contribution. If public works are undertaken, and especially if these are of such a kind that wages form a large proportion of their cost, a small increase in expenditure, as compared with what would be required to maintain the unemployed in idleness, may result in a comparatively large increase in employment and in production. It only pays private enterprise to employ an unemployed man, if the value of his work will be not less than his wages. But, on the same footing, it pays a public authority to employ him, if the value of his work will be not less than his wages *minus the cost to the authority of maintaining him and his dependants when he is unemployed*. The effect of a public works policy, which increases both production and purchasing power and reduces unemployment, is felt on both sides of the budget. It increases the yield of taxes at given rates and diminishes expenditure on the maintenance of the unemployed.

There is, therefore, considerable scope for a policy, by which public authorities will thus help to steady the demand for labour and diminish the great waste of productive power which trade depressions involve.[1] But such a policy, to be effective, presupposes the preparation in advance of detailed

[1] If the continuance of trade depression is mainly due to lack of "business confidence," a public authority may apply a psychological stimulus to trade by taking over, on conditions, certain risks which business men are unwilling to run. Thus it may guarantee loans for new developments, as under the British Trade Facilities Act, or guarantee payment for goods supplied, as under the British Export Credits scheme. Such guarantees, if wisely given, are for the Treasury the cheapest of all subsidies to employment.

schemes, and the power to act quickly, when the need arises.

§ 3. But public works should not be regarded merely as a device for steadying employment. They have other merits, and an important place, as was argued in Chapter XVIII, in policies designed to increase production. Used for this purpose, it was argued in Chapter XIX that, from the point of view of distribution, they are better financed by taxation than by loans. This last argument is reinforced by another, which leads us back to the problem of steadying employment. It is held by some economists, though this view of the matter is by no means universally accepted, that the trade cycle is traceable, through an increase in the supply of money, to an undue increase in the demand for consumption goods, which throws out of employment resources devoted to the production of capital goods, thus causing the familiar transition from boom to slump. Those who hold this view admit that these unfortunate results need not follow, if voluntary private saving were to increase sufficiently to prevent that " undue " increase in the demand for consumption goods which, according to this theory, from time to time upsets the balance of industry. But if the substitution of more voluntary private saving for more consumption would give stability, so equally would more compulsory public saving. If, therefore, this theory be true, the cure for instability is to be found in increased taxation, levied at the appropriate time, to finance new capital construction by way of public works.[1]

[1] An ironical conclusion, since most of those who hold this theory are rabid individualists, domiciled in London University but having their spiritual home in certain academic byways in Vienna.

§ 4. The discussion contained in this and the two preceding chapters indicates the wide range of objects which wise public expenditure may serve. We may bring this part of our enquiry to an end by emphasising once more the fundamental proposition, which in different aspects has been emphasised several times before. The central problem of public finance is no less, and no more, than the problem of securing the best disposal of the economic resources of the community, in so far as public authorities can influence this disposal.

PART IV

PUBLIC DEBTS

CHAPTER XXI

THE GENERAL CHARACTERISTICS OF PUBLIC DEBTS

§ 1. One method by which a public authority may obtain income is by borrowing. The proceeds of such public borrowing form part of public receipts, or public income. On the other hand, the payment of interest on, and the repayment of the principal of, the public debts thus created form part of public expenditure. The correlative of public debts is public assets. The debts of most national governments, however, greatly exceed their assets, chiefly because most of these debts are war debts. But some public authorities, especially local authorities, most of whose debts have been incurred in the purchase of land and material capital, have assets in excess of their debts.

A distinction is often drawn between "reproductive debt"—an absurd phrase—and "deadweight debt." The former is debt which is fully covered, or balanced, by the possession of assets of equal value; the latter is debt to which no existing assets correspond. Public debt, which is fully covered by public assets, is like the capital of a company, and the creditors of the public authority like debenture holders. The interest on reproductive debt is normally paid out of income derived by the public authority from the ownership of its property or the conduct of its enterprises. The interest on deadweight debt, on the other hand, must be obtained from some other source of public income, generally from taxation. It is significant of the usual relation of public debts to public assets in the modern world that there is no commonly recognised distinction between public assets which are subject to, and those which are free from, a mortgage of debt to private persons. If the assets of public authorities often exceeded their debts, such a distinction would be familiar.

§ 2. Public debts involve public loans, which may be classified in various ways. In the first place, a loan may be either voluntary or compulsory. A compulsory, or forced, loan is a rarity in modern public finance, since it combines the disadvantages, while lacking the corresponding advantages, of both a tax and a voluntary loan. The chief advantage of a voluntary loan, as compared with a tax, is that different lenders are free, according to their circumstances and inclinations, to subscribe as much or as little as they please. But this disadvantage is lacking in a forced loan, which must be compulsorily subscribed on the same basis as a tax. The chief advantage of a tax, as compared with a voluntary loan, is that it leaves behind it no trail of charges for interest and repayment of principal. But this advantage is lacking in a forced loan, though the rate of interest on the latter may be lower than on a voluntary loan.

In the second place, a loan may be either internal or external. A loan is internal, if subscribed by persons or institutions within the area controlled by the public authority which raises the loan ; external, if subscribed by persons or institutions outside this area. An internal loan may be either voluntary or forced ; an external loan must, except under military or other coercion, be voluntary. An internal loan only involves transfers of wealth within the borrowing community—which in this case is the same as the lending community; an external loan involves, first, a transfer of wealth from the lending to the borrowing community, when the loan is made and, second, a transfer in the reverse direction, when interest is paid or principal repaid. An external loan may be gradually transformed into an internal loan through the purchase by members of the debtor community of public securities held by foreigners. Similarly, an internal loan may be gradually transformed into an external loan by sales to foreigners of public securities held by members of the debtor community.

§ 3. In the third place, a loan may be for a long, or for a short, term. This is a distinction of degree. The extreme example of a long term loan is British "Old Consols," the principal of which need never be repaid. The extreme example, in British practice, of a public short term loan is the Treasury Bill, repayable after three months. It is common, in moderately long term borrowing, to fix two dates, after the earlier of which a public authority *may*, and at the later of which it *must*, repay the principal. Long term debt gradually turns into short term, as its date of repayment approaches. Like a boat which seemed securely beached on the shore, it is sooner or later floated off on the rising tide of time. Old Consols, alone of British government debts, lie securely above time's high water mark.

Hence the distinction often drawn between "funded" and "floating" debt, roughly equivalent to that between long and short term debt.[1] The near approach of the obligation to repay large sums is often a disturbing factor in the calculations of Finance Ministers. The process of "funding the floating debt" is designed to remove this factor by borrowing for a term of years in order to repay part at least of the floating debt which is "maturing" in the immediate future.

There is, indeed, another form of public debt which relieves Finance Ministers from any such preoccupation. This is the terminable annuity, involving a series of payments to a lender for a term of years, but no repayment of any capital sum at the end of the term. This naturally costs the borrower more per year during the term of the annuity than an ordinary loan, but less in the long run.

§ 4. The fact that a debt is not repayable before a certain date does not, of course, prevent a public authority from purchasing its own securities on the Stock Exchange at any time at their current price, and cancelling them. The phrase "not repayable" means not *compulsorily* repayable at par, or at whatever the price fixed for repayment when the debt was contracted. To make debts not repayable, in this sense,

[1] The use of the terms "funded," "unfunded" and "floating" is often confusing. Thus Funding Loan, issued in 1919 to fund part of the floating debt and repayable between 1960 and 1990 is classed officially as "unfunded" debt! A further example of confusion of terms may be cited here. A pernicious proposal has been made, though happily it has not been adopted, that the British Government should "fund war pensions," which means that it should borrow the money required to pay these pensions instead of paying them out of the proceeds of taxation. The use of the term "fund" in this connection is quite inappropriate, though it may convey to inexpert minds a vague and comforting suggestion of financial rectitude.

before a distant date is an additional inducement to lenders, if they anticipate that the rate of interest will fall. For the public authority is then binding itself not to take advantage of this fall in order to convert the debt into another at a lower rate of interest. For example, if a government borrows at five per cent. at par, and if, a few years later, the rate of interest falls to four per cent., it can then borrow at four per cent. and with the proceeds of this new loan, unless it has bound itself not to do so, can compulsorily repay the old, thus saving one-fifth of its annual interest charges, while the original lenders on reinvesting their money will only be able to obtain four-fifths of their previous interest on the same class of security.[1] On the other hand, to make debts repayable at an early date is an additional inducement to lenders, if they anticipate that the rate of interest may rise. For they will then be protected against capital depreciation and will be able, when repaid, to reinvest their money at the higher rate.

There are other special inducements which may be offered to lenders by a borrowing public authority, such as exemption from its own taxation of the income from its own securities, the right to tender these securities at a price above the market price in payment of taxes, the right of conversion into subsequent loans, if issued at a higher rate of interest, the right to repayment at a premium, and so on. Special inducements of this kind are substitutes for the higher rate of interest on the loan which would otherwise have to be offered in order to induce sufficient subscriptions. And most of

[1] For a further discussion of such "conversion operations" see Ch. XXIV.

them are bad substitutes. In particular, so far as internal debt is concerned, the exemption of public securities, or the income from them, from all future taxation is highly undesirable, hampering the discretion of future Finance Ministers and introducing tiresome complications into the tax system.[1]

§ 5. As a rule, public debts bear interest at a fixed rate. If, subsequently, rates of interest or prices fall, lenders secure an unearned increment. There is a strong case for making the rate of interest on new public debts vary in accordance with changes in the general rate of interest, or with changes in the general level of prices, or with these two sets of changes taken in combination.

To make the rate vary with the general rate of interest would make the date of repayment a matter of indifference to lenders. It would automatically secure the advantage of conversion to the public authority when the rate of interest fell, and to lenders when it rose.

To make the rate vary with the general level of prices would prevent an increase in the real burden of the debt as prices fell. This advantage, for reasons which will appear later, would probably outweigh the disadvantage of preventing a decrease in the burden of the debt as prices rose, and would remove one of the apparent advantages to a government of depreciating its currency by the issue of large quantities of paper money. It would also, in periods of falling prices, do something to satisfy the sense of justice of wage-earners, whose money wages were being reduced.

[1] See Ch. X, §6, footnote.

The proposal to substitute a variable for a fixed rate of interest would, however, probably encounter prejudice on the part of many investors, who are still ignorant or distrustful of the uses of index numbers.

§ 6. It has already been remarked that, so far as most national governments, and particularly European governments, are concerned, the bulk of their public debt is deadweight debt incurred for purposes of war. This is not a new development since 1914. The British Government for several hundred years has increased its debt by a large percentage at each successive war, by which our history is illuminated, and has never succeeded in wiping out these increases before the outbreak of the next war in the series. The British national debt of 1914 was, in part, incurred during the wars against the French more than a hundred years before.[1] Nor was the British Government peculiar in thus preserving from generation to generation financial mementos of "old unhappy far off things, and battles long ago." Other governments showed a like veneration for the past, each according to its antiquity and its historic capacity to fight and to borrow. But an historical explanation is not a justification. If past

[1] The British national debt was only reduced from £850,000,000 in 1817 to £840,000,000 in 1842, £800,000,000 in 1867, £660,000,000 in 1895 and £707,000,000 in 1914. The net reduction in these ninety-seven years was thus only £143,000,000. Of the £707,000,000 outstanding in 1914, some £210,000,000 represented new borrowings since 1817, including £35,000,000 for the Crimean War and £140,000,000 for the Boer War. But there remained some £496,000,000 of the debt of 1817, which had not been paid off in 1914. Moreover, if account be taken of the increase in the value of money during this period, both the real value of the annual interest charge in terms of commodities, and the real value of the principal of the debt, were actually greater at the end than at the beginning. This is a very remarkable fact which seems to have escaped the notice of many historians.

generations had been wiser, the present generation would now be happier and less heavily burdened. But reflections on the past are a digression. Here we are concerned with the present and future burden of public debts, and in the next chapter we shall study more closely the nature of this burden.

Chapter XXII

THE BURDEN OF PUBLIC DEBTS

§ 1. The nature of the burden of a deadweight public debt is often misunderstood. The direct burden of an external debt is, indeed, a simple matter. During any given period the direct money burden is measured by the sum of money payments, for interest and repayment of principal, to external creditors, and the direct real burden by the loss of economic welfare, which these payments involve, to members of the debtor community. If the direct money burden is given, the direct real burden will vary according to the proportions in which various members of the community contribute to the required money payments. If these are made mainly by the rich, the direct real burden will be smaller than if they are made mainly by the poor. Putting it another way, the money payments are used by the external creditors to obtain goods and services, which would otherwise have been at the disposal of members of the debtor community. The latter are, therefore, deprived of goods and services to this amount, and the resulting direct real burden will depend on the way in which this deprivation is distributed.

The indirect burden of an external debt, whether money burden or real burden, arises from the check to production due, first, to the taxation required to meet the debt charges and, second, to economies in those forms of public expenditure which would promote production. This indirect burden is similar in character to that of an internal debt and can best be discussed under that heading. The paradoxical idea is sometimes put forward, especially in connection with war indemnities, which are only a special case of external debt, that the obligation to make external money payments stimulates production and employment in the debtor community. If this were so, an external debt would give rise to no indirect burden, but to an indirect benefit, which might even outweigh the direct burden. But this idea is mistaken. The need to make external money payments on a large scale may, indeed, stimulate production, and hence employment, in trades working for export. This stimulus will be strengthened if, and so long as, the external value of the community's money is falling faster than its internal value.[1] But this is not a net stimulus to production and employment in the debtor community. It is only a stimulus to one set of trades at the expense of another, resulting in a diversion of resources, which will generally be harmful.

§ 2. The character of an internal debt is quite different. Here we are dealing, not with a debtor community in relation to a body of external creditors, but with debtors and creditors within the same community. Thus all transactions connected with an internal debt resolve themselves into a series of transfers

[1] This expansion of exports is also liable to check production and cause unemployment in the corresponding branches of industry in the creditor community and, indeed, in other communities as well. But that is another story. For a further discussion see Ch. XXV, §5.

of wealth within the community. It follows that there can never be any direct money burden, or direct money benefit, of an internal debt. For all the money payments cancel out. A, as a taxpayer, makes certain payments, for interest on the debt or repayment of principal, and these payments, minus a small proportion to cover the expenses of management of the debt, are received by B, who is a public creditor by reason of his holding of public securities. Often A and B are the same person.

The debt will involve a direct real burden or a direct real benefit to the community, according to the nature of this series of transfers from taxpayers to public creditors. Primarily it will bring burden or benefit, according as the transfers increase or decrease the inequality of incomes. The question, therefore, depends upon the distribution of taxation on the one hand, and of public securities on the other, among different members of the community. Roughly speaking, there will be a direct real burden, if the proportion of taxation[1] paid by the rich is smaller than the proportion of public securities held by them. There will be a direct real benefit if it is larger. If the British debt consisted exclusively of Savings Certificates held by wage earners, and if British taxation consisted exclusively of income tax and death duties on the wealthy, the British debt transactions would involve a large direct real benefit to the community. But the

[1] It is impossible, in an ordinary budget, to separate the taxes which go to pay debt charges from the taxes which go to pay for armaments or education. But we can calculate the proportion of the debt charges to the total expenditure, and can then legitimately assume that this same proportion of the taxes paid by any individual goes to pay debt charges.

actual facts are very different from this, both in this country and elsewhere. Owing to the large inequality of incomes, which is a feature of nearly all modern communities, public securities are held mainly by the wealthier classes, either directly, or indirectly in the form of shares in companies which themselves hold public securities among their assets. On the other hand, taxation, even if progressive, is seldom likely to be so sharply progressive as to counterbalance, among the wealthier classes, the income derived from public securities.[1] In the vast majority of actual cases, therefore, an internal debt involves a direct real burden.

Nor is this all. The transfers of wealth involved in the service of an internal debt are not only transfers from the poorer to the richer members of the community. They are also transfers, on balance, from the younger to the older generations, and from the active to the passive elements in the economic life of the community. There is a general presumption, on grounds of distribution, against the enrichment of the old at the expense of the young, and this is greatly strengthened when the instrument of enrichment is a War Loan, to which the old have subscribed in comparative safety, while the young have been risking their lives in battle. Here, if nowhere else in the sphere of public finance, the voice of equity rings loud and clear. There is also a general presumption, on grounds

[1] More precisely, the progressiveness of the tax system is not likely to be greater than the regressiveness of the grants paid, in the form of interest, to the holders of public securities. Repayments of principal are not grants, but purchase prices, and do not enter into the expenditure side of this calculation. But the corresponding tax payments do enter into the taxation side.

of production, against the enrichment of the passive at the expense of the active, whereby work and productive risk-taking are penalised for the benefit of accumulated wealth.[1]

§ 3. Again, as a general rule, an internal debt involves an additional and indirect burden on a community and, as already observed, an external debt does the same. One reason for this is that the taxation required for the service of the debt tends to check production, in so far as it reduces taxpayers' ability and desire to work and save. Another reason is that short-sighted " economies " in desirable social expenditure are particularly likely to be made, when heavy taxation is required to meet debt charges.[2]

So far as the evil effects of taxation are concerned, it might be supposed at first sight that these would be balanced, in the case of internal debt at any rate, by the good effects of expenditure to meet the debt charges. But this is not so.

In the case of an external debt, any effect of taxes in checking taxpayers' ability to work and save is clearly irremediable, so far as the debtor community is concerned. For it is the external creditors, and not members of the debtor community, whose ability to

[1] It has been objected to this analysis that similar injurious transfers are found elsewhere in modern economic systems, and that these evils are not, therefore, peculiar to the finance of public debts. This statement is true, but it cannot be regarded as an objection. It is rather an invitation to seek to remove these evils elsewhere, as well as here.

[2] Compare Chs. XVIII-XIX, where it is incidentally pointed out that certain sorts of social expenditure, education being the leading example, tend not only to increase production, but also to reduce the inequality of incomes. To reduce such expenditure is, therefore, to impose a two-fold burden on the community, first, in reduced production and, second, in increased inequality.

work and save will be increased through the receipt of the debt payments. In the case of an internal debt, the position in this respect is distinctly better. For, against the reduction of taxpayers' ability to work and save, must be set the increased ability of internal creditors. But even here there is likely to be a net loss to the community. For, where the debt involves a direct real burden—as in practice it is almost certain to do—it is probable that taxation will reduce personal efficiency more than the receipt of debt charges will increase it. There would thus be a net loss in ability to work, while ability to save would be unaffected by the transfer of income.

When we turn from effects upon ability, to effects upon desire, to work and save, the position is still worse. It has been argued in Chapter X that it is the taxpayer's elasticity of demand for income which determines whether taxation will, or will not, check his desire to work and save. Any loss to production through this cause is, again, clearly irremediable in the case of an external debt. In the case of an internal debt, what we have to consider is the effect, upon the desire of internal creditors to work and save, of the prospect of receiving year by year an addition to their incomes, irrespective of any work or saving which they may perform. Whatever their elasticity of demand for income, this prospect will not increase their desire to work and save. On the contrary, it will almost certainly reduce it and thereby cause a further loss to production and a further increase in the indirect burden of the debt.

There is only one argument on the other side, and it applies only to internal debt. If internal creditors, as a class, have a stronger desire to save than taxpayers, as a class,[1] it is possible that a transfer of wealth from the latter to the former may increase the effective desire to save of the community as a whole. This possibility counts for something, but not for much.

§ 4. Nor have we yet come to the end of the story. Nearly all deadweight public debts originate in time of war and it is a peculiarity of such times that both the general level of prices and the rate of interest are unusually high, the former owing to reduced production in many directions combined with floods of paper money, the latter owing to shortage of real capital combined with a large and inelastic government demand for loans. A public debt, thus originating as a war debt, is almost certain, for the reasons already discussed, to involve both a direct real burden and an indirect burden upon the warring community. Other things being equal, the larger the debt, the heavier the burden. Now, if the debt lingers on, unpaid or unrepudiated, into the succeeding period of peace, and if, as is likely when economic conditions become gradually less abnormal, both the price level and the rate of interest begin to fall from their war-time heights, the burden of the debt does not remain constant. On the contrary, it automatically increases. As prices fall, the amount of real wealth, which corresponds to a given money payment, increases, and thus the transfer of real wealth, by way of interest, from taxpayers to public creditors increases, and thus both the direct real burden and the indirect burden of the debt increase. And again, as the rate of interest falls, the market value of public securities rises, and thus the money cost

[1] Each internal creditor counting, in his class, in proportion to his receipts and each taxpayer in proportion to his payments.

of repayment of a given principal sum increases, and thus the transfer of real wealth, by way of such repayment, from taxpayers to public creditors increases, and thus the burden of the debt, in both its forms, increases.[1] And when the price level and the rate of interest fall together, these forces making for an increase in the burden of the debt reinforce each other.

§ 5. The argument of the preceding section points to the conclusion that deadweight public debts should not be lightly created. " The evil that men do lives after them " is a fit motto for those statesmen who, following tradition and the path of least resistance, rely upon internal loans and currency inflation, rather than upon straightforward taxation, as the chief means of financing war. Their only excuse can be that in a community, which is ignorant of economic truths or unduly dominated by narrow sectional interests, the war spirit thrives best and " civilian morale " is best maintained on short-sighted and unsound finance. And even this excuse is not always valid.

But for the carrying out of schemes of economic development in time of peace, finance by internal loans stands on a more legitimate footing. For public debts, which are the means of creating public assets yielding an income sufficient to cover the debt charges, throw no burden on the community. But even in such cases it would often be better to rely more on taxes and less on loans, so as to avoid the needless breeding of unearned income, and in order that, as the schemes matured, there should result, not merely no burden,

[1] Though against this must be set the fact that a fall in the rate of interest facilitates some reduction of the burden through conversion. See Ch. XXIV.

but a positive benefit due, in effect, to compulsory and collective saving.[1] Where, however, the total new expenditure on such schemes is large and very variable from year to year, the inconvenience of correspondingly large annual variations in taxation justifies the use, in moderation, of internal loans, provided these are repaid within a reasonable time. Likewise, as has been argued earlier, when an expansion of credit is desired, loans for public works are often the best means to this end.

The justification of external loans rests on different grounds. In time of peace external debts may legitimately be contracted by governments controlling large, undeveloped natural resources, the rapid development of which is too big a task for their own subjects to perform unaided. This is the broad justification of the external debts of the British Dominions and the South American Republics. For taxation, which is often preferable to an internal loan, is not a practicable alternative to an external loan. In time of war, again, an external loan is often the only practicable means of financing imports on the scale required. It is sometimes also the easiest, if not the only, means of re-establishing on a tolerable basis systems of currency and public finance, which war and revolution have shattered.

§ 6. We may conclude this discussion by examining two misconceptions, which have occasionally found influential support. The first is the idea that the burden

[1] New capital expenditure by public authorities is at present financed by taxation to a larger extent than is commonly realised and this method of securing compulsory collective saving is likely to be of increasing importance in the future. In so far as this is so, the objection to heavy taxation, that it tends to check voluntary individual saving, loses much of its force. Compare Ch. XVIII, §9.

of a public debt can be shifted, wholly or in substantial part, from the present to future generations. The second is the idea that the burden, if it exists, not only can be wholly escaped without repayment, but that it cannot be escaped by means of repayment. Both these false ideas work against a policy of repayment.

It is often suggested that we can " make posterity pay " the debts of our own generation. Even if we can, it does not follow that we should. For " posterity " has no share in the responsibility for those policies which have created our present debts and we are inclined, in any case, unduly to discount the future and, to this extent, to evade the moral obligation " to leave the world better than we found it." But, ignoring moral issues, *can* we " make posterity pay " ?

The suggestion is that this result can be secured by confining ourselves to paying the interest on present debts, but making no repayment of the principal. There is, however, some mental confusion here. Whom, if this policy is adopted, will posterity pay ? Not us, who will be out of sight and out of mind in the days of posterity, but part of itself. For what will happen will be that some members of posterity will pay other members. Future taxpayers will pay future bondholders and, unless some new factor intervenes to stop it, this process will continue indefinitely. The process will, however, be brought to an end at some point in the future, if a policy of repayment is consistently pursued, and this policy will mean that, over a given period, taxpayers, present and future, will pay bondholders, present and future, not only interest, but principal also. The burden of a public debt is not a fixed thing which can be thrown backwards and forwards through time and made to fall, at will, wholly on one generation or wholly on another. It is, so long as the debt remains, a continuing thing, the nature of which has been analysed in earlier sections of this chapter. The total burden of a given debt, through time, tends to be greater, the longer the period through which the debt endures. Repayment, therefore, tends to diminish this total burden and so to benefit posterity, while failure to repay tends to burden posterity. But failure to repay tends also to burden the present generation and the process of repayment brings present, as well as future, benefits. In securing the early clearance of a public debt, there is, in large measure, a harmony of interest between ourselves and posterity.

§ 7. I turn to the second misconception noted above. It is sometimes argued that the burden, if any, of an internal debt can be wholly removed by appropriate changes in the tax system, without any repayment, and also that a mere process of repayment removes no real burden. These two arguments are connected in the realm of practical advocacy, but may be separated in the realm of logic.

The first argument is logically valid as regards the direct burden, which consists, as we have seen, of the effects of certain injurious transfers of wealth, from the poor to the rich, from the young to the old, and from the active to the passive. A tax system is *conceivable*, under which, in conjunction with the debt payments, no such transfers would occur. Each taxpayer, for example, might pay towards the debt charges a sum exactly equal to that which he received as a public bondholder. We may, indeed, carry our imagination still further and conceive of a tax system, under which the poorer, younger and more active taxpayers paid less, while the richer, older and more passive taxpayers paid more, than they received as public bondholders. The direct burden of the debt would then be transformed into a direct benefit. But, in fact, such tax systems, though conceivable, are not realisable. We cannot hope, under the limitations of reality, to do more than substantially diminish the direct burden by means of steeply graduated taxation. Some direct burden will almost certainly remain and will vary, roughly, with the size of the debt. Nor is the argument even logically valid as regards the indirect burden, which consists, as we have seen, of certain checks, mainly psychological, to productivity and to desirable forms of expenditure. No changes in the tax system could wholly remove these checks, though they might greatly weaken them. The argument, therefore, falls to the ground.

The second argument stresses the fact that the repayment of, say, £100,000,000 of debt per year, is a burden on taxpayers, from which, in the absence of repayment, they would be free, and the further fact that, on repayment, these £100,000,000 are reinvested, so that the distribution of income, and the total of private property, remain unaffected. Repayment, therefore, it is argued, removes no burden, but, on the contrary, imposes one. But this is not a sound argument. For, as against the burden of £100,000,000 on taxpayers this year, must be set two gains, first, the continuing benefit to taxpayers of not having to pay interest on this sum in the future and, second, the continuing benefit to the community in securing, through the reinvestment of the £100,000,000, a larger addition to capital resources than would have accrued, if the £100,000,000 had not been collected in taxation, but had been partly spent on immediate consumption. Further, the distribution of income, and the *net* annual value of private property, will be affected by the way in which the £100,000,000 of taxation are raised. Distribution may, if we choose, be made less unequal and the *net* annual value of private property may be diminished. Thus this second argument against a policy of repayment, like the first, falls to the ground.

§ 8. The burden of a public debt, or, what is another way of stating the same thing, the benefit of its disappearance, may be thus exhibited. Assume that all public bondholders follow the example which an eccentric and high-minded minority has already set, and voluntarily surrender their War Loan scrip and similar public securities.[1] The immediate result, leaving moral uplift out of account, would be a diminution of inequality, and of the proportion of the community's wealth held by the older generation and by passive proprietors generally. There would also be some change in the relative position of various institutions and companies, according to the proportion of their assets which had previously consisted of public securities. But a further result would be manifested through the national balance sheet. On the expenditure side, a large proportion of the previous liabilities would simply vanish, since no more payment of interest or repayment of principal would be required. In many

[1] This has been done, not only in England, but, far more dramatically, in Fascist Italy, where Signor Mussolini on the Sixth Anniversary of the March on Rome, in October, 1928, burned publicly on the Altar of the Fatherland, before the Tomb of the Unknown Soldier, surrendered bonds worth £1,500,000.

modern communities the proportion of expenditure, that would thus be saved, would be in the neighbourhood of half the total. On the revenue side, there would be some consequential loss, chiefly under the head of income and inheritance taxes, since the public securities surrendered and the income therefrom would no longer be taxable. But the net result would be a Budget surplus, which in many cases would seem very substantial. This would be available, either to reduce taxation, or to increase various forms of expenditure, or partly for both purposes. A strong stimulus to production and a further marked diminution of inequality would thus be within easy reach of any competent finance minister.

The benefit from the disappearance of a public debt through voluntary surrender is thus obvious. If it disappears, not through voluntary surrender, but through repayment, repudiation or inflation, the situation is less simple, since the costs and disadvantages of these alternative procedures have to be set against the benefits obtained. These questions will be further considered in the next chapter, but the preceding discussion establishes a definite case in favour of repayment, as against allowing a public debt to linger on indefinitely.

CHAPTER XXIII

THE REPAYMENT OF PUBLIC DEBTS

§ 1. An obvious way of escape from the burden of public debts is to repay them. Another, which may seem even more obvious, is to repudiate them. Let us begin by considering this second possibility. If contracts between a public authority and its creditors are repudiated, while other contracts remain in force, a particular group of property owners is penalised, while all other groups are unaffected, and may even gain through subsequent reduction of taxation. There is a clear argument from equity against such a discrimination. If, on the other hand, all contracts involving payments to property owners are repudiated simultaneously, no discrimination against a particular group is involved and the previous argument from equity loses its force. But we are now contemplating a social revolution, the results of which might be held to be inequitable to property owners as a class. Some hold, however, that a *régime* of private property, especially if it involves great inequality, is itself inequitable.

Turning from considerations of equity to probable economic consequences, it is obvious that a public authority which repudiates its debts, whether as a mere incident in a social revolution or as an isolated act of policy, will have difficulty, at any rate for some time, in floating further loans. This is a strong argument against repudiation, except where the debt to be repudiated is larger than the loans likely to be required in the near future.

There is, however, another argument against repudiation. Particularly in the case of an external debt, there will be a danger of provoking aggressive action against the repudiating government on the part of the aggrieved creditors. The possible methods of aggression are many, overt military action, underhand support of enemies of the government, trade boycotts, campaigns of "propaganda," and so forth. All these methods were employed by the creditors of the Soviet Government in the years following 1917, and inflicted great economic injury upon the people of the Soviet Union. There is, therefore, on economic grounds alone, a strong *prima facie* case against repudiation.

But this case sometimes weakens with the lapse of time. Old memories of repudiation may grow faint, new lenders on tolerable terms may be forthcoming and the government, which repudiated old debts years ago, may, if it pays new debts faithfully, regain the goodwill of its neighbours. It is not obvious, nearly twenty years after the event, that, on a long view, the Soviet Government was not wise in its early repudiations.

§ 2. Since the Great War, and still more since the start of the Great Depression in 1929, there have been interesting developments both in the terminology and the technique of repudiation. This has been renamed "default," "suspension of payments," "transfer moratorium." "Repudiation" sounds provocative, wilful and unnecessary. These softer synonyms suggest inevitability, honest and regretful inability to pay, a chance of payment soon, though not at once. A "transfer moratorium" is a particularly soothing conception. The creditors' money is quite safe; it has been collected by the debtor government and lodged in a bank; unfortunately, for the moment, difficulties connected with the foreign exchanges make it impossible to pay it over.

On a variety of pretexts since 1929 many governments, and some lesser public authorities, have ceased, diminished or postponed payments on their external debts to private creditors. Payments of the inter-governmental debts, arising from the Great War,[1] have nearly all stopped, following a "gentleman's agreement" between some, but not all, of the governments concerned at Lausanne in 1932.

As regards internal debts, some governments have reduced the rate of interest on existing debts, either by compulsory conversions, as in Australia and New Zealand, or merely by decree, as in France. Strictly this is a partial repudiation. But it has usually formed part of a programme of economies, designed to balance the budget by deflation. It is not, therefore, a case of special discrimination against public creditors, but rather an attempt to make these share in the sacrifices imposed on other classes. And this attempt is defended on grounds of equity.

Inflation, far more thoroughly, has destroyed the value of fixed money claims, including public debts both internal and, where the debt is measured in the debtor's currency, external. This, too, has been called by some "repudiation." But, as in the preceding case of deflationary revision, there is no special discrimination against public creditors. All with fixed money incomes are hit equally hard, and all with sticky money incomes nearly as hard. And, unlike the preceding

[1] For a further discussion of these debts see Ch. XXV.

case, there is no change in the form of the debt contract, but only in its practical meaning.

The general conclusion is that, except in settled economic weather, loans, even to the most respectable governments, carry risks, and that sudden storms may wash away even the most reasonable and established expectations of creditors. And in recent experience it is surprising how little, in most cases, and for how short a time, the public credit suffers.

§ 3. We may now turn from repudiation, a topic the mere discussion of which may seem disturbing, to the more comfortable theme of the repayment of public debts. This is a fair weather theme. But even here there is not much immediate comfort for taxpayers, who are confronted with various disagreeable alternatives.

The chief decision, which has to be taken, is how fast repayment shall proceed. For the purpose of this decision, an external debt is analogous to the debt of a private person, but an internal debt is not. The rate, that is to say, at which an external debt should be paid off, depends upon the wealth of the debtor community in relation to the amount of the debt. The greater the wealth, and the smaller the debt, the faster should the debt be paid off, and conversely. The rate at which an internal debt should be paid off, turns upon different considerations, for in this case repayment involves, not a subtraction from the wealth of the community for the benefit of outsiders, but only a transfer of wealth within the community.[1] Here there is a strong

[1] The one, in the language of Ch. XVI, §5, is real, or exhaustive, expenditure, the other transfer expenditure. For this reason a learned British Judge (Mr. Justice Younger) was too summary when he said some years ago that the national debt was " eating up a large part of the income of the country."

argument for rapid repayment, whatever the wealth of the community and whatever the size of the debt. Indeed, in contrast with the case of an external debt, the argument for rapid repayment is stronger, the greater the burden of the debt, which means, in general, the greater its size. The analogy for the taxpayer is the choice between having an aching tooth out quickly (without gas) or letting it continue to ache.

If the debt is only repaid slowly, with the aid of a comparatively small sinking fund, the burden of interest payments will only decrease slowly and there will be, in addition, a long continuing burden due to the sinking fund payments. There is likely, therefore, to be a long sustained check to productivity and to beneficial public expenditure. If, on the other hand, the debt, or at any rate a large fraction of it, is repaid quickly, by means of special but short lived taxation, the burden of interest payments will diminish quickly, while the additional burden of taxation for repayment will be heavy while it lasts, but will not last long. The check to productivity and to beneficial public expenditure will, therefore, be greatly lessened in a comparatively short time. For, as we have seen in the last chapter, the effect upon the budget of large reductions in the debt charges will be to make possible considerable reductions in taxation, simultaneously with considerable increases in desirable forms of public expenditure.

On the other side, as against the policy of rapid repayment, it has been argued that the heavy taxation required, even if short lived, would cause panic in the business world, would ruin many businesses and would be administratively unworkable.

§ 4. The proposal to institute a special debt-redemption levy, or " capital levy " as it is often called, led, in several countries, to one of the major political controversies of the early post-war years. On this practical issue competent economists were divided among themselves, and some changed sides at short notice. A similar division, and instability, of opinion was shown in other circles, political, administrative and industrial, no less than academic. Of those who ventured to be vocal on this political issue, most British economists, following in the footsteps of Ricardo,[1] were in favour of a capital levy immediately after the war. But later most declared against it. In two British general elections, those of 1922 and 1923, it was the most favourite subject of debate. But since the appointment of the Colwyn Committee on National Debt and Taxation in 1923, and still more since the Report of that Committee in 1927 and the coming of the Great Depression in 1929, it has faded out of the foreground of public interest.

[1] Ricardo, who cannot be accused either of revolutionary opinions or of lack of business experience, strongly supported a capital levy after the Napoleonic Wars. He held that " a country which has accumulated a large debt is placed in a most artificial situation. . . . A country which has involved itself in the difficulties attending this artificial system would act wisely by ransoming itself from them, at the sacrifice of any portion of its property which might be necessary to redeem the debt. . . . This scheme has been often recommended, but we have, I fear, neither wisdom enough, nor virtue enough, to adopt it." (*Works*, p. 149.) Ricardo was right in his estimate of the wisdom and virtue, as he conceived them, of the politicians of those days. No capital levy was imposed. But the Victorians, even if they lacked wisdom and virtue, had a surprising run of luck, which Ricardo could not have foreseen. The real burden per head of the national debt was greatly reduced during the next hundred years by the unprecedented growth of wealth, population and gold production. But no such repetition of good fortune can be counted on to-day.

The great majority of expert British opinion judged that a capital levy was administratively practicable in this country, though some added a proviso that there must be a reasonable measure of co-operation by the banks and the general body of contributors. Many, especially in the earlier stages of the controversy, attached great importance to the reduction of our then unprecedentedly high annual taxation, which the carrying through of the levy would make possible, and to the removal of the risk that a heavy fall in prices would greatly increase the real burden of the debt. In later stages of the controversy the following arguments combined to change the minds of several high authorities who had previously supported the levy, and to create an adverse majority among the experts. My own opinion throughout the controversy has been, and still is, in favour of the levy as the best policy, on merits, for dealing with the debt. I, therefore, attach my own comments to the series of arguments which follow.

First, the evil effects of high annual taxation on business enterprise and production in general has been much exaggerated. I agree with this argument.

Second, annual taxation has already been much reduced, without the aid of a capital levy, since the end of the war. I consider that much of this reduction has been unjustified, having been at the expense of an adequate sinking fund and desirable public expenditure. The indirect burden of the debt, in the form of a check to such desirable expenditure, seems to me to have been very heavy in the post-war years. Successive " economy campaigns " against the social services have done much harm.

Third, the fall in prices, and the consequent increase in the real burden of the debt, against the risk of which the capital levy would, a few years ago, have been a partial safeguard, have actually taken place.[1] This weakens the case for the levy at the present time. I assent to the facts, but dissent from the inference. The facts show the wisdom of those who proposed the levy some years ago. But the risk of a further fall in prices remains. Moreover, the greater the real burden of the debt, the stronger the case for a drastic policy of early repayment.

Fourth, there is a serious danger of organised opposition to the collection of the levy. Such organised opposition by the banks and the wealthy classes generally would make the levy administratively unworkable. I am doubtful as to the reality of this danger, particularly as regards the banks, which have everything to lose from financial panic and confusion. I am inclined to think that the powers of Parliament, the Treasury and the Inland Revenue, if resolutely used, could overcome the resistance of a comparatively small number of unwilling taxpayers, wealthy and influential though these might be. Nor do I think it proper to withdraw a proposal, if sound on other grounds, in face of such a threat. Blackmail is a bad basis for government.

Fifth, the net saving from a levy on the scale proposed would not be more than about £50,000,000 a

[1] "Between March, 1920, and March, 1925," owing to the fall in prices, "the value of every pound paid in interest upon the debt increased by about 87 per cent." (*Colwyn Report*, p. 365.) Since March, 1925, first as a result of the return to the gold standard, and later in the course of the depression, prices have fallen still further.

year. The consequential loss of revenue would be much higher than was at first supposed. In view of this, the levy would hardly be worth while. I am not quite satisfied that the official estimates of consequential loss of revenue are not too high. But this factor is certainly more serious than I, and many others, at first imagined. *Pro tanto*, it weakens the case for a levy on the scale originally proposed. But I do not think that it disposes of this case and, on the other hand, it strengthens the case for a levy on a stiffer scale than that originally proposed, in order to secure a net saving that shall seem worth while.

Sixth, the prolonged trade depression, in which we still find ourselves, makes the time inopportune for a levy. I agree that this is a strong argument for the postponement of the levy, but not for its abandonment.

Seventh, psychologically the time for the levy has passed. As the war recedes, and public opinion becomes accustomed to the debt and its more obvious consequences, it is increasingly difficult to arouse sufficient interest or political driving force to put the levy through.

I think there is much truth in this view of things and I regret it. Though the war has receded and the years have passed, the debt has not passed, and its real burden, in terms of commodities, has doubled since prices reached their peak in 1920. So long as the debt has not substantially diminished, the case for the levy, as the best policy for dealing with the debt, is not, in my judgment, substantially weakened. But I recognise that my judgment on this point is not shared by many whose opinion I respect.

§ 5. I attach, I think, greater weight than most of these to the argument from equity in this particular case. I hold that one of the chief advantages of a substantial debt redemption levy would be, not only the abolition of burdens and the conferring of a net benefit upon the community, but also the shifting of a burden from the shoulders of the young, the enterprising and the oncoming, on whom taxation and the lack of educational and other opportunities now press heavily, to the shoulders of the old, the comfortable and the established, in whose ranks most of the largest contributors to the levy would be found. And this, if the adoption of the policy is not delayed until the generation of fighters in the Great War grows old, and until most of those, who were too old to fight, are dead, would be an act of rough justice as between the generations. For it would represent at least a part payment of a moral debt by those whom the good fortune of age kept safe at home, to those who experienced, over and above the loss of economic opportunities during a critical period of their lives, the perils and the torments of the battlefields. But, with each year that passes, even such delayed part payment grows more difficult to accomplish.

§ 6. The delay, which the adoption of the policy of a capital levy has already encountered, recalls the parable of the Sibylline books. The greater part of the debt need never have come into being at all, if we had taxed more courageously during the years of war. At the armistice the time was ripe for a big effort to reduce the debt and, if a levy on general wealth was then too big a project for timid minds to entertain, a levy on " war wealth " would have been worth achieving. But that opportunity, too, was allowed to slip and, as time passed, the reality of the distinction between war wealth and other wealth quickly faded. Since then, the coming of the trade depression has intensified timidity, while the fall of prices and of the rate of interest[1] have already greatly increased the burden of the debt. It may be that, in the end, we shall be driven back to the policy of a special debt-redemption levy, as the only way out of an otherwise intolerable financial situation. It may be, on the other hand, that the time for such bold policies of debt-redemption has, in truth, gone by, and that we must be content with more gradual and less dramatic alternatives. I now turn, therefore, to the consideration of these.[2]

§ 7. Barring out inflation, which has been considered above, and conversion, which will be considered in the next chapter, these alternatives consist of a number of varieties of the policy of the sinking fund. The phrase "sinking fund," the meaning of which is not self-evident, signifies simply a debt-redemption fund. The creation and maintenance of a sinking

[1] The fall of the rate of interest increases the capital value, and hence the cost of redemption, of the debt in all its forms, except those which are maturing in the very near future. On the other hand, it facilitates conversion of maturing debt.

[2] Having regard to the part which I have taken in the capital levy controversy, it would have been a foolish affectation to conceal my personal views on this subject, which were developed at greater length in my *Capital Levy Explained* (Labour Publishing Company, 1923), now out of print, and in my evidence before the Colwyn Committee in 1925. For a fuller expression of other views I recommend the reader to study the Report of the Colwyn Committee and the evidence of other witnesses before it, especially Professor Pigou, Professor Scott, Mr. Keynes and Mr. Pethick Lawrence. Professor Pigou has pointed out that a debt-redemption levy, to yield a given sum, might be assessed on the basis, not of a person's capital, but of his income. Administratively this would be easier. Earned income, if assessed at all, would pay substantially less than unearned income.

fund implies that some part of the public revenue is devoted to the repayment of debt. A sinking fund which is fed, not from revenue but from new borrowings, is not a true sinking fund at all. For in this case no net redemption of debt is taking place, but only a replacement of old debts by new.

A sinking fund may be definite or indefinite. Either a definite provision for repayment may be made, or an indefinite provision dependent on circumstances which are largely fortuitous, as, for example, when the sinking fund consists of the surplus, if any, of revenue over expenditure in a given year.[1]

Definite sinking funds may be classified from three points of view; first, according to the length of the period required to repay the whole debt; second, according to the distribution of the sinking fund payments over this period; third, according to the distribution of the sinking fund payments as between different forms of debt. Under each of these three heads something may be said as to the principles which should govern policy. Primarily, what follows applies to internal debt. External debt, as explained above, stands on a different footing.

First, as to the period to be allowed for complete repayment. The argument of the preceding sections of this chapter suggests that the period should be as short as possible. A special debt-redemption levy, which paid off the whole debt at one blow, would be the limiting case of a sinking fund with a very short period. Even where such heroic measures are for various

[1] A sinking fund, of course, may consist of two parts, one definite and the other indefinite, a fixed annual sum, plus the annual surplus, or minus the annual deficit, as the case may be. The post-war British sinking fund has usually been of this mixed type.

reasons impracticable, we are still left with a strong presumption in favour of a comparatively short period of repayment.[1] This presumption is further strengthened by another consideration. Where a debt is incurred by a subordinate public authority, for the creation or acquisition of tangible assets, in the form of capital goods, it is common for a condition to be imposed by a superior public authority, *e.g.*, by the British Parliament upon British local authorities, that the debt must be repaid within a fixed period. This period has some relation to the natural life of the capital goods and the sinking fund is, therefore, in such cases, equivalent to a depreciation fund. The principle, which in general is a sound one, is that, by the time the capital goods are worn out, the debt should be paid off. It is applicable to all reproductive, as distinct from deadweight, debt. War debts, however, have few tangible assets, if any, to be set against them. It follows that the appropriate period for their repayment is shorter than that appropriate to a debt incurred for productive purposes. It follows, also, that the proceeds of the sale of war stores should be earmarked for debt reduction and not treated as ordinary revenue. The appropriate period for the repayment of the British war debt may, perhaps, be estimated, on this basis, at about thirty-five years.[2] Mr. Churchill, on

[1] The danger that a large sinking fund may depress trade, by causing savings to exceed investment, and the way of escape from this danger, have been discussed in Ch. XVIII, §9.

[2] So Edwin Cannan argued in evidence before the Colwyn Committee, estimating that a cumulative sinking fund starting at £100,000,000 a year would do the trick. In Victorian days it was sometimes said that our national debt should be paid off before our coalfields were "exhausted." A vague conception, but based on the depreciation fund analogy.

the other hand, proposed a plan in his Budget speech of 1928 for repayment in fifty years, while the United States Government was then paying off its debt at a pace which, if maintained, would have extinguished the whole remaining debt within twenty years from 1928.[1]

Second, the period of repayment being determined, how should sinking fund payments be distributed over this period? Three types of distribution may be distinguished, according as the annual payments increase, or remain constant, or diminish with the passage of time. The first type includes the various species of "cumulative" sinking funds. A "fully cumulative" sinking fund implies a constant debt charge, for interest and sinking fund taken together, so that what is saved each year in interest is added to the sinking fund. The annual sinking fund, therefore, increases at compound interest.[2] A partly cumulative sinking fund, whereby part only of each year's saving

[1] The United States debt was reduced in the year 1927-28 by $907,000,000, *i.e.*, from $18,511,000,000 to $17,604,000,000. A continuance of annual repayments at this level would have cleared the whole debt by 1948. Alternatively, in 1927 the United States debt was only two-thirds of what it had been in 1919, when it reached its maximum. Therefore, one-third of the debt had been paid off in eight years. If this rate of repayment had been maintained, the whole debt would have been paid off in another sixteen years, *i.e.*, in 1943. In fact, it was reduced to $15,922,000,000 in 1930. But from that year onwards it rose rapidly again, owing to a series of budget deficits. Mr. Churchill's plan broke down, with a budget deficit, in 1929!

[2] It is interesting to notice, though it is as yet only on a tiny scale, the creation in this country in 1927 of the National Fund, started by an anonymous gift of £500,000 to accumulate, together with any other gifts which might subsequently be made, for the eventual redemption of the National Debt. To make this gift legally valid, the law against "perpetuities" and long accumulations was amended in 1927. On March 31st, 1934, the Fund, to which sixty-five other persons had made gifts totalling £14,000, stood, with accumulations, at £721,000.

in interest is added to the sinking fund, implies a steadily diminishing debt charge. Or again, a more than fully cumulative sinking fund might be adopted, whereby the annual sinking fund was increased by more than the annual saving in interest, and the annual debt charge consequently increased from year to year. The second type, that of a constant sinking fund, implies a steadily diminishing debt charge. So, *a fortiori*, does the third type, that of a diminishing sinking fund.

As between these three types, the third, if it is practicable to establish it at all, is more likely to be politically stable than the second, while the second has a similar advantage over the first. All sinking funds, planned to continue over a term of years, are standing temptations to politicians in trouble.[1] "Raiding the sinking fund" is a historic pastime. This temptation is weakened, if the debt charge is diminishing year by year. A fully cumulative sinking fund, under which no such diminution takes place, has always been found to place an impossible strain upon the financial rectitude of politicians. Such a scheme degenerates into a mere exercise in hypothetical arithmetic. The most that can be attempted, with any hope that it will endure throughout its planned course, is a partly cumulative sinking fund. The British debt, under Mr. Churchill's plan, would only have been extinguished in fifty years by a fully cumulative sinking fund maintained throughout that period. A constant sinking fund at the level of 1928 would have taken not less than a hundred and fifty years to pay off the British debt!

[1] It is, of course, a further argument in favour of a special debt-redemption levy that, by making a clean and speedy job of repayment, it removes these temptations.

Third, the annual sinking fund payments over a given period being determined, at any rate on paper, we have to consider their distribution as between different forms of debt. If the debt were homogeneous, there would be only one form and no such problem would arise. But, in fact, public debts are nearly all heterogeneous, containing a number of forms, with different rates of interest and dates of maturity. The sinking fund, in this case, may be wholly free, applicable at the will of the public authority to the redemption of whatever form of debt may be preferred at any given time; or it may be wholly attached, in definite sums, to particular forms; or it may be partly attached and partly free. The argument for freedom is that the public authority can then use a given sum to the greatest advantage, by concentrating it upon those forms which it is most advantageous, and cheapest, at any particular moment to redeem. The argument for attachment is twofold. First, specific sinking funds attached to special forms of debt tend to keep up the prices of the securities concerned, and thus to improve, from the borrower's point of view, the conditions of their initial issue, and to facilitate subsequent conversions into these forms. Second, attachment is a partial safeguard against subsequent "raiding." For a politician, subject to the temptation of raiding the sinking fund, will only venture, in very extreme cases, to cut down an attached sinking fund. And he will find it harder to justify a raid which involves new borrowing, than a raid which takes the apparently more innocuous form of diminishing a sinking fund which is free and unattached. It is probably best that the sinking fund should be partly attached and partly free.

I may refer, in concluding this discussion, to a proposal made by me to the Colwyn Committee, a proposal to which, though it did not find favour in their sight, I still adhere.[1] This contemplates the creation of terminable annuities by the Treasury, in compulsory exchange for a certain proportion of all inherited estates above a certain size. This proportion would be handed over by the inheritors in the form of War Loan scrip, other approved securities, or cash. The effect of such a plan would be the gradual transformation of public debt, the principal of which would be due to be repaid sooner or later, into terminable annuities which would automatically run off with the lapse of time. The relevance of this proposal to the preceding discussion is that its adoption might be used to create, not only a debt charge diminishing with time, but a sinking fund similarly diminishing. And we have seen that such a condition of things is more likely, than any alternative arrangement, to be politically stable and to secure, not merely that the repayment of debt shall be projected on paper, but that it shall be achieved in practice within a reasonable period.[2]

[1] Compare Ch. X, §8, for a reference to this proposal from the point of view of inheritance taxation.

[2] Terminable annuities were a device much favoured by Gladstone for reducing debt. But they were offered in the market, like other securities, and their annual value, therefore, contained a "redemption factor" or element of sinking fund, in excess of the annual interest on the initial present (capital) value of the annuities. Terminable annuities, on my plan, would contain no redemption factor.

Chapter XXIV

THE CONVERSION OF PUBLIC DEBTS

§ 1. It is sometimes possible to reduce the annual interest payments on public debts by conversion operations. Conversion is not repayment; it is only the exchange of new debts for old. But, if the interest on the new debts is less than the interest on the old, the immediate burden of debt is reduced. Whether the burden is reduced in the long run depends also on the other conditions of conversion. In this chapter I deal only with voluntary conversion, involving no breach, or unilateral revision, of loan contracts. I leave compulsory conversion, involving such revision, for some further mention in Chapter XXVI.

Voluntary conversion may take place, either when debt actually matures for repayment, or by the voluntary acceptance before the date of maturity of an offer made by the public authority to its creditors. Generally, a reduction of interest charges through conversion is only possible, if the credit of the public authority has improved between the date of creation of a given debt and the date of its conversion, or, in other words, if the rate of interest at which the public authority can borrow has fallen during this period. If, on the other hand, the rate of interest has risen, conversion operations will increase the interest charges. In this latter case we may speak of upward conversions, from lower to higher rates of interest, as against downward conversions from higher to lower rates.

§ 2. It is a common error to suppose that conversion operations have been an important factor in reducing the burden of public debts in the past. They have, in fact, been quite unimportant, chiefly owing to the comparatively small variations in the rate of interest over long periods. Thus in this country "during the nineteenth century conversion gave very little relief. . . . The only refunding operation that made a saving commensurate with the effort involved was Goschen's in 1888 and 1889,"[1] and this only resulted in a reduction of less than £1,500,000 in the annual interest charge at that time, and a further, but smaller, consequential reduction in 1903. Similarly, the effect of conversion on the interest charge was practically negligible after the Great War until 1932.[2]

In that year £2,000,000,000 of War Loan were converted from 5 per cent. to 3½ per cent., making an annual saving in the interest charge of £30,000,000. In absolute terms this is the biggest feat of its kind in financial history. But relatively the saving in the interest charge is little more than one-tenth. The success of this conversion exceeded many expectations. But the way was well prepared for it by a combination of three factors, bad trade, a Treasury embargo on new loans, and heavy purchases of gilt-edged securities by the banks. All these three forces drove down the rate of interest, and the first two drove down employment also. There is a constant tendency for the British

[1] Stamp, *Wealth and Taxable Capacity*, p. 186.

[2] In the Report of the *Colwyn Committee on National Debt and Taxation* (1927), p. 61, it was estimated that there had only been a reduction of £1,500,000 a year on an annual total of more than £300,000,000. Between 1927 and 1932 reductions through conversion continued to be trifling.

Treasury to be more preoccupied with the prospects of conversion, as of economies generally, than with employment. This is a constant drag on useful action, and shows a perverted sense of values.

A few minor conversions followed this major operation, and exhausted current possibilities. For some time there will be no more large and favourable maturities. For a number of years to come, as regards conversion, we have now shot our bolt.

A reduction in the annual interest charge through conversion does not represent a net saving on the budget. It represents a gross saving, from which must be deducted a consequential loss of revenue. For, if the holders of public securities are receiving a smaller income by way of interest, they are liable to pay less income tax and surtax, and less, perhaps, of certain other taxes. In this country at the present time such consequential loss of revenue would amount to between a quarter and a fifth of any savings in interest charges by conversion. On the other hand, not the conversion itself, but the fall in the rate of interest which makes it possible, raises the yield of taxes assessed on capital values, such as death duties.

§ 3. A conversion offer by a public authority may contain conditions which, though they facilitate its acceptance by private investors and may even facilitate an immediate reduction in the burden of the debt, yet increase this burden over a term of years. The issue of new public securities at a heavy discount, but to be redeemed at par, is the most obvious example. Such an issue not only increases the nominal capital of the debt, which, it is often contended, is of no real importance, but increases the sum which will have to be repaid in the future. For such securities will gradually rise to par, as the date of repayment approaches, even if the rate of interest does not fall. And, if it falls, they will rise all the faster. Such issues, therefore, are popular with investors out of proportion to their yield in interest, for they carry a practical certainty of capital appreciation which, in most countries, is free of income tax. But, for this very reason, they increase the ultimate liability of the State and are a thriftless discounting of the future, for which, equally with the present, the statesman is a trustee. They are condemned, as unsound finance, by most competent authorities, but they have been a common feature of British post-war conversion operations. A very gross example was the 3½ per cent. Conversion Loan issued in 1921, when Sir Robert Horne was Chancellor of the Exchequer, and not redeemable before 1961. £163 of this loan was given in exchange for £100 of maturing debt. This loan was quoted at the start at 63 and by 1932 had risen above par, thus having realised in eleven years a capital appreciation of more than 50 per cent.[1]

Another form of the same objectionable device is the issue of new public securities at or below par, to be repaid at a substantial premium. Similar objections apply to other special inducements to lenders, such as exemption of interest from income tax. A clean and beneficial conversion will either reduce the interest

[1] "The Conversion Loan had a mixed reception in the City yesterday. . . . It was argued that to put British credit on a 5¾ per cent. basis for at least forty years was extravagant finance. But the greater the truth of this criticism, the greater are the advantages of conversion." (*The Times* City Editor, April 27th, 1921.)

charge without appreciably increasing the capital sum to be eventually repaid, or will reduce the capital without appreciably increasing the interest, or will reduce both interest and capital simultaneously. It follows that, though new issues at a heavy discount should be barred, there is no objection in principle to taking advantage of a fall in the rate of interest, in order to make a new issue at a premium, to be repaid at par, provided that the annual interest charge is not appreciably increased. But, in fact, such issues are not made, for they appeal neither to the investor, who dislikes the prospect of capital depreciation, nor to the finance minister intent upon his next annual balance sheet.

To compare the merits of two alternative conversions of the same debt, we must compare the total burden over a given period, adding the sums required for repayment of principal to those required for payment of interest, and making a further allowance for untaxed capital appreciation, if any. Such a comparison, made at the time of conversion, will, of course, involve estimates of future price movements.

§ 4. The relation between sinking fund policy and opportunities for beneficial conversions, has been disputed. Thus it is believed in the City of London that a large sinking fund strengthens British credit, or, in other words, tends to lower the rate of interest at which the British Government can borrow and to raise the market value of British Government securities, thus facilitating conversion. This belief is a simple deduction from the fact that a large sinking fund implies a large demand, operated by the Treasury, for British Government securities on the Stock

Exchange, or, alternatively, large repayments of maturing debt which release private funds for reinvestment in a similar type of security.

But it has been argued, on the other side, that this belief is an insular delusion. There is a world rate of interest, it is said, for gilt-edged securities and this rate cannot be appreciably influenced by variations in a sinking fund in any one country. Even a sinking fund, which was very large relatively to the British Budget, would be very small relatively to the total world supply of gilt-edged securities. The international mobility of funds seeking safe investment, and the magnitude of the world market, will reduce any British sinking fund to insignificance. Opportunities for conversion are almost solely dependent, therefore, on a fall in the world rate of interest.

This dispute turns on questions of fact, and the facts, on the whole, seem to be on the side of the City. There is not yet, in any real sense, a world rate of interest. There is only a force, much weakened by existing restrictions on capital movements, which tends to diminish wide differences between national rates of interest. The rates at which various national governments borrow, on comparable terms, differ considerably. It follows that a large sinking fund is a genuine aid to conversion, though a still more powerful aid would be a fall in the general level of rates of interest, which are related, though not equal, throughout the world.

But conversion is no substitute for repayment, if our aim is a substantial reduction of the burden of public debts. It is only a somewhat weak auxiliary, and such strength as it has is partly dependent on a vigorous policy of repayment being simultaneously pursued.

§ 5. The floating debt raises a special problem. By definition it is in a continual state of conversion. But should it be converted into fresh floating debt, or funded into debt at moderate or long term? The decision at any given time turns partly on the relative height of the short and long term rates of interest. If the former is above the latter, there is a clear economy in funding; in the contrary case such an operation will increase the interest charge. But, if the short term rate seems likely to rise, funding may be an economy in the long run, though not immediately.

The decision also turns partly on the size of the floating debt. A large floating debt may embarrass a government, subjecting it too much and too continuously to the caprice of lenders. On the other hand, too rapid a reduction of the floating debt may, by reducing unduly the volume of short term securities, cause an undesired restriction of credit.

CHAPTER XXV

INTER-GOVERNMENTAL DEBTS

§ 1. A special class of public debts are those owed by one national government to another.[1] These are external debts for the debtor governments, and the communities they represent, but public assets for the creditor governments and communities. Such relationships between governments arose as a result of the Great War on a scale and in a variety unparalleled in previous history.

Most of these inter-governmental debts fell, as regards origin, into two groups. The one consisted of debts imposed by the Peace Treaties upon the defeated, in favour of the victorious, States. The other consisted of debts imposed, by arrangements made among themselves, upon the poorer, in favour of the richer, victors. The former might have lost more lives, but the latter had lent more money, in the " common cause." Similar arrangements, provisionally made between the defeated States, were swept into oblivion when defeat overtook them. In an examination, from a strictly economic point of view, of inter-governmental debts, their origin may be disregarded. Historically some may be debts for services, other for disservices, rendered. But the question is, not on which side did men, or did their fathers, fight years ago, but are they debtors or creditors to-day ?

1 As to which compare Ch. XXIII, §2.

§ 2. What is the process, and what are the economic effects, of actual payments?

There are two separate aspects of debt payments, whether on account of interest or principal, from one government to another. There is, first, the aspect of public finance and, second, the aspect of private finance or private trade. So far as public finance is concerned, the position is very simple. A debtor government, A, transfers purchasing power to a creditor government, B, receiving in exchange only a receipt. In A's national balance sheet there is, in consequence, an item of expenditure, in B's an equivalent item of revenue. A is accordingly compelled to increase taxation, or to borrow more, or to reduce other expenditure, while B is enabled to reduce taxation, or to borrow less, or to increase expenditure. And, apart from remote reactions, this is all.

§ 3. But the second aspect is less simple. A must obtain from individuals the purchasing power to be transferred, B must pass on the purchasing power received to other individuals, and the purchasing power, in the course of transfer, must be changed from A's currency into B's. These three processes give rise to a number of transactions within the sphere of private trade. The third process, which may influence the rates of foreign exchange, will be considered separately. But the first two may be taken together.

Their effect must be as follows. Over a period of years the debtor community must build up an "export surplus," or, in other words, must part with a quantity of exports unbalanced by imports. The creditor community must likewise accept an import surplus. But the period, during which these surpluses will actually emerge, may differ from the period during which inter-governmental debt payments are being made. In particular, the former period may begin to run at a later date than the latter, and may run longer. This divergence will be caused by further external borrowing by A, or by its nationals, or, on the other hand, by further external lending by B, or by its nationals. Thus the German Government paid reparations under the Dawes Scheme for several years, while the German trade balance showed, not an export, but an import, surplus. This was because large loans were made by American and other foreign investors to German municipalities and private enterprises. The emergence of an export surplus might be postponed indefinitely by continuous imports of capital based on new loans from abroad, but only at the cost of heaping up an indefinitely large ultimate liability. As this ultimate liability grows, relatively to the resources of the debtor State to discharge it, new external loans will become more and more difficult to obtain. The emergence of an import surplus might likewise be postponed indefinitely by the continuous export of capital on a sufficient scale. But, in fact, as recent history shows, there is an element of economic instability in such postponements.

§ 4. I turn to the third process, which operates through the foreign exchanges. The unilateral transfer of purchasing power from A to B, where currencies differ, causes an increased demand for B's currency in terms of A's. This tends to lower the value of A's currency and to raise that of B's. If, by means of a gold, or gold exchange, standard, or by other means, any currency is effectively stabilised, the tendency for its value to fluctuate, in terms of another currency which is also effectively stabilised, is held in check, and the effect of debt payments is reflected solely in the trade balances of the two communities. There is then no separate and appreciable effect of debt payments on the rates of foreign exchange. But, if there is no effective stabilising mechanism for A's currency, and the effectiveness of any mechanism will depend upon the strain to which it is subjected, there is danger of a serious depreciation in the value of this currency, with evil consequences both to debtors and creditors.

The possibility of such a danger was recognised by the authors of the Dawes Scheme, who provided for a "transfer fund" into which the German Government should pay its reparation obligations in marks, but out of which payments should only be made in francs, pounds and other creditor currencies, so long as the stability of the mark was not endangered.[1]

§ 5. The paradox has been maintained by certain writers that, as between nations, it is not only more blessed, but economically more advantageous, to give than to receive. War indemnities, it has been held, damage the recipients, and it has even been suggested that they may benefit the nations which are compelled to pay.[2] This argument conflicts with the common-sense view that to obtain something for nothing is an economic gain, and that to part with something for nothing is an economic loss. It also implies that the ownership, by some of its members, of investments

[1] In earlier times the thing looked simpler. Ancient Rome, when she demanded tributes of corn from Egypt "did not ask whether Egypt had an export surplus or not; she made her have one." (Cannan, *Economic Journal*, Sept., 1933, p. 377.)

[2] Compare Ch. XXII, §1.

abroad is a source of economic loss to a community. It points to the conclusion that a flow of imports, unbalanced by exports, is to be deplored, while a flow of exports, unbalanced by imports, is to be welcomed. But this conclusion stinks of the crudest protectionist and mercantilist fallacies. Moreover, while misconceiving the private trade aspect of debt transactions, it wholly loses sight of the public finance aspect.

The paradox, indeed, in its general form, rests upon gross intellectual confusions. In its conflict with common sense it is an obvious loser. But, in certain special circumstances, it contains an element of truth. A creditor community may suffer a wasteful disorganisation of its economic life through the payment of debts due to its government. For a large and sudden increase of imports, or decrease of exports, may cause serious depression and unemployment in industries producing those commodities, of which the imports increase or the exports diminish. This is the more likely to happen the more immobile, as between different employments, are the labour and capital affected, and the more similar is the national economy of the debtor community to that of the creditor. Thus the payment of reparations by Germany, by means of an increased export of coal, will tend to cause unemployment in the British coal industry, particularly since labour in this industry is in a high degree immobile. It is a matter of indifference, so far as this argument goes, whether the German coal is sold in this country or, as is more likely to be the case, in foreign markets previously supplied by us. Similarly, the receipt of debt payments by the United States, which result in a decreased export of American cotton, will tend to cause depression among American cotton-growers, particularly if they cannot easily turn to the cultivation of other crops. It is possible, of course, that the decreased foreign demand for British coal or American cotton will be replaced by an equivalent increase of demand in the home market, due to the additional purchasing power received through the debt payments. If this happens, there is no resultant unemployment. But such precise coincidences are rare. Again, if the national economies of the debtor and creditor communities are widely dissimilar, the risk of unemployment is much reduced. Increased imports of rice or of tea into this country, for example, would have no direct tendency to cause unemployment, for we have in this island neither rice fields nor tea plantations.

If the receipt of debt payments causes industrial disorganisation and unemployment in the creditor community, the cost of these evils must be debited against the direct advantage of the receipt. And it is conceivable that, in some exceptional circumstances, the result may be a debit balance. But this result is, in general, unlikely, particularly if the debt payments continue over a sufficiently long period to allow the disorganisation gradually to disappear. Moreover, disorganisation, due to a large and sudden change in a community's trade balance, is likely to be just as serious when debt payments cease, as when they begin. It might, therefore, be argued that, once begun, they should continue, in the interests of stability, for ever.

Looking at the question from the other side, we may allow that an increase of exports from a debtor community, or a diminution of imports competing with some of its domestic industries, may cause a stimulus to certain branches of its trade. But this is seldom a stimulus to its economic life as a whole, but only to some branches at the expense of others. And against any such stimulus is to be set the direct loss of making the debt payment. A balance of economic advantage here is almost inconceivable.

§ 6. Another fallacy, which has obtained some vogue, may also be noticed. It is sometimes said that the imposition by B, the creditor community, of a heavy tariff on imports from its debtors, such as A, prevents the payment of an inter-government debt from A to B. This is not true, even if the tariff diminishes the imports of B from A, and even if we exclude the possibility of capital exports from B. For B may still obtain a sufficient import surplus, in spite of diminished imports from A, either by sufficiently increased imports from elsewhere, or by a sufficient reduction of its own exports. Further, if the possibility of capital exports is admitted, payment of the inter-governmental debt may take place, while B has, not an import, but an export, surplus. The creation of new private debts abroad may outweigh, in B's trade balance, the effect of the repayment of old public debts. But repayment may, none the less, be proceeding steadily.

It is possible, moreover, that the imposition of a tariff by B may result, not in A and other debtors paying less, but in their actually paying more, in terms of goods and services, than they would otherwise have paid. For the incidence of the duties imposed by B may be largely upon A. This is likely, indeed, to be the case. For the fact that A must make unilateral payments to B reduces the elasticity of supply of exports from A to B, and this tends to shift on to A the incidence of duties imposed upon such imports by B.[1] It is likely, for example, that duties imposed by the United States Government on imports from its debtors were largely paid by the latter, and it is possible that duties imposed on German exports by her creditor governments were partly paid by the Germans. This does not mean that debts due to the United States, or due from Germany, could not be paid. It means, on the contrary, that something additional was paid as well.

§ 7. In the preceding discussion modern inter-governmental debts have been studied exclusively in the light of economic principles. But it is important that the economist should not, by too great concentration on theoretical analysis, lose altogether his sense of wonder. The course of events since 1918 in regard to these debts is one of the most astonishing things in economic history. It was an amazing prospect which confronted us, the opening of a strange new chapter in international relations.[2] I have given expression

[1] See the argument of Ch. VII, §§4-5.

[2] Thus the United States during the early 1920's had been settling with her European "war-debtors," one by one. No fewer than thirteen of them, from the Baltic to the Adriatic and from the Black Sea to the Atlantic, had been made to toe the line. Payments had been arranged which between 1926 and 1930 would aggregate more than a billion dollars, rising for the period between 1951 and 1955 to nearly two billion dollars and running on for another thirty years at the same level. On the other hand, Germany's total reparation liability had been officially fixed in 1921 at the fantastic figure of 132 billion gold marks and, even if she had paid the full Dawes annuities of two and a half billion gold marks from 1928-29 onwards for evermore, she would always be paying less than the annual interest on her official debt, so that her total liability, far from diminishing, would be continually increasing by the addition of unpaid compound interest! But the Young Plan, which in 1929 replaced the Dawes Plan, reduced her liabilities to what then seemed quite tolerable figures.

elsewhere to some general reflections on this subject[1] and I think it permissible to reproduce them here.

"Facts keep moving on. Huge paper obligations, which seemed a few years ago like unsubstantial economic nightmares, wholly incapable of enforcement, have been rapidly assuming solid shape. Reparations, on a large scale, are being punctually paid by Germany, and passed on by the recipients, with additional payments from their own resources, to the United States. Let us look at the picture from the other angle. In America, as Professor Moulton tells us,[2] 'a cycle of discussion and negotiation has practically been completed. Between 1921 and 1926 a whole series of debt and reparation settlements has been negotiated, and practically all the important outstanding obligations have now been funded and regularised with definite annuity payments provided. Aside from the Russian debt, only a few minor obligations remain unfunded, although the French debt agreements with both the United States and Great Britain have not yet been ratified.' As a result, a large part of Europe, victors and vanquished alike, has bound itself to pay tribute, direct or indirect, to America for more than sixty years, and has actually begun to pay. Within this framework of obligations, the poorer nations, in most cases, pay tribute to the richer, the nations which lost most lives in the war to those which lost least.

"For the United States the war must appear in retrospect as a beautiful idyll of thrift, a gigantic process of profitable foreign investment, the creation

[1] In my book, *Towards the Peace of Nations*, pp. 64-6.

[2] In his *World War Debt Settlements* (Allen & Unwin, 1926).

of a sure source of income from Europe, which will continue to flow across the Atlantic till the present century is almost at an end. Unborn Americans will wax fat on the labour of unborn Englishmen and Germans, Frenchmen and Italians. Already American investors are lending to Europe the money with which she is to pay what she owes to American taxpayers, so that America is able to charge interest twice over on the same debts! Mr. Wells in the second volume of *The World of William Clissold* has a passage which depicts this situation. 'A golden incarnation of Vishnu, the creditor spirit, rules America, as they see it from these broken European countries, rules America absolutely, sitting upon a Treasury full of gold. Indeed, the American Vishnu sits, in this vision, like a golden weight upon all the world, smiling gold stoppings at the figure of Hope.'

"To some this situation will seem morally monstrous; to others it will appear as a solemn and majestic vindication of the sanctity of contract. But, however this may be, there are grave doubts as to its stability."

That was in 1928. But the phase of actual payments was short. In 1934, in another book,[1] I wrote of these inter-governmental debts that "the crisis is washing them all away. The 'solemn engagements' of the Germans at Versailles in 1919, of Mr. Baldwin at Washington in 1923, of the French and Italians to Mr. Churchill in 1925 and 1926, all these and many others like them, are swirling down the stream, following, after an interval of some fifteen years, the promissory notes of the last of the Romanoffs,

[1] *Unbalanced Budgets*, pp. 450-1.

which the Bolsheviks, from the first hour of their arrival in power, bluntly refused to honour.

"As regards war debts to foreign governments we are all Bolsheviks now. Little face-saving devices—little token payments at Washington, to ease the final bump and dodge a declaration of default, or little slipshod undertakings at Lausanne to pay something more some time in the vague future—make no important difference. Neat schedules of payments, running on till 1984, or even longer, are now only scraps of paper. But for the crisis, and the increasing burden on unbalanced budgets of these tributes fixed in terms of money, this strange system of one-way traffic between State Treasurers might have endured a little longer." It ended when it did, because the Great Depression brought the great excuse to debtors whom it irked to go on paying.

CHAPTER XXVI

BALANCING THE BUDGET

§ 1. The common conception of a "balanced budget"[1] is that, over a period of time, revenue exceeds, or at least does not fall short of, expenditure. If expenditure exceeds revenue, the budget is said to be "unbalanced."[2] In Chapter III, § 1 of this book, I touched this question in passing. In this chapter I shall explore it more in detail.

That budgets should be balanced is often regarded, not only as an unquestioned precept of finance, but as a moral precept as well. It is enunciated by orthodox financial experts with a cold puritan pride. In this country this moral sentiment, reinforced by a primitive and widespread fear, artificially stimulated, of the consequences of an unbalanced budget, reached a high pitch in 1931. By means of large economies and more taxation the budget was duly balanced. But in 1933 this sentiment had so far weakened that an influential

[1] The word "budget," as applied to public finance, was traced by Cannan to an anonymous pamphlet, entitled *The Budget Opened*, attacking the policy of Walpole while Chancellor of the Exchequer and likening him to a clown opening his bag of tricks and deceptions. The phrase stuck and in time turned anodyne. "Opening the Budget" is now the most official Parliamentary language.

[2] This is common usage. But it would be more logical to call the budget "balanced," only when expenditure exactly equalled revenue, and "unbalanced" when, as would practically always be the case, either exceeded the other. We might then distinguish between an "overbalanced" and an "underbalanced" budget, according as revenue was greater or less than expenditure. See my Chapter II in Part I of *Unbalanced Budgets* for a discussion of the definition of "balancing the budget."

campaign was set on foot to persuade the Chancellor of the Exchequer deliberately to unbalance the budget in order to increase employment. He was not persuaded. But the campaign rallied much support.[1]

§ 2. I turn from moral sentiments to economics. The budget is to be regarded as balanced if, during a given period, expenditure does not exceed revenue. Three preliminary questions arise. What should be included in " expenditure " ? What should be included in " revenue " ? What length of time should be chosen as the accounting period ?

[1] I draw on the columns of *The Times* alone. The campaign was opened by a leading article on January 25th, 1933, advocating large tax reductions, the gap to be filled by borrowing on Treasury Bills and Ways and Means Advances from the Bank of England. On March 10th, a letter appeared signed by thirty-seven teachers of economics, from twelve Universities, arguing that, though " it is a general maxim of financial prudence that all Government expenditure should be financed by taxation, . . . it would be pedantic and injurious to regard this as barring the Government from giving assistance to the well-accredited policy of price restoration in present conditions." The budget estimates should be divided into expenditure on current and on capital account, the latter should be financed by loan and taxation should be reduced. A leading article on the same day blessed this letter. Then followed a series of articles by Mr. Keynes, afterwards republished in the pamphlet, *Means to Prosperity*, urging a large loan expenditure for development, and the unbalancing of the budget now, in order the better to balance it later. He was cautiously supported by Sir Josiah Stamp, in an address reported on March 23rd, who held that, when savings exceeded investment, it was legitimate to unbalance the budget temporarily, provided foreign opinion was not thereby scared, while Sir Basil Blackett, in an address reported on March 31st, boldly declared for unbalancing the budget by tax reductions and temporary borrowing and " did not disguise his opinion that, in present circumstances, the Treasury had been unduly influenced by old-fashioned orthodox views regarding the wickedness of budgeting for a deficit." A leading article on the same day recalled the budget of 1922-23, when Sir Robert Horne took a shilling off the income tax, reduced other taxes and suspended the sinking fund, and was rewarded by a reduction in unemployment and a budget surplus the next year.

As to expenditure, we should certainly exclude all debt repayment, even under statutory, or attached, sinking funds. If, during the period chosen, there is any net repayment of debt, the budget may reasonably be said to be balanced.[1] Likewise all borrowing for "reproductive" purposes, such as loan expenditure for public works, should be excluded. On the expenditure side, the division of the budget into two parts, a current budget and a capital budget, is not difficult. Greater difficulties arise on the revenue side, though in some countries they have, after a fashion, been surmounted. But the division is a purely formal operation. It has only a psychological value, in helping to prevent scares of an unbalanced budget based on a misunderstanding of the nature of expenditure. Where new capital expenditure is financed, not by loan, but by taxation, the budget is, to this extent, balanced with an extra margin. This should be regarded by the Puritans as extra sound finance.

As to revenue, we should exclude all receipts which are of the nature of capital, such as the proceeds of sales of public property, or sums drawn from reserves accumulated out of previous surpluses. For the diminution of public capital assets is equivalent to an increase in the deadweight public debt. But there is no ground for excluding revenue derived from taxes assessed on private capital, such as death duties.[2]

It follows from these considerations that we may define a budget as being balanced, if during the

[1] The May Committee on National Expenditure in 1931 blundered badly on this point. They estimated a prospective budget deficit of £120,000,000, but included in this total the current sinking fund of £50,000,000.

[2] Compare Ch. X, §7.

accounting period there is no increase in the *net* deadweight public debt.

What, however, should be the length of the accounting period? There is no special virtue in a year, though this is the most usual period. "It is a mouldy fallacy," says Professor Jacob Viner, "that, regardless of circumstances, the government must balance its budget in each year. Why not in each month, or week, or hour?"[1] Where administration is weak, or financial control apt to be slack, there is something to be said for a shorter period than a year. But, in general, there is much more to be said for a longer period. It may be argued, for example, that there is some gain in keeping rates of taxation stable over a longer period, so that, if expenditure fluctuates within moderate limits, annual deficits and surpluses may roughly balance over a term of years. Similarly a variable sinking fund may be used as a buffer to keep rates of taxation stable. But, so long as the sinking fund does not become negative, the annual budget remains balanced, though with a variable surplus. If, on the other hand, expenditure is stable, and still more if it is higher when trade is bad than when it is good—as with expenditure to maintain the unemployed and, in terms of commodities, with all expenditure fixed in terms of money, in so far as prices rise with good, and fall with bad, trade—variable rates of taxation to balance the budget annually mean rates varying inversely with general prosperity, and hence with taxpayers' ability to pay. Thus it has been argued

[1] In an address on *Inflation as a Possible Remedy for the Depression*, delivered at, and published by, the University of Georgia, May, 1933.

that " our existing budgetary procedure is open to the serious objection that the measures which will balance this budget are calculated to unbalance the next, and *vice versa*."[1] Some American economists have proposed that the accounting period should coincide with that of the trade cycle, surpluses being used to repay debt in years of boom, and deficits met by borrowing in years of slump. But such a plan assumes both foreknowledge of the course of trade and power to resist demands, whether for tax relief or more expenditure, when trade is good. These are large assumptions.

None the less, there is a strong case for lengthening the accounting period beyond one year, or, at least, in judging, and encouraging public opinion to judge, a series of annual budgets as a whole, rather than separately. This conclusion goes some way towards answering the question, " Should the budget be balanced ? " Clearly, in the long run, it must be, unless we are prepared to contemplate an increase, unlimited both in time and in amount, of the dead-weight debt. And such a prospect is clearly intolerable, even if lenders were willing. But, in the short run, measured in terms of a year or two, the budget need not be balanced. This proposition is true in two different senses. First, an annual deficit or two will not, of themselves, cause any great disaster.[2] And, second, public policy may sometimes deliberately and legitimately incur temporary budget deficits in the

[1] Keynes, *Means to Prosperity*, p. 13.

[2] Of Mr. Churchill's five budgets from 1925 to 1929 two at least, and perhaps three, were unbalanced. But there was no catastrophe. From 1929 onwards the great majority of budgets all over the world have been unbalanced. But this is a mere symptom of deeper disorders. In itself, it has been a relatively unimportant incident.

pursuit of larger aims, notably an increase of employment through an expansion of credit.

But there is an important qualification to be made. Budget deficits, even in the short run, must not be excessive. The practical question is, not only how long, but how much, a budget is unbalanced. If deficits are either so frequent or so large as to give the sense of a financial situation out of control, the results may be very damaging. And these results depend, not only on the facts of the situation, but on opinions, whether false or true, about the facts.[1] It is a fallacy, as I have pointed out above,[2] that an unbalanced budget necessarily leads to inflation. It will only do this, if the government resorts to the printing press to cover the deficit, either directly to meet its own expenditure or indirectly to support inflationary bank loans to itself. If the government covers the deficit by ordinary loans or by the sale of public assets, there is no inflation.

Some measure of inflation may, of course, form part of policy, and appropriate steps be taken to promote it. But it must be kept within bounds and under firm control, and must meet with early and visible success, or it may result in a flight from the currency and other symptoms of distrust. To deal effectively with these is troublesome, though, as experience in several countries shows, not technically very difficult, given

[1] This question of opinion and of " confidence " is interesting, but I cannot pursue it here. On its relation to the British "financial crisis " of 1931, see Lord Snowden's *Autobiography*, Vol. II. He states (on pp. 946-7) that, in the course of his vain and, as I think, misguided efforts to keep this country on the gold standard, he secured a loan from the Federal Reserve Bank of New York, but only when the latter had been assured that " the Bank of England approved the programme of economies," which the Chancellor of the Exchequer had submitted to this higher authority.

[2] See Ch. XV, §8.

strong and confident administration and an economic situation which, in spite of superficial troubles, is fundamentally sound.

There remains, of course, the general argument against all budget deficits, that they increase the net deadweight public debt and that this is an economic evil.[1] And this argument must be given its due weight.

§ 3. The cause of the world-wide epidemic of unbalanced budgets in the Great Depression is simple. It is the steep and rapid fall of prices, aggravated by the decline in production and the rise in unemployment, which have accompanied this fall. Whether this fall of prices be regarded as a cause or an effect of the slump, it is unquestionably the cause of budget deficits. It diminishes public revenue from almost every source. The yield of taxes based on the price of goods, whether customs or excise, falls as these prices fall. When, with declining production, the quantity of taxable goods declines, the yield falls further. The value and volume of business transactions fall, and with it the yield of stamp duties based on these transactions. The money income of many taxpayers falls, and with it the yield of income tax. If the tax is on a progressive scale, the yield falls more than in proportion to the fall in income. Taxpayers, being poorer, tend to delay tax payments. Finally, the profits of State enterprises fall with the decline in the purchasing power of their customers. As against all this, the fall in the rate of interest, which usually accompanies bad trade and falling prices, cheapens the floating debt and facilitates conversion of other debt as it matures and, by raising

[1] See Ch. XXII.

the value of gilt-edged securities, raises the yield of taxes based on capital values, such as death duties. But these are very insufficient compensations to the budget.

The fall of prices, on the other hand, has no immediate effect on that large part of public expenditure which consists of fixed money charges. It has some effect, though much even of this is delayed, upon public expenditure which varies with prices, such as the purchase of stores, or wages and salaries on a cost-of-living sliding scale. But, as against this, the cost on public funds of maintaining the unemployed, however low the level of maintenance, rises as their number increases.

Expenditure, in short, is much more rigid than revenue. This works both ways. Just as a fall in prices breeds deficits, a rise in prices breeds surpluses. Whatever its other effects, from the point of view of balancing the budget, a moderate measure of inflation has much to commend it.

§ 4. To stop budget deficits, or at least to keep them within reasonable bounds, there are, indeed, two possible types of policy which may be adopted. The first is deflationary, the second inflationary or, if a term be preferred which emphasises the fact of past deflation, reflationary. The first accepts the fall in prices, together with the possibility of further falls, and, on this basis, seeks to reduce expenditure and increase revenue. It aims at balancing the budget by direct means. The second seeks to reverse the fall in prices, and relies less on economies than on stimulating trade and thus increasing revenue. It aims at balancing the budget by indirect means and is generally willing to leave it out of balance for a while, rather than risk further deflation. Logically these two policies are quite distinct. In practice, some governments have tried to compromise, or have wobbled to and fro, between them.[1]

The first policy has been pursued, under orthodox financial guidance, in many countries. It has generally led to a further fall of prices in a " deflationary spiral." It has involved, in its most drastic forms, a wholesale breakage of contracts, both public and private, by legal process, including the compulsory conversion of public debts and the revision of established expectations, including cuts in the salaries and wages of public servants, in pensions and many other social service benefits. Sometimes also the authoritative reduction of prices by decree. It is doubtful whether it has anywhere succeeded in its object. Where it has seemed to have succeeded best, in Australia and New Zealand for example, in both of which it was pursued with great energy and boldness, external factors of an inflationary character finally turned the scale, rising export prices, especially for wool and wheat, and an exchange depreciation of 25 per cent. Since it has sought to balance the State budget by unbalancing the budgets of private persons, the deflationary policy has caused great immediate privations and aroused deep popular resentments. And thus in Germany it helped to kill democracy.

In this country, and in some others, economies in public current expenditure were accompanied, under

[1] The practice of the governments of twelve European countries, and of Australia, New Zealand and the United States of America, has been examined in detail by the authors of *Unbalanced Budgets*.

the influence of the government, by economies in public capital expenditure and in private expenditure, both capital and current. This was a stupid blunder, due to gross mental confusions over the meaning of " economy " and of " balancing the budget." For loan expenditure on public works, as pointed out above, stands outside the ordinary budget and there is no public economy in checking private expenditure, either capital or current, during a trade depression. On the contrary, the effect of this blunder was to slow down the circulation of money, including bank deposits, and thereby to reduce prices, prolong stagnation, increase unemployment and diminish public revenue. Such conduct was exactly wrong. It worked against the success of the policy which it was designed to aid.

The second policy is " expansionist," as the first is " restrictionist." It has been tried by fewer countries and affords less evidence, as yet, either of practical success or failure. It involves, in the absence of a generally accepted international monetary system, the national abandonment of the gold standard and the acceptance of exchange depreciation. It aims at raising prices and generally includes large loan expenditures for public works and sometimes also for current public expenditure. It seeks to speed up the circulation of money, to stimulate trade by increasing purchases and to avoid the more brutal and socially dangerous " adjustments " of the deflationists.

§ 5. These two contrasted policies for escaping from unbalanced budgets correspond to two wider policies for escaping from the Great Depression. Given an excess, at many points in the industrial field, of costs of production over selling prices—and this is the essential characteristic of depression—the first policy seeks to reduce costs, the second to raise prices. At first sight both seem equally reasonable. On closer examination each has its own difficulties. But, given the actual institutions and temper of the present age, the second seems the less difficult. It meets with fewer human frictions and other obstacles inherent in our present economic arrangements, and it gives easier play to the more obvious forces making for recovery. But we are here on the fringe of problems lying far outside the sphere of public finance as commonly delimited; the causes of industrial fluctuations under modern capitalism, the effects of alternative monetary policies, the possibilities of economic planning, projects of great changes in the social and legal framework of economic activity. On all these subjects new thoughts and new experiences multiply fast. They will bear their fruits.

NOTE ON BOOKS

Every writer, who aims at organising a general discussion of Public Finance, must be conscious of a conflict between two personalities, those of the practical and of the analytic man. Moreover, in seeking to compose this conflict, he is in danger of getting the worst of both worlds, missing both the perfection of theory, boldly guided by pure reason, and the wisdom of statesmanship, cautiously guided by administrative officialdom. Public Finance lies very close to practical politics. It is, in this sense, the most live branch of economics. Its precepts and its formulæ may change, at the wave of a politician's wand, into the clauses of an Act of Parliament. Here, more easily than anywhere else in economics, theory and practice may either play into each other's hands, or remain at cross purposes. Studies in Public Finance have, for this reason, a special fascination, but for the same reason an excess of abstraction is apt, in this sphere, to seem especially unreal and an excess of conventional rule-of-thumb especially half-witted.

It is a peculiarity of English economists that, unlike their American, French, Italian and German brethren, they seldom write general treatises on Public Finance. Bastable's *Public Finance,* until recently the only large systematic book on the subject published in England in modern times, is out of date in many respects, as a result of later developments both in theory and practice. On the other hand, much has been written by English economists on the subject of taxation and a good deal on the subject of public debts. But, as I have pointed out above, the theory of public expenditure has been greatly neglected. Professor Pigou's *Study in Public Finance* is an important book, but only professes to cover selected parts of the field. Valuable fragments of a theory of public expenditure will also be found in his *Economics of Welfare,* Parts V and VI, in Sidgwick's *Principles of Political*

Economy, Book III, and in Dr. W. A. Robson's *Relation of Wealth to Welfare*. Sir Josiah Stamp's *Fundamental Principles of Taxation, Wealth and Taxable Capacity* and *Current Problems in Finance and Government* are well worth reading. A good, though very brief, general introduction to the subject will be found in Mrs. M. E. Robinson's *Public Finance*. Mr. Findlay Shirras' *Science of Public Finance* is on a larger scale, but is somewhat dull and traditional. It has been described by an American reviewer as "Bastable served with Indian curry." On the other hand, Edgeworth's papers on taxation in Vol. II of his *Papers Relating to Political Economy* are an intellectual delight, and many later writers owe more to his originality than they always realise.

Other books dealing with special aspects of Public Finance are Cannan's *History of Local Rates in Relation to the Proper Distribution of the Burden of Taxation*, my own *Inequality of Incomes*, Part IV, Chapters VII-XI, with special reference to inheritance taxes, Mr. Wedgwood's *Economics of Inheritance*, Mr. Sykes' *British Public Expenditure*, 1921-1931, Mr. Burton's *Finance of Local Government Authorities*, Mr. J. A. Hobson's *Taxation in the New State*, Mr. Chorlton's *Rating of Land Values* and, more on the administrative side, Higgs' *Financial System of the United Kingdom*, Sir Hilton Young's *System of National Finance* and Mr. R. G. Hawtrey's *Exchequer and Control of Expenditure*. On the historical side Buxton's *Finance and Politics*, Mallet's *British Budgets* (in three volumes, the second and third in collaboration with Dr. George, bringing the story up to 1933), and Professor Rees' *Short Fiscal and Financial History of England* may be consulted. Dr. H. B. Spaulding's *British and American Income Tax* is an interesting comparative study, and Professor Adarkar's *Principles and Problems of Federal Finance* is an able book by an Indian economist.

Unbalanced Budgets, a study of the Financial Crisis in Fifteen Countries by myself and other authors, Mr. Durbin's *Credit Problem*, Mr. Keynes' *Essays in Persuasion*, Professor Robbins' *Great Depression* and Sir Arthur Salter's *Recovery* present a variety of facts and opinions concerning recent problems.

Turning from books to government publications, the student will derive profit, and perhaps also some amusement, from comparing the answers to an official examination paper set to various civil servants, professors and other eminent persons in 1899, published in the blue book on the *Classification and Incidence of Imperial and Local Taxes.* These examinees were fortunate in being allowed ample time for their answers and unlimited access to books and papers! Reference should also be made to the Reports of, and Evidence before, the *Select Committee on the Income Tax* (1906), the *Royal Commission on the Income Tax* (1920) and the Colwyn *Committee on National Debt and Taxation* (1927), and to the Report of the May *Committee on National Expenditure* (1931). The annual *Finance Accounts* and the Annual Reports of the *Commissioners of Inland Revenue* and of the *Commissioners of Customs and Excise* contain statistical details.

American general treatises include Adams' *Science of Finance,* Professor Plehn's *Introduction to Public Finance* and Professor Lutz's *Public Finance.* On taxation Professor Seligman's writings, especially *Essays in Taxation, Progressive Taxation* and *Studies in Finance* should be read, and the chapters on taxation in Professor Taussig's *Principles of Economics.* The leading modern French authority on Public Finance is Professor Jéze, whose *Science des Finances* should be consulted. Good Italian books are Professor Einaudi's *Corso di Scienza della Finanza,* Professor Graziani's *Istituzioni di Scienza delle Finanze* and Professor De Viti De Marco's *Primi Principii dell' Economia Finanziaria.* Rignano's *Socialismo in Accordo colla Dottrina Economica Liberale* and *Una Riforma Socialista del Diritto Successorio* contain his proposals for the taxation of inherited wealth. An English translation, with an introduction by Sir Josiah Stamp, is entitled *The Social Significance of the Death Duties.* In German Wagner's *Finanzwissenschaft* is already classical and Professor Lutz's *Finanzwissenschaft* is one of the most widely read modern treatises. A good book in German, by a Magyar author, is Professor Béla Foldes' *Finanzwissenschaft*. *Public Finance in Soviet Russia* by Sokolnikoff and others gives a good picture of the special problems of the Soviet Union.

Modern Swedish economists are some of the best in the world, combining theoretical with practical strength in a unique degree and making notable contributions to the study of public finance. Unfortunately they are little translated, but Dr. Brinley Thomas' *Monetary Policy and Crises, a Study of Swedish Experience* contains some account of their leading ideas.

Further references, both to books and to articles in periodicals, will be found in the *Public Finance* section of the *Select Bibliography of Modern Economic Theory*, compiled by Mr. Batson and published in the London School of Economics Series.

INDEX